CONTAINMENT AND CHANGE

CONTAINMENT AND CHANGE

by Carl Oglesby

and Richard Shaull

INTRODUCTION BY

Leon Howell

The Macmillan Company

Collier-Macmillan Limited, London

Library of Congress Catalog Card Number: 67-13593

FOURTH PRINTING 1969

The Macmillan Company
Collier-Macmillan Canada Ltd., Toronto, Ontario

Printed in the United States of America

Contents

Introduction

THE TWO ESSAYS in this book, discussing revolution in today's world, differ as widely in analysis, prescription, and response as the experiences and viewpoints of the writers themselves. Yet a common concern for America's role in this revolution, at home and abroad, links the two essays.

This book began in February 1966, when the two men took part in an informal discussion of these questions at Union Theological Seminary in New York City. They had never met before. One had been involved in the American domestic movement toward a more just society; the other had spent many years in Latin America in close association with Catholic and Protestant student movements. Public and private conversations that night revealed an identity of concern and a difference of perspective which opened the way for an interesting confrontation and discussion.

Anxious to have these discussions available for a much wider audience, the University Christian Movement asked that their ideas be expanded into essays. They are presented here as two efforts to understand and respond to a crucial problem of our time, in the hope that a larger conversation will be encouraged.

LEON HOWELL
University Christian Movement

PART ONE

Vietnamese Crucible

An Essay on the Meanings of the Cold War

by CARL OGLESBY

I

West Meets West: The Vietnam Nexus

Western destiny is "the knowledge of causes and secret motions of things, and the enlarging of the bounds of human empire, to the effecting of all things possible." —FRANCIS BACON

THE ANCIENT ORACLES of the Mediterranean West opened the bellies of oxen and in the smoke of their burning entrails understood the past and foresaw the future. Modern America, fruit of that same Western line, has contrived now to open the underbelly of old-young Asia; and in the smoke that arises from that sacrificial gash on the South China Sea she reads her past and sees omens of her future not half so obscurely as she might wish. Not only her soldier-sons face pitfalls and punji spikes in those jungles. It is this Western America of ours herself, her confusion not at all hidden by her fury, who has been ambushed in Asia by her own oracular past.

Crisis after crisis these past twenty years had seemingly numbed us to crisis, emergency becoming in our time man's ordinary state. But Vietnam is no Berlin or Korea or Cuba. Vietnam seizes us in a new hold, fingers a new nerve, persuades us that this war is a most distinguished and fateful event. Of course, it has certain allies in this persuasion. American racial problems worsen even as our leaders try hardest to end them. Urban disaster deepens even as our leaders attack it head-on with their best available will and ingenuity. The militarization of our political economy accelerates even as our leaders find themselves most lonely in the grand defense of Western liberty. A new sectarianism turns us angrily against one another at home, and the West European states begin to individuate themselves within the Alliance even as our leaders demand more unity, global and domestic. But the war alone would be ominous enough. No one pretends anymore to see its limits. Everyone is forced to admit that it seems to be "open-ended"—an eternal war.

Men have died before now. Why should Vietnam disrupt Western composure so deeply? We have the same explanations for this war that we had for all the others. Why do these explanations now seem so banal and inappropriate, so unworthy of the moment? Why are so many Americans—so many more Europeans—not satisfied to hear that the liberal West has again gone forth on a new march of the old holy war against totalitarianism? Why are so many of us no longer rejuvenated by the old tales? It cannot be the hardships of the war that make the difference, Americans never having been afraid of the hardships of violence; nor the elusiveness of victory, Americans always having been ready to do what is needed to win what must be won.

The problem seems to be that we are no longer sure what "victory" means. The Western liberalism that formerly produced such convincing and useful definitions of victory and defeat, presented with this war, stands mute.

Since the old truths refuse to function, since in neither Vietnam nor Mississippi do the old pleasure-pain remedies solve our problems, we begin to wonder in the back of our minds if they ever really solved anything before. Maybe they were only postponements or quarantines, these successes of the past. Maybe there now seems to be no more time for postponement, no more places of quarantine, no more excuses for not coming to a judgment.

This war is moving into our history in a unique way. It is not the first of its kind. But it is the first to be so big, so protracted, and above all so well observed: a whole nation beholds itself in the act—the act being (with whatever justice) the incineration of a whole other nation. Has any other culture ever possessed itself so openly—so *carnally*—as ours does now? We can scarcely return unchanged from this spectacle to dream the old dreams, take comfort in the old verities; we cannot worship again in the old church because we cannot now deny that there is blood on the altar, that the priests' hands are not steady. With this war, history becomes the intimate affair of each one of us, a private act for which each of us has to account personally.

No culture has been more violent than has our Western

culture. It was the West which framed the vaultingly arrogant concept of the "savage"; the West which gave the horizon itself a distinctively political meaning, maintaining that what it could not yet see existed in order to be made visible to it at some future time, to be subject to it, civilized by it, or, if found to be an obstacle to its "enlarging of the bounds of human empire," destroyed by it. There has been no moment when the people of the West, who have been customarily granted the reprieve of ignorance, have stood so specifically exposed to a clear view of their culture's capacities for violence. This essay on Vietnam is thus an essay on the West.

No less in the dark nor any more in the light than anyone else, I write as a partisan who has been educated by other partisans. It could hardly be otherwise. One is not born with a political commitment. One receives certain values, tries to apply them with honesty and as much skill as one can muster, and tries to have the courage to accept whatever personal commandments the results may imply. The pattern of argument in this essay essentially follows the process by which I came to be the particular sort of partisan that I am. The effort is to probe the specific for the principle it embodies and the untrue for the truth it palliates; to move through the superficial platitudes about Vietnam toward firmer, more well-bodied generalizations about the Cold War and the longer term conflicts within the West and between the West and the East of which the Cold War appears to be the current and climactic episode.

Thus, the chapter following engages in a brief skirmish with the official explanations of our "Free World" war for Vietnam, explanations which I take to be rather transparently irrelevant. I dismiss them so abruptly in part because they have been argued through enough by now, but largely because they suffocate a less pious but much more solid line of argument that lies below them, an argument which the good Cold Warrior might make if his commitment to pontifical banalities had not silenced him. The main purpose of Chapter II is to reconstruct that argument.

Chapter III is a critical analysis of the Cold Warrior's better story, an attempt to pry open the ideology of Cold War anticommunism to find out not only what historical mistakes it contains but more importantly what political truths those mistakes exist to conceal. The resulting reinterpretation of the Cold War (Chapter IV) is applied in Chapter V to the case of Vietnam. Chapter VI moves to the other side of the line of battle; its purpose is to put some human flesh on the too abstract enemy whom we too hastily condemn—the rebel. The last chapter, standing on what comes before it, is an attempt to reconstitute the main lines of the main issues that Westerners should try to confront—an attempt, that is, to make more explicit the general theme which I have already suggested: that the Vietnam war is a revelatory Cold War crisis, and that the Cold War itself is a terminal crisis of Western identity. It is not really the East that the West encounters in Vietnam; it meets itself.

II

The Cold Warrior's Story

Secretary Rusk is no dope; why does he keep on saying this?
—Senator Clifford Case[1]

One might ponder the official reasons Washington gives for our fighting in Vietnam, and think: These reasons are so bad that we must have fallen into the hands of fools. But one might also think: These reasons are so bad that there must be *other* reasons.

The second thought is better.

Other reasons exist. There seem, in fact, to be several grades and varieties of *raisons de guerrilla* that overlie one another like so many geologic strata, the softer reasons lying at the surface, and the harder, the stronger ones, below it. So we must do some strip-mining, peel away the top propaganda layer to expose the firmer underlying layers of ideology that give the propaganda its ground-base and purpose. That is the objective of this chapter: to move the analytic focal point past the white lies of warfare politics into the ideological substrata where the less pious, more honest war reasons are embedded. With Senator Case, I am unwilling to conclude that Dean Rusk is a dope. If Rusk pretends to be convinced by arguments that should convince no one as intelligent as he, then he must have been convinced by other arguments which for some reason he prefers not to develop. I think the more convincing arguments can be reconstructed; the Cold Warrior's story can be pieced together. But first his propaganda has to be cleared away.

We are legally obligated to fight. It is obvious that there are no unambiguously binding agreements, the SEATO pact having even more escape clauses in it that has NATO's. It is still more obvious that no strong state will hesitate for a moment to violate a treaty which it judges to be harmful to its national interests. If we fight, it must be because we think we *must* fight, not because we have been trapped by a legal instrument.

We are responding to an emergency plea from the Vietnamese people. We have never heard from the Vietnamese people. We have heard only from those elite Vietnamese sympathetic enough with our own politics to have been allowed their hour in the Saigon Presidential Palace.

Our global reputation is at stake. Maybe it is, and maybe that is important. But this argument cuts both ways. No less than President Johnson, the dissenters consider themselves to be the partisans of America's prestige, which they define differently. The only question is, What kind of reputation do we want our country to have?

We are resisting an invasion: (a) The National Liberation Front of South Vietnam is the political creature of North Vietnam. The best development of this argument can be found in a lengthy, highly detailed essay in the April 1966 issue of *Foreign Affairs*, "The Faceless Viet Cong." The author, George A. Carver, Jr., is identified as a former AID official in Saigon. In view of AID's notorious intimacy with the CIA in Vietnam and the wealth of what appears to be privileged intelligence to which Carver has had access, one has to wonder if his piece is not, more or less, a CIA document. Since it might be just that, it is only prudent to be skeptical about Carver's "facts."* But where exactly does skepticism leave us in a case where the "facts" are so in-

* Several samples of CIA historiography might be cited. For one, the Bay of Pigs: Murray Zeitlin and Robert Scheer (*Cuba: Tragedy in Our Hemisphere*, 1964) have established that the CIA badly tampered with the texts of Castro speeches that it presented to State Department and White House analysts; that is, the CIA appears to have consciously falsified the supposedly objective information on which our policy-makers were basing their plans. And the CIA's contention just before the invasion that the Cuban people were prepared to join in revolt against Castro is bizarre if we do not assume that the CIA's purpose was to involve the United States in a situation from which few administrations could have decided to withdraw. In January 1964, for another example, the CIA leaked the "information" that the U.S.S.R.'s 6 to 10 percent annual growth rate had fallen in 1962–63 to 2.5 percent, a decline that most Western experts found unbelievable. Paul Blackstock (*The Strategy of Subversion*, 1964) writes that this report "was widely interpreted as an attempt to influence U.S. allies not to extend large export credits to the U.S.S.R." (p. 187).

accessible? For all we can ever know for sure, Carver's elaborate description of the genesis of the National Liberation Front (NLF) might be little more than a Borgesian fantasy; it might also be complete and perfect truth. What tests can we make? We could compare Carver's version with Wilfred Burchett's,[2] but Burchett is no less a partisan than Carver. French scholars Bernard B. Fall, Philippe Devillers, and Jean Lacouture are more trustworthy by any ordinary academic standard, and all three describe the NLF in ways that differ much more from Carver than from Burchett; but they might be wrong. What does one do with a "proof" which cannot be checked?

Accept it. Concede that Hanoi, with that vicious skill by which we know our Enemy, intrigued to create and retain control over the NLF. This concession allows us to ask Carver what he knows about that *other* intriguer, Ngo Dinh Nhu, and that *other* "creature" organization, Nhu's Committee for the Liberation of North Vietnam. I know very little about this mysterious and unjustly ignored committee except that it was conducting paramilitary operations in North Vietnam shortly after Ngo Dinh Diem's consolidation of power in 1956. One conjectures, however, that it may have been trained by some of the U.S. Special Forces personnel who were infiltrated into South Vietnam (on civilian passports) in the mid-fifties, that it may have been financed directly by the CIA, and that it may have been involved in the famous Vinh farmers' rebellion of November 1956.* No scholarship in the world will tell us which of these two "liberation creatures" was invented first, which was the first blow and which the counterblow.

But much more important than questions about the bureaucratic origins of the NLF is the question, Why did it grow? Suppose that the North Vietnamese regime promulgated certain decrees through an underground in South Vietnam: Why did so many South Vietnamese people respond? How could it be that this illegitimate invasion from without was experienced by so many South Vietnamese as an entirely

* The detail about U.S. military infiltration is documented in ex-Special Forces member Donald Duncan's memoir in *Ramparts*, February 1966. My other information about Nhu's committee was picked up in conversations with U.S. officials and with a former Vietnamese member of it in Saigon and Hue in July 1965.

legitimate revolution from within? Because there was terror? There was terror on both sides; why did only one work? Because there was a tightly disciplined secret organization? There were tightly disciplined secret organizations on both sides; why did only one work? If we know anything at all about popular wars (a study of our own revolution would tell us a great deal), it is that they cannot be summoned into existence through the decrees of remote bureaucrats. Such decrees can give them tactical and sometimes even strategic form; but their substance and their momentum are massive popular resentment, alienation, and distress. Popular wars are cultural phenomena; they are never the product of a black diplomacy. And to the extent that any government official must be given the credit or blame for the popular war that now ravages Vietnam, that official would be the late Ngo Dinh Diem himself. In the late 1950s, President Diem violently suppressed all political opposition, Communist and non-Communist alike. That suppression forced the initial episodes of defensive insurgency. Diem proceeded to shatter the traditional village base of Vietnamese society by imposing the famous resettlement programs; simultaneously, he was reconstructing the landed oligarchy and the comprador classes which the Vietminh had broken down. This new feudalism exploded the initial insurgency into a social revolution. Diem sought or tolerated or could not resist more and more military aid from the United States, and he allowed himself to become unambiguously associated with the well-meaning Americans, who were even taller, whiter, and better armed than their French predecessors. This new imperialism exploded the social revolution into a patriotic war of liberation. Step by step, as if it were his real intention to do so, Diem reassembled the cultural-political matrix from which the Vietminh movement had sprung, even down to the details of surrounding himself with Vietnamese officers who had fought on the side of the French and upper-class Catholics who for generations had identified themselves not with the peasants of Vietnam but with the salon elite of the French Riviera.

George Carver, the CIA, the State Department, and the White House probably know as well as anyone else (we shall return to this) what it is that creates popular wars, just as they quite probably know that the issuing of orders in Hanoi has precious little to do with the way those orders will bite in South Vietnam. If revolt is needed, it will come, orders or no; and if it is not needed, no orders in the world can instigate it. In view of the mountainous fact that South Vietnam revolted, Carver's fine-spun arguments about "puppet" and "creature" organizations lose all their body.

We are resisting an invasion: (b) North Vietnamese troops are fighting in the south. Compelling enough if one knows nothing else, this line of argument finally seems the most dishonest of all. Americans are shown a number and handed a gun. That is not enough. There are other numbers, other facts. One is that our militarization of South Vietnam was solidly under way by the end of 1954, well before the period of French control was to have ended, and long before there was any substance to the infiltration-from-the-north charge.[3] What comes before cannot have been caused and cannot be excused by what comes after.

But much more surprising than this omission is the inconclusiveness of the infiltration statistics themselves. With all the official furor, one is prepared to hear that our enemy consists mostly of northern troops, just as in the Korean War. But the case turns out to be different. In midsummer 1966, total NLF strength was officially estimated at 282,000 men, an increase of 52,000 since the beginning of the year.[4] (This figure, incidentally, is politically menacing. In this same period, we claim 31,571 "kills," the largest total yet for any six-month period. The old pattern repeats itself: The more there are who die, the more come to fight.) Of these 282,000, about 50,000 are supposed to be northern infiltrators—and the great majority of these 50,000 are said to have entered the south since the systematic American bombing of North Vietnam commenced in February 1965. Thus, North Vietnamese, who may think they have a good reason to fight, still account for no more than 18 percent of the total NLF force. The Administration's performance on other statistical matters (these same "kills," for example) gives us no right to believe that this estimate is not inflated for maximum political effect. But even if it is not, we are still left with no "outside-aggressor" explanation for fully four out of five active military partisans of the revolution. The invasion argument seems undermined by its own best evidence. Certainly that evidence does not seem to justify our own force level, which now surpasses North Vietnam's "invader" force by better than 6 to 1.

We might dwell a moment on the political strategy of this

preoccupation with "foreign" troops. It conceals two crucial assumptions.

The first is that an army's claim to nationalist revolutionary status is bogus if a substantial number of its troops are foreign. But this is clearly incorrect; and of all people, we Americans should know that. Recall the extent to which our own revolution was directly and indirectly supported by France, Spain, and Holland. Recall our national feeling for Lafayette. Recall the 3000 British freighters the French helped sink in support of our revolutionary cause. Recall that General Washington's troops were outnumbered at Yorktown by their French comrades under General Rochambeau. Recall that Washington chose to fight the battle of Yorktown largely because Admiral de Grasse promised to sail from the West Indies to land 3000 French troops with cannon on James Island, and that Washington won that battle largely because de Grasse searched out, engaged, and defeated the British fleet protecting Cornwallis' rear. This is of course not to say that the American and Vietnamese revolutions are alike. It is only to say that the presence of outside troops or the making of alliances or the interference on either side of third-party states proves nothing whatsoever about the internal political nature of the conflict. Some Czechs supported Hitler's Wehrmacht; that does not make Hitler a Czech revolutionary. Some third parties support Nguyen Huu Tho's NLF; that does not make Tho an aggressor's agent.

The second concealed assumption of the invasion argument is that between North and South Vietnam a politically ordinary invasion is possible. That is, the argument assumes that there are two separate and sovereign Vietnams, one of which could aggress against the other's territory. Thus, the Administration has depicted the 17th parallel—the 1954 Geneva Conference's "temporary military demarcation line"—as a permanent national frontier, permanent at least for the duration of the Cold War. Cold Warriors may argue that such a division is legal enough if it is right and right enough if it is necessary. Law serves power. We shall look very closely later on at this necessity and this rightness; but whether the division is defensible or not on political grounds, it will remain incorrect to say with the Munich-bemused that the two halves of Vietnam relate to one another as Germany and Czechoslavakia of 1938. Vietnam is divided now, rightly or wrongly, strictly at the insistence of the United States, and strictly because there was a revolution in China which the United States finds appalling.

If we fail to contain Them here, we shall have to contain Them someplace else. In 1779, Lord North concluded that England's attempt to subdue the Americans had gone on long enough, was too expensive, and should be broken off: The Americans should be granted their independence. North conveyed these sentiments to George III. The king was dismayed. He answered that the American contest was the most important that any country had ever yet been engaged in and rebuked North for "weighing such events in the scale of a tradesman behind his counter." The king made it clear to North that if America succeeded, "the West Indies must follow them, not [toward] independence, but must for its own interest be dependent on North America; Ireland would soon follow the same plan and be a separate state, then this Island would be reduced to itself, and soon would be a poor island indeed, for reduced in her trade merchants would retire with their wealth to climates more to their advantage, and shoals of manufacturers would leave this country for the new Empire."[5]

Every master of a global empire since has found occasion to dust off what we now call the domino theory. The theory's implicit description of the way in which the demand for change emerges and is shaped by international events is primitive, paranoid, and mechanistic. But its most fundamental assumption still seems sound: Nationalism is a threat to imperialism. Toward the end of Chapter IV, we shall be taking this argument very seriously in a much rephrased form. For the moment, we need only note that its popular version begs or circles all the really important social questions on which Westerners generally and Americans in particular are in such need of enlightenment. Is stability more important than social justice? Can change be managed within the status quo? Can Western acquisition of global economic hegemony coexist with the just aspirations of small states? Can the progress of that acquisition be reversed without violence? The domino theory has nothing to say about the very conditions and problems that give it the lame life it has. It pretends that there are no questions at all to ask about our extremely advanced international positions; with infuriating arrogance it depicts Vietnam and all the other dominoes as possessions of the Free World (read, the United States) which, being possessed by us, are ours to lose; and implicitly denying that men revolt for human cause, it implicitly outlaws rebellion as a criminal if not diabolic act. Generally, it evokes the images of a very legendary threat, wants us to believe that there is a Gate and that the Enemy is at it—or about to be. There *is* a struggle in the world. That struggle very much *does* involve America. And that struggle needs to be understood. But the domino theorists beat the drums of anticommunism, and the war is on. A good people have been given no chance to wonder who their enemy is and why their enemy fights; have been given no time to think through the astounding implications of a foreign policy which has crept upon them without being explained or debated, a foreign policy which Gary Porter, borrowing from Walter Lippmann and George Ball, has aptly termed "globalism—the ideology of total world involvement."[6]

From fighting for freedom to stopping Them now, these reasons for war are little more than the slogans of a hard-sell sales campaign, an unchecked federal executive hawking his wares on the public money. By these slogans, the nation's heart is warmed for the sacrifice, the young men are summoned, the heroes are decorated, the dead are buried, a diffuse and sometimes easy-going nationalism is given point and passion.

The slogans also do something more subtle: they rivet our attention on Vietnam itself. Even when we grow critical, these slogans manipulate our thought, invite us to reenact in our solitude the birth of rebellion and its spread, to master the sense of Hoa Hao and keep the Cao Dai straight, to labor over the fine meanings of treaties and their clauses, to probe statistics for their secrets and their prophecies, to lampoon certain brown-robed figures and commiserate with others. We Americans debate and debate, always sucked again into that Southeast Asian vortex. What does Ho Chi Minh want exactly? Is Le Duan stronger than Vo Nguyen Giap or Pham Van Dong? What factions struggle within the NLF? Is Mao alive or dying or dead? What new shapes will this confetti of statistics, names, and dates take on in the future? What will *Asia* do? Meanwhile, in stunning contrast to this problem for an undiscovered calculus, America stands all but aloof in the serene simplicity of her purpose, as if the only hard part of her Vietnam policy were the purely technical chore of applying, in Asia's turbulence, her elemental desire for justice. Even the critics do not tamper much with the idea that justice is what America wants. Instead, good, learned men bend themselves over and again to one more perusal of the Vietnamese puzzle, the better to prove to someone that we have or have not been mistaken in our choice of Vietnamese beneficiaries.

This is wrong. The subject matter of a serious political analysis of Vietnam is America. What is it that the good American Cold Warrior must see behind his propaganda? What persuades him to deceive other Americans? Why does Secretary Rusk, who is no dope, "keep on saying this"?

This can be answered. We need only review the past two decades, guided in that review by the most commonplace assumptions of Cold War anticommunism, America's leading political ideology.

Think of 1945. Two enemies faced each other across a devastated Europe. Their wartime alliance had perhaps done as much to deepen as to dissipate their long-standing and apparently well-founded mutual distrust.

The United States saw Soviet Communism as threatening Europe with another long revolutionary convulsion. The war had broken main-beam social institutions almost everywhere. In East Europe, Italy, Greece, Turkey, Yugoslavia, and France there were powerful figures who would surely not be satisfied with defeat of the Axis and return to the prewar social order. They wanted social change. At the center of Europe's desperation, trying, it seemed, to deepen it and use it, was the Communist party, a centralized international bureaucracy whose European elements were under Moscow's discipline. America had spilled her blood and treasure throughout both Europe and Asia to preserve certain values and institutions and an idea of society that simply were not idle matters with her. She wins these simultaneous wars only to see those values threatened again, perhaps more menacingly by Stalin in 1945 than by Hitler in 1940.

For her part, the exhausted Soviet Union also found herself still threatened. Condemned by the West from the earliest years of her revolution, the victim of a massive Western military intervention which only stretched out and deepened the horrors of her civil war, ostracized throughout the twenties and thirties from the political and economic affairs of Europe, convinced that she had been offered up sacrificially to the Wehrmacht through Chamberlain's appeasement policy, battered internally for four years by the brunt of Hitler's power and cheated of relief by Churchill's delaying of the second front, her principal cities smoking and her farmlands wasted, her industry crippled from war and her people dazed and numb with suffering, as many as 20 million of them killed and five times that number degraded by the Nazi occupation, she looked out over that Germany whose invasion she had so expensively repulsed only to see another enemy, this one more powerful than the first.

And the rumor ran through Europe, even as Nazi Germany was about to fall, that those five years of war would prove to have been mere prelude to that more fundamental, fateful, and "historical" of wars, the one that must be fought to make the whole world safe at last for democratic capitalism. In spite of the comradeship of the Grand Alliance, who did not know what was coming?

But the Russian-American war was not fought. It was transfigured. Stalin's seizures within East Europe to build a buffer zone against aggression from a rebuilt Germany would be allowed, even legitimated in state documents—at least for awhile. The West would emplace its own iron across the curtain and bide its time, convinced, in Franz Borkenau's words, that "the inner law of the Stalinist terror [would] drive Stalin's Russia . . . to total catastrophe not only for the terroristic regime, but also for the nation ruled by it. . . ."[7] Over the next decade, the democratic West watched horrified as East Germany and Poland and Hungary stood up only to be crushed. And Russia's horror must have been at least as great as she watched the New Germany come alive with steel and guns, the calculated assembly on her political frontiers of a totally encircling military alliance, and the growing influence in her enemy's camp of the very boldest advocates of "rollback" and "liberation."

On both sides of the frontier, even the most disinterested and innocent learned how to live on alert. The war that did not take place became a way of life.

By about 1950, the territorial lines of the European Cold War had been fitfully agreed upon by the two master powers.

George F. Kennan's famous "X" article of 1947 had laid the basis for a tenable Western diplomacy: Communism was not fascism; it did not assert the inevitability of nationalistic conflict, but rather the inevitability of self-caused capitalist decay; hence, it did not consider itself to be committed to a timetable for conquest; it need merely allow time and economic logic to do their work; it was patient. So the capitalist West might be patient, too, since the Marxists were wrong. Capitalism could very well take care of itself. No preventive war was needed. It was only important to remain vigilant and disallow recklessness and opportunism, to push back where the Russians pushed out and so hold the line until the communist nonsense should finally disprove itself. Certain key duets were sung in certain graveyards: In April of 1947, the Truman Doctrine passed sentence on the Greek left, and in May, the Hungarian right paid the piper; in early 1948, the Marshall Plan tempted Czechoslovakia from one orbit to another, and the Red coup of February followed like a reflex. And from crisis to crisis, the wary understandings of our own day were taking shape, each side at least pretending to remain confident of final victory, convinced that the other side's evil blinded it to the lessons of history, the laws of economics, the facts of human nature, and the wave of the future.

But at some point it was possible to say that the metabolism of the European Cold War had changed. It is hard to fix a date for what is not an event but a process, but perhaps 1962 is in some rough sense a watershed. In that year the Soviets accepted what at least seemed to be the humiliation of the Cuban missile showdown, America accepted on some perhaps conditional terms the permanence of the Cuban revolution, and both sides together were about to produce the limited nuclear test-ban treaty. It was in that year that an East-West strategic power balance became undeniable, and that the Chinese launched their all-out ideological attack on the Soviet Union.

Today, we are the often bewildered witnesses of a Soviet foreign policy that can tolerate with little apparent anguish our nuclearizing of West Germany, our mounting violence in Vietnam and our Dominican theft; and of an American foreign policy, equally bizarre by Cold War standards, that can applaud the Soviets for their diplomatic success at Tashkent, that can call openly in a wartime State of the Union message for more trade with the European Red bloc (even offering these countries most-favored-nation treatment), that can even be caught casting furtive glances at the Soviet Union as a possible mediator of a Vietnam settlement, and that meanwhile says nothing at all when this same Soviet Union undertakes the arming of our North Vietnamese enemy, makes the most energetic and effective diplomatic incursions on our Asiatic influence sphere, and promises at the Tri-Continental Conference in Havana to supply arms to Latin American revolutionaries.

All this is evidently quite all right with us. Our anger is now reserved for China—the same China which, compared with Russia, does nearly nothing for the Vietnamese but make speeches, has not a single foot soldier, base, or port in foreign lands, and which poses no military threat to the United States whatsoever.

With the Soviet Union, we have gone from confrontation to *détente*. The relationship is no longer defined by its anger and uncertainties. Its bitterness has lost the old edge, become blunted by the mundane securities of daily usage. Direct military collision is feared and avoided equally by both sides, crises are referred to hot lines instead of war rooms, and one sometimes wonders if there is not something still springier in the air: a slow convergence of political aims. The European Cold War no longer finds Russians and Americans peering at each other through gunsights. Instead, we have had the experience of virtually integrated aid programs in Afghanistan and India. We are in open solidarity on the vexatious Kashmir question—and behind it, perhaps in essential agreement on the China question. We congratulate one another routinely on our superscientific exploits in the allegedly nonpolitical vicinity of the moon. In the Soviet Union, the Great Capitalist Collapse is no longer anticipated daily: Eugene Varga's heresies of the middle forties have quietly become the orthodoxies of the middle sixties. Over here, our own political *cognoscenti* have evidently received a new signal, for we have some signs that an Advanced Propaganda is abroad. We are permitted to think that Brezhnev and Kosygin are skilled bureaucratic technicians, a breed apart from the devils of only yesterday. We are told how one Professor Libermann, in the name of the profit motive, has bearded the Marxist economists in their den.[8] And C. L. Sulzberger of *The New York Times*—a privileged source of information—has wondered if the explicit Soviet-American animosity has not become only a façade for a more fundamental implicit alliance.[9]

A substitute for war has evidently been found. Most often, to be sure, with a devious motion, power nevertheless moved to understand itself in distinctively new ways, moved to accept in new ways the existence of other power. This was not a mere renovation of nineteenth-century sphere-of-influence politics whose aim was dominance. The aim now was thought of as "conflict management." The demands of power slowly lost their nearly metaphysical status. Positions became negotiable, attitudes mutable, antagonisms conditional instead of absolute. Politics is detheologized in our time; it becomes secular and pragmatic.

The fact that the seemingly predestined war did not take place is perhaps what now beguiles us. How did we manage to come through? By what luck or wisdom was the inevitable reduced to the problematic? The problematic to the improbable? Above all, can we capture the secrets of this alchemy that changed graves into bombshelters and bombshelters into houses?

The political intuitions produced in our statesmen by twenty years of European Cold War can no doubt be made explicit in a number of different ways; it is not as if there is one definitive exposition. But we can proceed from the broadly held assumption that the mutually qualifying aims of American policy are the avoidance of war and the creation of a stable global society in which liberal values will predominate. To the extent that pursuit of these aims is steadily less obstructed in the present European *détente*, one can generalize our experience there in terms of a conflict-management theory which consists of four very basic propositions:

First, each side must commit itself to the view that global war is an unsatisfactory means of securing global objectives, since what such a war might win is under all conditions drastically less than what it will most certainly lose.* This commitment *must* be established. But unwise nations may not

* For example, Secretary McNamara's words: "Now people realize what hardly anybody realized five years ago—*that it's impossible to win an all-out nuclear exchange.* Once you realize this, you arrive at certain rational conclusions." (Quoted in Stewart Alsop, "His Business is War," *Saturday Evening Post,* May 21, 1966, p. 30.)

understand that. So it sometimes becomes essential for the wise nations to produce that commitment among the unwise. The wise do this by producing military power, and by so exhibiting that power before the eyes of the unwise that they cannot possibly misconstrue the message: You will pay badly for any foolishness. Power plus the credibility of its use equals deterrence, which makes all nations pacifists and creates time and room for diplomatic maneuver. The Strategic Air Command was not trying to be ironical when it made its motto "Peace is our profession."

Second, a global truce line must be unambiguously drawn. The establishing and maintenance of this line are top-priority matters. Under most conditions, in fact, no objective is more important than its protection. One must be prepared even to go to war to keep it intact. The other side must understand that. (The two Cuban crises may mean that in some geopolitical settings, a position on one's own side of the line can be allowed to decay, but it will still remain forbidden territory to the major opposition power.)

Third, it is through the process of defining and securing the truce line that the *rival powers build up a store of information about each other, develop and habituate themselves to a modus vivendi, and begin to create a communication system* —initially, of course, irregular, informal, and unreliable— which with time grows more trustworthy, broader, and more secure. Most important perhaps during this phase is what passes unspoken between the two sides, the quiet unadvertised awareness that this experience of adversity is shared, that what frightens one diplomat's nation frightens another's. This experience gradually builds up a fulcrum for a new balance of trust. We begin to know this enemy of ours. We begin to learn how to dance with him. We begin to trust him not to expect too much. In his actions, we recognize our motives. We grow sensitive to his special internal problems and even begin to have favorites within his house. We see him return occasionally to the temple of his nation's myths and enact there for the benefit of the unsuspecting masses— and those narrow-eyed ascetics, the generals—the eternal drama of his patriotism, heroism, tribal loyalty. We hear harsh words; our names are implicated; certain threats and accusations begin to have a seasonal fashion; but we understand: He is protecting his budget, vying for power, neutralizing an opponent. We are all men of the same world.

Finally, the dividend of this patience is that the common interests so necessary to a more productive relationship will have had time to incubate. This is the crux of the distinctively *liberal* understanding of power politics. There is an underlying faith that men will be able to work together usefully in the world if they can only escape the shibboleths of man's past. There has to be a time, then, when history stops insistently repeating them. There must be a stillness among us. If history is the interruption of war by truces, or if it is the continual reconfiguration of boundaries and the power clusters they stand for, then the Cold War is a time in which history does not take place, a dictated twilight in which movement is restrained, a cease-fire and stand-fast, a suspension of those forces that kept the wheel in its sorry motion. Over and over again these twenty years, opportunities appeared which tempted both sides to break the unnatural charm. On both sides, of course, there are those who live in a state of perpetual, wanton surrender to this temptation; there are still others who weaken when the strains are great; but on balance the anchor men on both sides resisted and restrained them. And because of that, there begins to be a bit of hope.

This is not a bad vision, this bit of hope. Maybe it is even a bit more of hope than we deserve. But, one way or another, the drift of Soviet-American relations since World War II—at least, one may so imagine—suggests a way in which the vision might be realized everywhere: Make up your minds to have no big war; draw clearly in the world's good honest dirt a line which you will neither violate nor see violated; in the joint superintending of that line, learn a few things about one another, stop dreaming apocalyptic dreams, stop evangelizing the millennium, face the fact that the future is no nation's private property—and so make peace.

Look now at Asia in this wisdom's light.

Red China and America glower at one another across the Pacific—rather, across the Formosa Strait, the Yellow Sea, the Sea of Japan. We are enemies, no question about it. There even seems to be something familiar in the situation. As we had cooperated with the other Western democracies in attempting to reverse the Russian Revolution, so we had tried (but even harder) to reverse the Chinese Revolution. As we had interrupted our quarantine of Russia to make common cause against Nazi Germany, so we had tried to combine the Chinese Communist and Nationalist armies for common cause against fascist Japan. As our chief European enemy became in defeat our chief friend, and our chief wartime friend became in victory our major foe, so with Japan and China in the Pacific. Frustrated again in our second attempt at a major counterrevolution and nursing an ugly shame for having failed, we confronted in the Korean War years a question quite like the European question of 1946: Shall we annihilate Red China? Or shall we have an Asian Cold War too?

For a while, there was a political half-light in the world. The peak of the China debate coincided with a vindictive pietism about the Free World in the State Department and a militant anticommunism in Congress. Dissent was heresy. Reputations were burnt in a long fainting national exorcism whose recrudescence seems to remain a permanent possibility with us. But we finally found ourselves in possession of a Pacific Cold War. By 1954, we were copying our European policy in Asia, treaty for treaty, bastion for bastion. China was just another Russia and would have to be dealt with in the same way. The Asian West Europe was, of course, fragmented badly, scattered all over the Pacific from Japan to New Zealand and stretching out along the continent's edge from Korea to West Pakistan. We stared perplexed for a while at this geopolitical Rorschach test, but gradually we found its Gestalt, discerned its pattern and meaning.

The first principle of the European wisdom was applied: We shall seek no war with China, the primary reason being (as with Russia?) that her army was too big, her land too vast. To prove that we meant what we said, General MacArthur was retired, and the Korean War was cautiously made to disappear. The second principle now had to be established: The truce line had to be fixed. We hold here, they there. No violence must be done to this line; it is the only hope we have that Chinese people decades from now can at last clasp hands with American people. Nor does this line represent an unfairly one-sided division. Korea remains only divided. Chiang Kai-shek remains present but pent up. We wring our hands for the rich ruling clergy of Tibet, but make no move to intervene: Tibet becomes the Asian Hungary. Peking can trust us to make no sudden moves against the northern half of Vietnam. Let the socialist government there make what it can of its opportunities. But let there be no incursions on this border. Let Cambodia "lean to one side" in her neutralism; but let there be no disturbances in Thailand. This line must hold. Accept this line, Red China, and we can begin to talk of other matters—of doctors and reporters exchanged, of your participation in disarmament talks, of a somewhat freer economic arrangement with our industrial protégés in Japan, even of your membership in the United Nations. Of course, there will be difficulties. But with a little patience and skill, there might easily be an Asian *détente* too. The unnegotiable condition of every prospect, however, is that the line of truce in the Asian Cold War must not be broken. Until that fact is accepted, there is little use in talking about the future.

The Cold Warrior who sees Asian affairs in this way might be forgiven his exasperation with both China and the American peace movement. He does not need to be reminded of the carnage in Vietnam. Many of his kind have seen it much closer up than the unblooded peaceniks ever will. He is, after all, a man, this Cold War dialectician; he has sons and daughters and he prefers life to death; no one has any right to assume that he is less anguished than the next man by the sight of scorched earth, burnt flesh, and torture. From our observation post outside the Establishment, where we suppose for some reason that the visibility is better, we critics inform him that his war is not helping the Vietnamese. If he were not gagged by the official pretense that it is, maybe he would reply to us: "Of course. I know that. Do you take me for an idiot?" We inform him that his bombing raids in the countryside and whorehouse abandon in the cities are laying that nation waste, and that this physical and cultural slaughter, by a familiar psychology, is only making more Vietnamese turn Communist. Maybe he wants to say: "What could be more obvious? I struggle with this problem day and night. But why can't you see," he might say to us critics, "that Red China has to yield to the partitioning of Vietnam? Of course that's hard for many Vietnamese to take. But is it really more than history demanded of the Germans, whose society was, after all, mature and a million times more integrated than Vietnam's? And don't we have a perfect precedent in Korea? This tiny sliver of a country that has been partitioned for most of its life—at one time into three parts by the French and before that into hundreds of parts by its own warlords—is its present temporary partition really so high a price to pay, if in return for what we purchase stability in Asia? And if the price of refusing partition is the undermining of that truce line upon which we build all our hopes for an Oriental reconciliation? Be realistic," he says to us idealists; "This is not a perfect world by any measure, and it just so happens that history is all against us. We are doing everything we know how to do to change man's fate by making peace *practical.* We do this not only in the teeth of Red China and these scandalously persistent Vietnamese guerrillas, but here at home we must also fend off you soft-heads who want an impossible peace and those hard-heads yonder who want an unthinkable war."

The point has been made by Zbigniew Brzezinski, director of the Research Institute on Communist Affairs at Columbia University, consultant to the State Department on policy planning, and one of the foremost of our Cold War scholars:

> The long road to international morality leads through the creation of international order, and international order necessitates, first of all, the creation of international stability. We can only create international stability if all the major powers in the world accept the principle that in the nuclear age no side can change the political *status quo* through the use of force and through direct challenge to another side. We restrained ourselves from doing that in Hungary, in spite of our policy of liberation. The Soviets learned that lesson more painfully in Cuba. That lesson is still to be learned in many parts of the world, but I believe that the cause of peace, the cause of global reconciliation, the cause of international adjustment, requires, first, the creation of stability, and stability in Asia will not be achieved by American disengagement or Chinese expansion.[10]

Some of us object: You have not proved that this Vietnam war is China's fault. Far from it. Even now, your gravest charge concerns a few aircraft flying from Hanoi and a few thousand technicians who only repair American-bombed roads and railroads at the Yunnan border. This war in Vietnam is at bottom a revolution, we say, and it came not from China's export commisariat, but from the torpid colonial feudalism of that society. No one at all sensitive to the history of Vietnam could ever question this.

But for such an argument, there may now be a quite intriguing answer.

SHERIDAN SQUARE
PAPERBACK CORNER
10 SHERIDAN SQ. N.Y.C.

-5 MAY 70

$001.45 —
$001.95 —
$000.21 —

MDS MDS MDS

$003.61 B TOTL

It is important to be clear first about what the answer would *not* be. It would *not* be that China is directly at fault for this war; *not* that Hanoi is acting on Peking's orders; *not* that Hanoi commanded and is directing the performance of a puppet in the south; *not* that the NLF, instead of being revolutionary, is only a new-fashioned invasion force.

On the first point, we have the oblique evidence of Secretary Rusk's repeated word that China, though her words infuriate, has acted most "conservatively" and with great "restraint." Maxwell Taylor has been even more expilicit about the alleged master-puppet relationship between China and North Vietnam. "To Hanoi," he told the New York Rotarians early in 1966, "China is the traditional, distrusted enemy."[11] This must mean he is at least skeptical about the often insinuated, never proved surrogate theory, and when Taylor is skeptical others must be hardened nonbelievers. The skepticism extends to that other link as well, the one which the commoner wisdom sees between Hanoi and the southern rebels. During the "peace offensive" of the 1965–66 holiday season, *The New York Times*' highly respected Max Frankel reported from Washington:

Even more perplexing to officials here is their inability to judge the degree of Hanoi's influence over the Vietcong. They have judged that influence to be considerable in military terms, but they do not know whether North Vietnam could negotiate an end to hostilities even if they wanted to.[12]

And on the same point, Bernard B. Fall:

One does not fight for eight long years, under the crushing weight of American armor, napalm, jet bombers and, finally, vomiting gases, for the sheer joy of handing over whatever one fights for to some bureaucrat in Hanoi, merely on the say-so of a faraway party apparatus. . . . There are some doubts among many observers as to whether the apparent intransigence of Hanoi does not in reality hide its relative inability to "deliver" the NLF bound hand and foot at a problematical conference table. Having sold out the guerrilla movement twice before, in 1954 and 1956, it may find the task difficult, if not altogether impossible.[13]

The security of the official invasion-from-the-north propaganda line requires official discretion on the point, but slips occur. Piece these together, and it grows clear that the War Room may very well know what the picket line knows: We face revolution, not invasion. In February 1966, for example, Ambassador Lodge said, "For years now in Southeast Asia, the only people who have been doing anything about the little man at the grassroots—to lift him up—have been the Communists."[14] But well before that, General Edward Lansdale, our ace counterinsurgent and one of the key figures on our Vietnam team, had published a most revealing essay in the establishmentarian *Foreign Affairs*, issue of October 1964. "The Communists have let loose a revolutionary idea in Viet-Nam," he wrote. "It will not die by being ignored, bombed, or smothered by us. Ideas do not die in such ways." All Lansdale seemed to have against the Communists who let this revolution loose, in fact, is that they are bound to betray it: "The tragedy of Viet-Nam's revolutionary war for independence was that her 'Benedict Arnold' was successful." He is, of course, thinking of Ho Chi Minh, the revolutionary senior of Mao Tse-tung. If Ho is Benedict Arnold—a strange idea—then who is George Washington? We may have been tempted to speculate about a certain Texan, but Lansdale punctured the hope: "The Vietnamese need a cause and we have not supplied it." The surest-fire official profundity about this war is that it is "political" and not military—a deep insight which was explained to us year after year while the troop build-up accelerated and the war cargo grew into millions of tons and our "social reform" programs persisted in their efforts to enrich the rich, chattelize the poor, and modernize South Vietnam's oligarchic feudalism.

The most arresting evidence on this matter is that we have convinced ourselves that we must field a rebel force of our own. To this end, some 42,000 "revolutionary cadres" are being trained by a CIA-advised advanced guard at Vung Tau, which, as bad luck would have it, happens to be the old French resort town of Cap St. Jacques. The idea was very well explained by one of the camp's directors, Captain Le Xuan Mai. He and his superiors, he said, had

> come to realize that the people of Viet-Nam are sold on revolution. In a backward country like Viet-Nam, where the people have had nothing but misery and injustice, the people are prepared to listen to any promises of a better life. So they listen to the Communists. They've had no alternative. The goal of the cadres we are training here is just that—to fulfill the promises of the Communists that they are unwilling to carry out.[15]

The psychological dislocations this program creates must be enormous. These "revolutionary cadres" of ours wear black pajamas, just like the NLF; are practiced in group self-criticism sessions, just like the NLF; taught how to set up village governments, just like the NLF; and through these means are expected to "capture the revolution" from the NLF leadership. Will they also assassinate the hated Saigon-appointed village chiefs, just like the NLF? Will they drive off the big landowners and distribute their land to the tillers, just like the NLF? For free, just like the NLF? Will they also say "Vietnam for the Vietnamese," just like the NLF, and fight the new tall palefaces to prove they mean it? Then who is the enemy? Who is the friend? Whose black pajamas is this Captain Mai really wearing?*

Such puzzles aside, we may at least have found a different picture of Washington's beliefs about the war. It may not really be the inside view, then, that Comrade Mao made a secret decision years ago and passed it through the mountain gates of Yunnan Province into the hands of Ho Chi Minh, who sent it on south to a hidden headquarters deep in Nam-Bo, where the old Vietminh guns were hanging fire for the high sign.

The answer might simply be: So what?

Or it might be that *this does not matter*! American policies cannot be asked to react to speculations about chain-of-command structures; they must react to *events*. And the very plain fact of the matter is this: If the Chinese *did* control Hanoi, and through Hanoi the National Liberation Front, *then the situation in Vietnam would look exactly as it does.* Whether we confront in Vietnam a replica or an extension of the Chinese will, whether this revolution is an intentional or accidental copy of China's policy or the thing in itself, makes absolutely no difference at all. China is the threat. The appearance of her spirit within the forbidden zone, on the wrong side of the global line of truce, at whatever time and through

* After the above was written, it developed that his black pajamas were his own. Described by Saigon as a "third-force nationalist," Mai was dumped and Saigon took the Vung Tau project out of the CIA's hands. The explanation was that Mai was insufficiently loyal and too quick to accuse the central government of corruption and indifference to the people. Where will Mai be discovered next?

whatever agency, must be denied. Thus, to speak of the historical "origins" of the war is politically frivolous. In substance, in aspiration, and in effect, Chinese-like or plain, straight Chinese, this war remains indistinguishable from the war the Chinese want. The consequence is that it must be treated as though it *were* a Chinese war.

This leads us to the quite unexpected but nevertheless entirely reasonable complaint that even if China does *not* control Hanoi and the NLF, *it nevertheless remains true that she should be controlling them.* The politics of Cold War peacekeeping makes it essential for major powers to control the events within their spheres of influence. For a major state not to have control over minor confederate states is inexcusable. Without that control, the means through which conflict can be managed no longer exist, and statesmen are faced with an unpredictable environment. Less control means less stability and hence greater danger for everyone; less certainty about the perceptions and inclinations of the other side forces diplomacy to be more guarded and restrictive and edgy. For all its old bitterness about West Germany, for example, the Soviet Union would no doubt be horrified to discover an East German plot to spring an invasion over the Wall, or even a few good blows of sabotage beneath it. And the same would hold for us: Park will very well stay put in South Korea; Chiang will grumble his bellyful in Taipeh but he shall go no further. We guarantee this. China must learn to make similar guarantees. It thus becomes essential, *in the name of peace*, for China to commit the expansionist crime of which she stands accused. And the American refusal to accept the NLF as the responsible agent in this war begins to seem not so obtuse at all; it appears instead to be an almost exquisite diplomatic brilliancy, for this refusal is perhaps a concealed attempt to extend a *responsible Chinese authority* into North Vietnam and over the Communist parties to the south.

Surely this sounds too Machiavellian. But on January 30, 1966, in what was described as a "major" foreign policy speech, George Ball, then Under Secretary of State, said:

> A main focus of the [East-West] struggle has shifted recently from Europe to Asia because the Soviet Union, having grown powerful, has begun to have a stake in the *status quo*. The purpose of the

forcible containment of Communist China is to induce a similar change in its outlook. . . . This is the issue in Viet-Nam. This is what we are fighting for. This is why we are there.[16]

One would not fight Vietnamese rebels in order to "induce a change" in China's outlook unless one believed either (*a*) that China controlled those rebels, or (*b*) that China, whether she controls them or not, bears the ultimate responsibility for their behavior. We have already noted that Washington probably rules out the first premise. That leaves us with the second. To inform China that she is responsible for these Vietnamese events is quite openly to demand of China that she take control over those who make them. That is, our Vietnam policy warns China that she must expand her influence, accept the discipline of the Cold War, and impose that discipline on her Vietnamese friends.

But the war continues. Either China has not got the message, has got it but chooses to ignore it, or has got it but can do nothing about it. These uncertainties invite us to derive a final speculation: that an underlying aim of American policy may in fact be to stimulate the penetration into Southeast Asia of *Soviet* influence. China, the reasoning may go, has been given chance after chance to prove herself a realistic and responsible world power—clue after clue whose meaning she is either too inexperienced to understand or too insane to accept. Having proved herself ineducable, having flunked the grammar of modern power politics, she may not be trusted. Russia, that old and trusty scholar who knows all the rules, must be brought in to rescue the increasingly grave situation.

Consider the 1965 Kashmir affair in this light. Both belligerents in an old-fashioned border dispute were warring upon one another with arms of American manufacture and supply. Pakistan is a formal military ally of ours. India is a major long-term recipient of American military and economic aid. Both Pakistan and India are Commonwealth states. The natural mediator of a dispute between them would be the United States; if not the United States, then England; if not England, then the United Nations. But a Russian makes the Kashmir peace in a conference held at Tashkent, in Soviet Asia. Perhaps the United States was afraid of the consequences of bungling a mediation, and so preferred that another take the office. Perhaps Britain also considered the affair too delicate, even unresolvable. Perhaps the UN machinery was too cumbersome for such a crisis. But these explanations do not explain the extent to which the United States not only accepted, but loudly applauded the Soviet diplomacy. We quite likely have our own good reasons for wanting Russia's prestige to rise in Asia. It is not wild to conjecture that this Russia whom we once accused of waging the Indochina war as part of the plot to take over China*—this very same Russia that makes North Vietnam's skies more hazardous for our pilots—is quietly invited to mediate. "Recently," said Secretary Rusk in his March 1966 China statement, "a leading official of a Communist state said to me that the most serious problem in the world today is how to get Peking to move to a policy of 'peaceful co-existence.' "[17]

It is easy to picture that conversation between two gentlemen adversaries, each no doubt remotely aware that an accident of birthplace gave them both their politics and mission, that in a very human sense they are interchangeable. One overhears their intimate conversation from a distance that might as well be galactic, but everything about it seems to shine with clarity: the slow, measured click of heels on marble, the hand of one at the other's elbow, their heads slightly inclined together, while between them flows the wisdom that all the categories of men really want the same thing—all rich men and all poor men, all strong and all weak. I see the same maturity in each face, identical frowns of concern. I heave a sigh of relief. I also shudder.

We explore one level of the Cold Warrior's Vietnam story and discover a stronger box within the propaganda box. Uncritically, we accept the most elemental Western assumptions about the origin and progress of the Cold War. Manipulating by means of this ideology the main political features of the war for South Vietnam, we find ourselves in the possession of a conflict which no longer seems so senselessly holy. The war may now seem to be merely practical.

* For example, Ambassador William C. Bullitt was arguing in late 1947 that any promises Ho Chi Minh made "would be broken as soon as he should receive orders from Moscow to break them. . . ." Ho's movement was designed to "add another finger to the hand that Stalin is closing around China." Twenty years later, the hand is as good as new; it only belongs to a different arm. Substitute Peking for Moscow, Mao for Stalin, and Southeast Asia for China, and we have a contemporary document.

If the Cold War is really what most Americans consider it to be, then the Cold War is necessary. If it is necessary, then it may very well be necessary for America to maintain her hold over South Vietnam.

So we have to reach inside our Cold War truths to see if they do not conceal some other truths. We have to be very naive and ask: What is this Cold War all about? And is it really necessary?

III

Open Doors, Falling Dominoes

Westward the course of empire takes its way; . . . Time's noblest offspring is the last.
—BISHOP BERKELEY

THE COLD WAR is a section of history made coherent by an ideological framework of implicit and explicit beliefs about history and values in terms of which events are infused with form and intelligibility.

The Cold Warrior's story of the preceding chapter pivoted on one very basic assumption: that the United States is not to blame for the current East–West encounter. This is probably the central and most sustained single assumption of America's Cold War anticommunism. From the Truman Doctrine to the Vietnam war, from the Marshall Plan to the Alliance for Progress, our policies have paid homage to that assumption and derived their legitimacy from it.

This assumption of innocence is held in place by two cooperating beliefs about recent history. The first is that Stalin started the Cold War. The second is that the United States had nothing to gain from the Cold War and did nothing to provoke it. In the sections that follow in this chapter, I want to elaborate two connected heresies: first, the heresy that both these beliefs are false; second, the heresy that our Cold War foreign policy of containment is most basically a response to the fact that non-Western political cultures are for the first time threatening to contain *us*, to resist or restrict that long-term expansionary onslaught of the West upon the East which is the overarching theme of modern history.

The Russian–American Encounter

Our survey can be brief. It is behind us, this mercurial past, and apparently the main use of knowing something about it is to be put on guard against the common wisdom that takes United States–Soviet relations to have begun in the vicinity of 1945, and that holds the igniting act of the Cold War to have been Stalin's territorial seizures in eastern Europe. These seizures, the reabsorption of tsardom's Baltic states, a moment's nervousness about Iran and the Dardanelles, and the communization of China are the original crimes for which the Soviet Union is condemned as an imperialist aggressor. Because we suppose our foreign policy to have taken shape as a response to that threat, we believe our aims to have been defensive and our occasional violence provoked.

Expose this belief, in the first place, to a few elemental facts: Stalin's postwar European policy was framed neither in secret nor unilaterally; the zoning of central Europe was an obvious problem of the war and the peace; its solution was forged in quite ordinary ways by the Grand Alliance powers together; Russia could hardly have been expected to tie down for four savage years and then at immense human cost to defeat the large part of Hitler's power without winning a right to that frontier security that was a traditional Russian goal (not at all a "Communist" one). Above all, one simply has to grasp the fact—we happen to be stuck with it—that the between-wars behavior of the West had given the U.S.S.R. precious little evidence of good Western intentions. A quick review:

The Tsar fell in 1917, tsardom having decayed from within and World War I having pulverized its shell. Under Western pressure, the Social Democrat Kerensky government elected to continue Russia's part in the war despite the fact that her troops were being sent into battle with clubs in their hands. This decision and the decision to postpone convening of the Duma enflamed popular resentments and thus set the stage for the Bolshevik Revolution, a relatively bloodless palace coup. Lenin shortly concluded the Brest-Litovsk peace treaty with Germany. Under confused circumstances, a mass uprising of Czech legionnaires on their way from Russia to the still open Western front led finally to the formation of an anti-Soviet government at Omsk under the monarchist Admiral Aleksandr Kolchak. Six months after the European armistice, when the West could no longer pretend that its aim was to hold the Eastern front open, the massive Western intervention in behalf of the White counterrevolution was on full force. Kolchak received half a billion dollars worth of material support from Britain. By March 1919, the French, British, Italians, Romanians, Serbs, and Greeks had poured 850,000 counterrevolutionary troops into south Russia. From April 1920 to March 1921, the Poles were battling in the Ukraine to secure "the permanent weakening of Russia." In the Baltic, British commanders and tanks and American gasoline nearly made a success of the White campaign against the Soviet stronghold of Petrograd. In north Russia, a total of 5500 American and 37,000 British troops supported the White regime and, under War Minister Winston Churchill's direction, nearly linked up with Kolchak's army. Throughout this time, the Allied Supreme War Council's naval blockade deprived the Red government of the use of all seaports.

When the five-front Western intervention succeeded only in rebuilding the Soviet army and guaranteeing that the Soviet government would be harshly totalitarian, Western opposition still did not end. It merely took up other instruments, the weapons of political quarantine and economic isolation, having quite early used its considerable economic resources to annihilate the Red Bela Kun government in Hungary.

This was Western practice during the crucial period in which the Russian Revolution was struggling to consolidate itself and begin the process, difficult under even the best of circumstances, of creating Soviet nationhood and modernizing the economy.

All of Europe was shaken by the Russian Revolution; Germany in particular teetered from time to time like an uncertain domino until the arch anticommunist came to power in January 1933. But Western relief soon became anxiety as it appeared that there was more to this Hitler than a fire in the Reichstag. October 1933: Germany follows Japan out of the League of Nations, munition plants already roaring. Almost a year later: The League accepts a new member, the U.S.S.R. (Said Sumner Welles: "When the Soviet Union entered the League, even the most obstinate were soon forced to admit that it was the only major power which seemed to take the League seriously."[1]) A month afterward: French Minister of Foreign Affairs Jean Louis Barthou, a strong and rather lonely proponent of collective security, is assassinated in Marseilles. March 1935: Germany decrees universal military conscription, violating both the Treaty of Versailles and the Locarno Treaty. In the League, Russia's Commissar for Foreign Affairs Maxim Litvinov argues for prompt collective-security arrangements. London's answer is a naval treaty with Hitler which allows Germany to build a submarine fleet the size of Britain's. Less than a year later, Ethiopia falls to Mussolini. March 1936: Hitler occupies and remilitarizes the Rhineland. Litvinov—a sad figure—again begs for League action. He is supported by Poland, Czechoslovakia, Yugoslavia, and Roumania (which is perhaps ironic). Britain votes No. It is explained in the West that Hitler's "Real Aim," a good one, is to crush communism. July 1936: The slow assassination of Republican Spain commences. The democracies impose arms embargoes on both sides equally and practice "nonintervention" in this "civil war" fought with German warplanes and 100,000 Italian troops, leaving it to Stalin to send the Loyalists that meager, tardy, and pernicious "aid" and "advice" that may have hurt their cause as much as the "neutrality" of the democracies.

The prevalent theory was that Germany's *Lebensraum* lay only in the east. March 1938: Hitler storms Austria, Neville Chamberlain having made his government's position clear enough the month before when he said, "We must not try to delude small and weak nations into thinking that they will be protected by the League against aggression."[2] In May 1938 something new happens: President Eduard Beneš orders partial mobilization of Czech troops against the Nazi buildup at her borders. Hitler retreats! The democracies proceed to reproach Beneš for his rashness. His mistake is corrected by those more mature than he the following September at Munich, where certain famous deals are made. The Czechs, allowed to hear their fate, protest; Chamberlain yawns.

Stalin had been convinced by this time that Russia's only hope for survival lay not in collective security with the West, but in some time-gaining accommodation with Hitler. And the same five years had convinced many in East Europe that the West was not its ally: As D. F. Fleming suggests, it was perhaps not at Yalta but Munich that postwar Europe was partitioned.[3]

Comes the war. A generous America, soon drawn into the fight, mounted a powerful production offensive and developed plans for opening a Western front against Hitler by late 1942 or in the spring of 1943. The Russians, whom British intelligence had predicted would collapse within six weeks of Hitler's attack, were finally taking on the full force of German power. They somehow survived the terrible victory of the battle of Stalingrad.

Where was the promised relief of the second front in France? Thanks to Churchill, the Allies substituted the war for North Africa, which neither Roosevelt nor Stimson and Marshall found desirable. There followed the long bloody struggle up the Italian peninsula, the military wisdom of which was also dubious. Churchill, thinking increasingly of the political configuration of postwar Europe, argued for an attack on the "soft underbelly" of the Continent. If successful, such a strategy would emplace Western armies in East Europe, closing off the increasing likelihood of a Red Army drive across the Carpathian Mountains in the Balkans, maybe even across the Danube. Maybe beyond. The American General Staff judged that such a strategy was militarily wrong. But up to the last moment before the invasion of France in June 1944, more than two years after the Western front was to have been opened, Churchill was still arguing for a Turkish campaign.

Against this backdrop, what shall we make of Stalin's postwar foreign policy in Europe?

Recall that the foreign policies of nation-states are essentially continuations of their domestic policies. Recall that the Leninist theory of economic development had consistently led the U.S.S.R. toward a semiautarkic domestic policy and hence toward a semi-isolationist foreign policy.* At Brest-Litovsk, Lenin had surrendered a third of Russia's crop area, more than half her industrial strength, and 62 million

* The New Economic Policy (NEP) of 1921 was not a reversal of this commitment to self-sufficiency. To be sure, NEP recognized the importance of the internal "private capital sector" (which by 1924 was accounting for 40 percent of domestic trade) and externally allowed for concessions to foreign capitalists. But the British-French assumption that NEP was a thermidorean return to capitalist normality was punctured by Bolshevik rejection of their plan for investment in Russia, and again punctured by the 1922 Treaty of Rapallo in which Germany implied recognition of the Bolshevik nationalizations.[4]

A similar autarkic isolationism is evidently practiced by revolutionary China, whatever the cant about "Chinese Communist expansionism." Ironically, Western hostility toward both revolution-

people in order to be let alone by Germany,[5] and the U.S.S.R.'s entry into the League in 1934 was less the onset of a new positive internationalism than a new response to the threat Hitler posed to Russian solitude.

At the end of World War II, Russia's need for economic development was greater than ever. To a continuing need to modernize and develop, Soviet planners now had to add the need for massive repair. But for the still struggling U.S.S.R., this need was now situated in a wholly new political environment.

Germany's violence produced a number of radical changes in Europe. For one: All the old powers were severely reduced and the United States had expanded into a position of unchallenged political and economic ascendency. But abrupt as this change was, it was perhaps finally no more than an acceleration and a temporary overstatement of a process already well under way. What was wholly unique and much more profound was the compulsory appearance on the scene of international politics of that new world power, the "de-isolated" Soviet Union. It was Hitler's attempt upon her and Hitler's failure to make that attempt good which tore the U.S.S.R. out of her shell and forced her to play that major-power role for which she seems to have been so poorly prepared.

Consider that the one and only base of Stalin's international authority in the aftermath of the war was the Red Army, which flexed its muscles over a bombed-out urban and rural Soviet economy and a starving, demoralized, and disoriented people. This presents us with what is surely one of the major political anomalies in the modern history of the West. In a culture in which international political power traditionally flows from an advanced industrial base, we confront here

---

ary regimes expressed itself as a quarantine which in fact cooperated with and intensified their drives for self-sufficiency. Of course, this circle is really a wheel which turns in both directions: As the Soviet economy matured and Soviet planners gained confidence, the political doctrine of coexistence emerged, trade doors began to open wider, and the West slowly began to abandon its economic and political quarantine. Barring war, the same process—economic advance of the backward state, commercial reconciliation, political tolerance—will very likely determine the evolution of United States–China relationships, although a great many useless adventures will be enacted along the way, and a great lot of human blood will be unnecessarily shed.

the sudden appearance of a "major power" whose industrial base was immature in the first place and devastated in the second. It may be a revealing exaggeration to say that in 1945 the nation-state of the U.S.S.R. consisted of an army, nothing else. That army was Stalin's sole source of diplomatic strength. Industrially, agriculturally, socially, his nation—and it was very nearly not even a nation—was not to be compared with the Western states. It is perhaps by understanding the peculiar airiness of Soviet power in the immediate postwar period that we can make most sense of the eccentric turns that Soviet diplomacy takes—the flirtation with Eugene Varga's most un-Marxist ideas on living with a capitalist West (a kind of "right deviationism"), the rebuilding and installation to power of right-wing political parties in East Europe, the vacillating policy on reconstruction loans from the United States, the abandonment to their own devices (and worse) of Communist-led revolutionary and resistance movements in other European countries. The one development that seems to run most counter to the view that Stalin's power was exclusively military was the fairly rapid demobilization of the Red Army. But perhaps even this fact supports it: An army without an industrial base is not a proper army. Thus, it was an urgent Soviet necessity to reconstitute the Soviet labor force—and therefore to demobilize. At the same time, it was also a Soviet necessity (a traditional one, but much intensified by still vivid memories of Hitler) to maintain territorial security—and therefore not to demobilize.

It was these two connected and in important ways competing aims—internal repair and development and territorial security—that directed Stalin's foreign policy. It was the U.S.S.R.'s weakness vis-à-vis a united West that set the basic conditions under which he would have to pursue those aims. How was Stalin to get development capital, time, and political security?

We know that he wanted and at least half expected to get (it was discussed at Yalta) a massive development loan from the United States. At Potsdam he discovered that there would be no such loan. But this in itself was not crippling. There was another prospective source of major reconstruction capital—war reparations from Germany, which Stalin proposed to collect and distribute on a Four-Power basis (that is, without dividing Germany). The United States, however, opposed this, for a very good reason. Very early and very clearly, we had recognized our own future economic need for a rebuilt market place in Europe. We also understood that we would have to finance the rebuilding of that market place.[6] German reparations to Russia would thus have been financed by the United States, and the United States had no intention of financing the revolution. So a bargain was struck, in which each of the Allied powers would collect reparations from the particular zone which its army occupied. The following exchange at Potsdam in July 1945 is clear as to the political implications of this bargain:

MR. MOLOTOV: My understanding, Secretary Byrnes, is that you have in mind the proposal that each country should take reparations from its own zone. . . .

THE SECRETARY [BYRNES]: Yes. . . .

MR. MOLOTOV said, Would not the Secretary's suggestion mean that each country would have a free hand in their own zone and would act entirely independently of the others?

THE SECRETARY said that was true in substance.[7]

Stalin's subsequent exchange with Truman is no less clear:

PREMIER STALIN: . . . with regard to shares and foreign investments, perhaps the demarcation lines between the Soviet and Western zones of occupation should be taken as the dividing lines and everything west of that line would go to the Allies and everything east of that line to the Russians.

THE PRESIDENT [TRUMAN] inquired if he [Stalin] meant a line running from the Baltic to the Adriatic.

PREMIER STALIN replied in the affirmative.

[BRITISH FOREIGN SECRETARY] BEVIN said he agreed, and asked if Greece would belong to Britain.

PREMIER STALIN suggested that the Allies take Yugoslavia and Austria be divided into zones.

MR. BYRNES said he thought it was important to have a meeting of minds. Mr. Bevin's question was whether the Russians' claim was limited to the zone occupied by the Russian Army. To that he understood Mr. Stalin to say "yes." If that were so he was prepared to agree.

PREMIER STALIN replied in the affirmative.

THE PRESIDENT [TRUMAN] said that he agreed with the Soviet proposal.[8]

Thus, Russia would collect reparations from the poorer of the two halves of Europe; and the fiscal authority which this bargain conferred upon the Russian occupation government absolutely necessitated the concomitant political hegemony which Molotov must have envisaged when he used such phrases as "a free hand in its own zone" and "entirely independently of the others."

The American aims appear to have been twofold: first, to obstruct or delay the repair of the Russian economy by denying Ruhr Valley-based, American-financed German reparations to Russia; and second, as Byrnes was later to tell Congress, "the maintenance of the open door in the Balkans."[9] It seems now that these aims contradicted and defeated one another. Obstructing Russian reconstruction required that Russia be denied West German reparations. This ruled out Four-Power treatment of Germany, implicitly necessitated the partition of Europe, and thus foreclosed to the West its "free entry into the Danube Valley and Eastern Europe for the goods and capital of the Western countries."[10] On the other hand, Western failure to internationalize the development of the Danubian economy led to the reconstruction of the Soviet economy: It left Stalin with a free hand to manipulate East European resources in the service of Russian economic needs. Truman and Byrnes, who at Potsdam had learned of the Manhattan Project's success, were perhaps acting on the supposition that America's A-bomb monopoly would have a coercive political power (which it ultimately proved not to have), and that once coerced into opening the East European door, the Soviets would be incapable of countering the United States' immense industrial and economic authority. Without the Bomb—in Stimson's famous phrase, "rather obstentatiously on our hip"—our position on German reparations to Russia might have been more accommodating. Accommodation on that point might have led to an East European door at least less conclusively bolted shut. But our bargain-from-strength diplomacy seems to have force-fed Stalin his ever ready distrust—and the Cold War in Europe was irreversibily on. Stalin was not simply offered East Europe; it was thrust upon him. This is not to say that he did not want it. One can also want what one is forced to take, and there is an irreducible possibility that Stalin really did see himself as an empire-maker in the long, mixed tradition of Caesar, Prince Henry the Navigator, Isabella of Spain, the Virgin Queen, and Napoleon. But let someone try to prove it. To argue that Stalin was bent on conquest and so maneuvered for the hegemony in East Europe that Russia finally acquired is to substitute for a very rich reality a myth as troublesome as it is banal.

Stalin seems to have been neither an imperialist nor even very much of a Marxist. Certainly he was no revolutionary, and it is not by applying the tenents of revolutionary Marxist-Leninism that we can make the most sense of his diplomacy. For him, a practical politician if there ever was one, the dream of a universal socialist society was not nearly as compelling as the prospect of an industrialized and unitary Soviet nation-state; and under his control Lenin's Third International, far from being a force for initiating the world-wide revolution, was only an arm of the Soviet Foreign Office (a body, by the way, this Comintern, whose subservience to the wild vicissitudes of Soviet *Realpolitik* has given it one of the most ridiculous histories known to modern man).

Stalin was a nationalist. The Bolshevik idealism, sometimes banal and sometimes vivid, was for him a rhetoric, a grab-bag of phrases to be used roundly when they served or cooperated with national needs (as he saw them) and discarded without ceremony when they did not. Stalin really comes alive as a man with some genuine passion only when he speaks as a Russian nationalist, as in the following (1931):

> To slacken the pace means to lag behind, and those who lag behind are beaten. We do not want to be beaten. . . . Old Russia . . . was ceaselessly beaten for her backwardness. She was beaten by the Mongol Khans, she was beaten by Turkish Beys, she was beaten by Swedish Feudal lords, she was beaten by Polish-Lithuanian gentry, she was beaten by Anglo-French capitalists, she was beaten by Japanese barons; she was beaten by all—for her backwardness. For military backwardness, for cultural backwardness, for political backwardness, for industrial backwardness, for agricultural backwardness. She was beaten because to beat her was profitable and went unpunished. You remember the words of the pre-revolutionary poet: "Thou art poor and thou are plentiful, thou art mighty and thou art helpless, Mother Russia." . . .
>
> We are fifty or a hundred years behind the advanced countries. We must make good this lag in ten years. Either we do it or they crush us.[11] *

Try to imagine, then, what the world of 1945 must have looked like from the viewpoint of this Russian nationalist.

* Stalin was better at prophecy than history; "ten years" was exactly right, but he forgot to mention Old Russia's victorious wars.

Before him towered a demanding United States, history's most violent nation (Hamburg, Kassel, Dresden, Tokyo, Hiroshima, Nagasaki—unparalleled), in the prime of its superpower. Behind him lay the unburied bodies of 20 million Russians and the burned farms and gutted factories of the Soviet economy. In his mind was the memory of unambiguous Western opposition to the Soviet Union. What were his choices? It apears that he had two: (1) He could accept the American plan of European partition, take no action to close the door on East Europe, and hope that the inevitable American penetration of the Danubian economy would be carried forward with a sympathetic eye on the U.S.S.R.'s economic needs and political sensitivities; or (2) he could accept the partition and close the door. Two unappealing alternatives. Given Western diplomacy since 1918 and such current clues as the abrupt termination of U.S. lend-lease to Russia (but not to France and Britain), the first was probably out of the question (hence, too, his later refusal of Marshall Plan aid and his perhaps maladroit rejection of the Baruch atomic energy proposal). The second alternative was also bad. It destined Russia for conflict with the United States at a time when peaceful relations were very much in Russia's practical interest, just as peace had been in Russia's interest in 1918 and 1905. It divided Europe at a time when the U.S.S.R. had an interest in a reconstructed Germany over whose politics and economy she could exercise some control. But this course at least offered some advantages which the first did not. It put a defenseless (if needy) East Europe at Moscow's disposal, and the international tension it was certain to generate would justify Stalin's police-state consolidation of power, enforcement of national unification, and forced-draft economic repair.

Thus, if Stalin accepted the bitter United States–U.S.S.R. contest that came to dominate Europe's politics, it was not because he enjoyed dooming the Poles or the Czechs to servitude, but (1) because he wanted to secure the Soviet Union from collapse, and (2) because the peculiar configuration of Soviet and Western weaknesses and strengths limited his possibilities to that one course. That is, the West refusing aid and rejecting Four-Power German treatment, Stalin seemed to have just one policy alternative that would satisfy at least partially the basic aims and requirements of Russian nationalism, and that policy was the creation of a nonmilitant, forcibly stabilized system of tributary buffer satellites positively controlled by the U.S.S.R. but unprovocative to the United States. A principle that we shall develop when we discuss rebellion (in Chapter V) is applicable here: Neither men nor nations customarily do more for good or bad than they believe they have to do.[12] The uniformly powerful West wanted—and believed, as we shall presently see, that it had to obtain—a guarantee against the spread of revolution and (what I shall argue is mainly the other side of the same coin) a guarantee of economic and political access to all of Europe. The unevenly powerful Soviet Union wanted development capital without strings, heavy German machinery, and some reprieve from militant Wagnerism. The aims of both sides were concentrated in opposing ideas about the control of Germany. The Cold War in Europe emerges in all its complex eventfulness from that elemental opposition.

Some will surely see in this a left-handed if not a leftist whitewash of Stalin. Even if one had a mind to try it, such a thing would easily consume four or five miracle-studded careers, there being too many unforgettable patches of shame in that man's story: the sorry spectacle of the purges; his slaughtering of the kulaks; his willingness to watch and even support the attempted destruction of the Chinese Revolution; his cynical manipulation of the Spanish Loyalists; his toleration of British and American dismemberment of the Greek Revolution. My aim is neither to condemn nor absolve this figure who for us is hardly more than a distant moral abstraction, but only to reconnect that abstraction with a few of the dominant concrete realities of that time; and then to suggest that Stalin's record in the early Cold War is less that of a fairy-tale monster on the prowl for sadism's blood and imperialism's plunder than that of a small, cold, very practical nationalist in a tight, dangerous situation. Stalin accepted the Cold War. He seems to have had little choice. Accepting it, he waged it in the years that followed with moments of ferocity and deceit that come close to validating America's stereotype of him. But that does not prove that he *created* it. The terms of that eerie battle were mainly set by the power that held the initiative and commanded the heights, and those powers were England in the rear and the United States far out in front. The Lion was securely coddled, the

Eagle was soaring in its prime, and the Bear was not dead but down. Let the Cold Warrior find it more difficult to persuade us that the Bear dictated the rules. The Truman Doctrine of 1947, as Secretaries Stimson and Wallace plainly said, fell not far short of an act of war. The Marshall Plan was offered to the Soviet Union out of complex and no doubt defensible motives. But it came too late. In Stalin's view, to accept it then would have been the same as to accept the economic and ultimately the political hegemony of the United States in Eurasia. Since he therefore had to refuse it, and since he probably believed that the United States expected him to refuse it, he could see the Marshall Plan as nothing but an American commitment to the resurrection of superpower in Germany—the old enemy rearmed.

Further: Throughout the Eisenhower-Dulles years, the U.S. policy of "defensive containment" remained consistently on the brink of fulfilling its worst implications; at any moment "liberation" might have broken out. And even today, when no one claims that the "threat" in Europe is increasing, when the reverse is obviously the case, we continue to seek the total military integration of the Atlantic concert, continue our efforts to arrange that integration in terms of a Washington-Bonn axis, and through our endlessly redecorated proposals for a multilateral nuclear force continue to perpetuate our demand for a West Europe bristling with atomic hostility toward the East.

In a word, we do not deserve the Cold War history which we have only *imagined* is ours. We do not need to compound the error of the late forties and fifties by pretending in the sixties, as our good Cold Warrior does, that containment in Europe was only a policy for the interim, intended all along to be discarded in favor of coexistence when its duty-time was out, and that we are even now acting out the same restrained and heroic role in Asia. Containment sometimes ached to become liberation. If we now find ourselves beginning to coexist in Europe, it is because containment failed. And if it failed, that does not seem to be because its failure was decreed by anyone from Byrnes to Rusk or Truman to Johnson. It failed because its back was broken in Moscow, which brutally engineered the Russian recovery, and its heart in Paris, to which the news of that recovery somehow got through.

The same harrowing salvation *may* be brought upon us via

Peking and Tokyo. But, in the first place, waiting for such a salvation is no way to live, and, in the second, the long odds humanity faced in Europe were as nothing compared with the odds in Asia. European peacemakers, the rational men of Europe, never had to contend with a Vietnam war. Besides which, we Americans knew Europe in a way in which we probably never will know Asia; we culturally referred ourselves to Europe, and perhaps half suspected all along that the Russians were at heart just as European, just as white, as we. In Asia, even less informed than in the first Cold War, we continue uncritically to convict Mao Tse-tung of all of Stalin's Cold War crimes, both real and legendary, and every starving, landlord-ridden, angry Asian patriot who dares pit himself against our Free World dream of benign dominion rekindles our violent pietism, our politics of confused resentment and frustration. And there is no one around in that mysterious part of the world to mediate the conflict—no one but us and the yellow people. The trouble with Asia is that nobody can save us there but ourselves.

How is it that we find that salvation so hard even to begin? Why do we superpractical Americans keep trying to navigate uncharted Asian territory with an erroneous European road map?

But maybe there is something more to the Cold War than well-intentioned mistakes about history. Maybe these mistakes are purposeful, intended only to palliate an unbecoming truth. Maybe our ideology of Cold War anticommunism is a beauty mark.

The Frontier Around Us

Big overviews and bad oversights make easy partners, but that provides no ground for agnosticism in the face of disaster. Grant that American history is subject, like all national histories, to the accidental, disjunct, and eccentric forces that sometimes catch hold of events and drive them in unpredictable directions. More important, grant that ours is not the only history on the planet. Our government and people did not produce the drama of Napoleonic Europe. But that drama produced the setting in which Jefferson's emissary to France, aiming only to procure New Orleans and the right to navigate the Mississippi River, found himself staggering home with the whole Louisiana Territory on his back. It was not our government and people that produced the drama of Leninist and Stalinist Russia. But that Russia has been America's main preoccupation for at least the past quarter-century. Our own history is more than met halfway by the independent history of others.

Nevertheless, we have a national style, an internalized system of motives and expectations which fundamentally predetermines our response to our opportunities and problems. My argument is that this system is today basically what it has always been; that our history is organic and thematically continuous; that whatever our capacity for elaboration and surprise, we still have had one and only one metabolic center; and that if we want to understand the Cold War, we first have to understand that center.

In his *Common Sense* paper of January 10, 1776, Thomas Paine wrote:

'Tis not in the power of Britain to do this continent justice; the business of it will soon be too weighty and intricate to be managed with any tolerable degree of convenience by a power so distant from us. . . . To be always running three or four thousand miles with a tale or a petition, waiting four or five months for an answer, which, when obtained, requires five or six more to explain it, will in a few years be looked upon as folly and childishness. . . . I have heard it asserted by some that, as America has flourished under her former connection with Great Britain, the same connection is necessary towards her future happiness. . . . I answer roundly that America would have flourished as much, and probably more, had no European power taken any notice of her. The commerce by which she hath enriched herself are the necessities of life, and will always have a market while eating is the custom of Europe.[13]

It was not simply that we *could* go it alone. Our colonial relation to mercantile Britain put such a very good future so far out of reach that we would either go it alone or not at all. The exploitative nature of Britain's rule had been masked during the French and Indian War by the influx to the colonies of good British war money and the fellowship of combat against the then despised *Gens de mauvaise Foy* and, just as importantly, against those redskin tribes which continually allied themselves with whomever was most against their paleface fur-trade competitors. But whether artisan or entrepreneur, farmer or trapper, the American pioneer was always mindful of the westward reach of opportunity; and the obstacles that checked him were chiefly those set in his path by the mother country. When the British mercantilists were debating the question of Mississippi Valley development, for example, one strong line of argument was that the settlers should be very carefully watched. General Thomas Gage, royal governor of Massachusetts, urged that it was to Britain's "interest to keep the Settlers within reach of the Sea-Coast as long as we can; and to cramp their trade as far as it can be done prudentially. Cities flourish and increase by extensive Trade . . . and they soon come to make for themselves what they used to import. I have seen this Increase, and I assure your Lordship that Foundations are laid in Philadelphia that must create jealously in an Englishman."[14]

The American "people's war of liberation" was fought because the American colonials wanted to expand into the North American continent and develop its wealth for themselves, and, as a corollary, because they could no longer tolerate their indebtedness to England and the restrictions which England had lately placed upon them. It is not an accident that George Washington was both one of the colonies' richest planters and one of the most deeply indebted to British merchant interests. The radicals Paine, Sam Adams, and Jefferson made powerful arguments about national freedom and national slavery; but it was the more practical argument about money and land that won the Revolution the decisive support of early American conservatives. That was the unifying and denominating cause.

Jefferson's presidency perhaps represented both the last chance for self-contained agrarian democracy and the final plunge into our own form of expansionist mercantilism: the same Louisiana Purchase that doubled our continental growing space and provided land for an inward-looking nation of free farmers also made it certain that we would have much to sell to the rest of the world. It was the plantation owner's land that created the skipper's sea. The dynamics of the long wave of resentment, convulsion, uncertainty, and decision is quite clear in this passage by the historian Curtis P. Nettels:

If [after 1763] the British imperium would not allow them to grow and expand, if it would not provide a solution of the central problem of the American economy, the colonists would have to take to themselves the right and the power to guide their economic development. They would find it necessary to create a new authority that would foster American shipping and commerce, make possible the continual growth of settlement, and above all stimulate the growth of domestic manufacturing industries. Thus another result of English mercantilism was the American Revolution and the creation thereafter of a new mercantilist state on this side of the Atlantic.[15]

Jefferson's idealism had represented the only strong challenge to that new mercantilism. Physical expansion was necessary to procure new farmland, but he wanted the country to seek no territory whose protection required a navy: Navies (he might have felt the same about air forces) were too expensive —"a wicked waste of the energies of our countrymen"[16]— they produced politicking-prone bureaucracies, and they tended to affiliate too closely with the commercial interests that supplied them. That is, like Eisenhower some 150 years later, Jefferson feared the growth of a military-industrial complex. But his democratic idealism, perhaps internally compromised by what Alfred Beveridge would later call his "land lust," was at last no match for his practical imagination: Jefferson very well understood the needs of an aggressively commercial people and those events in Europe which seemed to justify our disdain for Old World intriguers and warhawks at the same time that our commerce with them was making us rich.

The internationalist stance was taken once and for all. True, we went eagerly westward into the continent, slaughtering and cheating Indians as no Henrik Verwoerd or Ian Smith ever slaughtered and cheated the blacks of Africa. But we went into that frontier with our heads up, faces turned always to our trade positions, first in Europe and not much later in the Pacific. The War of 1812 failed to make good our grandiose ambitions concerning Canada, but it established our access to the sea and our claims to the land west of the commercially strategic Mississippi. In 1819, John Quincy Adams affirmed that "the United States and North America are identical." In the same year, we finally succeeded in annexing Florida. By the half-century mark we had taken a big piece of Mexico and the Oregon country and had made ourselves master of the entire land mass. In the 1860s, prepared for it by the Missouri Compromise, the Kansas and Nebraska Act, the Kansas civil war, we underwent our major national trauma to settle the dispute between the planters and the industrialists about how the West was going to be developed and, at bottom, about who was going to run the country.

We expanded. We exploded. The same energy that took us across rivers, prairies, and mountain ranges also took us across oceans. We were never isolated and never isolationist. From the beginning, we had a Department of State and we were always directly interested in the power struggles of the commercial European states. John Jay's treaty of 1794, whose acquiescence to British naval interests had certain neocolonialist implications, represented a countercurrent that nearly cost George Washington his reputation.* It was a mistake soon corrected and not often to be repeated. In 1823, Monroe's famous doctrine laid the groundwork for North American hegemony in Latin America. Three years later, Secretary of State Clay affirmed "a lively interest in the execution of the work" of making "a cut or canal for the purpose of navigation somewhere through the isthmus that connects the two Americas, to unite the Pacific and Atlantic Oceans. . . ."[17] In 1854, the Ostend Manifesto, noting that "self-preservation is the first law of nature," declared that "Cuba is as necessary to the North American republic as any of its present members," not merely because it guarded "the natural and main outlet to the products of this entire population, the highway of their direct intercourse with the Atlantic and the Pacific States," but also because there was a Danger afoot in the World. The Manifesto made this danger plain to see; its reverberations with present ideology make it especially interesting:

> We should . . . be recreant to our duty, be unworthy of our gallant forefathers, and commit base treason against our posterity, should

* Frank Monaghan records that "the wrath of the republicans was boundless. Without neglecting 'that damned arch-traitor, John Jay,' they heaped abuse on Washington as the man who 'had completed the destruction of American freedom'. . . . In Virginia, 'A speedy Death to General Washington' was toasted; in New York the Thanksgiving Proclamation of Governor Jay was denounced because it ventured to include the preservation 'of the valuable life and usefulness of the President of the United States' as one of the subjects worthy of a prayer of thanks. . . ." (In William A. Williams, *The Shaping of American Diplomacy*, Rand McNally, Chicago, p. 68.)

we permit Cuba to be Africanized and become a second St. Domingo with all its attendant horrors to the white race, and suffer the flames to extend to our own neighboring shores, seriously to endanger or actually to consume the fair fabric of our Union.[18]

We need only read "St. Domingo" for "Cuba" and vice versa, "communized" for "Africanized," and "Free World" for the less euphemistic "white race," and we have a statement that is not only contemporary but almost newsworthy. If there is an important difference between then and now, it is that this "anti-Africanism" of the Ostend Manifesto is more obviously a sham than the anticommunism of the Truman Doctrine, although that may be only because we can see 1854 more clearly than our own time. In both cases, the specter of an encroaching Menace is used as moral shielding for a quite simple ambition of business. But when we finally came to blows with Spain at the end of the century, first supporting, then turning against the revolutionaries of both Cuba and the Philippines, we had no time for pietistic hogwash; we were openly in the business of protecting business. In December 1896, President Cleveland, "anti-imperialist" as he was, viewed the developing Cuban crisis as follows:

The spectacle of the utter ruin of an adjoining country . . . would engage the serious attention of the Government and the people of the United States in any circumstances. In point of fact, they have a concern with it which is by no means of a wholly sentimental or philanthropic character. . . . Our actual pecuniary interest in it is second only to that of the people and Government of Spain. It is reasonably estimated that at least from $30,000,000 to $50,000,000 of American capital are invested in plantations and in railroad, mining, and other businesses on the island. The volume of trade between the United States and Cuba, which in 1889 amounted to about $64,000,000, rose in 1893 to about $103,000,000, and in 1894, the year before the present insurrection broke out, amounted to nearly $96,000,000.[19]

Our war-won control over the Cuban economy and our annexation of Puerto Rico were not separate from, but were part and parcel of our internal development. It was a prairie wind that blew those Yankee clippers through the Pacific, where we annexed Hawaii and the Philippines, all the way across what General MacArthur was much later to call our "peaceful lake" even to the ports of Old Cathay. By the middle of the nineteenth century, superenthusiasts had already called for the annexation of Formosa; our capitalists had made formidable penetrations into the economies of Japan and Korea; and to name the names of those whose control of the Turkish opium monopoly made them rich is to name the most glittering array of dope-pushers ever seen: Astor, Peabody, Perkins, Sturges, Cabot, good and proper Bostonians, blue-noses all.[20] ("Take away your opium and your missionaries," said Chinese Foreign Affairs Minister Kung, "and you will be welcome.") "Americans looked toward Asia in the middle of the century," writes Foster Rhea Dulles,

> as they would not again until its close. . . . That great country remained the key to the period's expanding interest in the Pacific world. We came near to annexing the Hawaiian Islands as a way station on the road to China, and Commodore Perry's expedition to open up Japan was in part inspired by the need to obtain coaling depots for the new steam vessels on the long voyage to Chinese ports.[21]

By the early 1900s, with suppression of the Boxer Uprising behind us, cotton had supplanted opium as our major export to China, and the American Asiatic Association, a combine of southern crop growers, New England millers, New York bankers, and assorted entrepreneurs had interlocked with the American-China Development Company to promote vigorous government support for the Open Door Policy. There is no need here to debate the real intent of the open-door notes of John Hay. It is conceivable at least that, had it been actually implemented by all the European states involved in the China rape, the Open Door Policy might have made Western imperialism more tolerable for the Chinese people. It is even conceivable that the British and Americans who strove to realize an open-door situation *cared* about the Chinese people. Apart from such speculations, however, there stand three hard commercial facts. The first is that we were in China. The second is that we wanted to get in deeper. The third is that the spheres-of-influence diplomacy practiced quite well by Great Britain (the Yangtze provinces), France (some of the southern provinces), Germany (Shantung), and Russia (the Liaotung peninsula) made us uneasy about our position and its future extension. The Open Door Policy, in its essentials, merely admonished the European mercantilists to abandon those gunboat privileges which we happened not to share. Its outer principle was that American business could hold its own in any fair competition in an open market. The inner principle was that American business happened to find itself at the moment on the short end of the concessions stick. The Open Door Policy—just as with our often double-standard opposition to "economic nationalism"—was a politically expedient way to formulate our expansionist Asian objective.

America had become what is called a Major World Power and was quite prepared to act like one. It cannot be surprising that we had our champions of very plain, even blazing imperialism. Perhaps one of the plainest was Senator Henry Cabot Lodge, who said in 1895:

> We have a record of conquest, colonization, and expansion unequalled by any people in the Nineteenth Century. We are not to be curbed now. . . . For the sake of our commercial supremacy in the Pacific, we should control the Hawaiian islands and maintain our influence in Samoa.[22]

Plainer and more blazing than Lodge was Senator Albert J. Beveridge, whose prose is too marvelous not to quote at length (1898):

> Shall the American people continue their march toward the commercial supremacy of the world? Shall free institutions broaden their blessed reign as the children of liberty wax in strength, until the empire of our principles is established over the hearts of all mankind? . . . Has God endowed us with gifts beyond our deserts and marked us as the people of His peculiar favor, merely to rot in our own selfishness? . . . Hawaii is ours; Porto Rico is to be ours; at the prayer of her people Cuba finally will be ours; in the islands of the East, even to the gates of Asia, coaling stations are to be ours at the very least; the flag of liberal government is to float over the Philippines, and may it be the banner that Taylor unfurled in Texas and Frémont carried to the coast.
>
> The Opposition tells us that we ought not to govern a people without their consent. I answer: The rule of liberty that all just government derives its authority from the consent of the governed, applies only to those who are capable of self-government. We govern the Indians without their consent, we govern our territories without their consent, we govern our children without their consent. . . .
>
> Distance and oceans are no arguments. . . . Steam joins us; electricity joins us—the very elements are in league with our destiny. Cuba not contiguous! Porto Rico not contiguous! Hawaii and the Philippines not contiguous! The oceans make them contiguous. And our Navy will make them contiguous.[23]

All nations and all movements produce their windstormers. A good deal more surprising—even stunning—is the following 1907 passage from the hand of one of our great liberal statesmen, Woodrow Wilson:

> Since trade ignores national boundaries and the manufacturer insists on having the world as a market, the flag of his nation must follow him, and the doors of the nations which are closed must be battered down.[24]

In May 1914, Wilson's Secretary of Commerce, William Redfield, told the National Council of Foreign Trade, "Because we are strong, we are going out, you and I, into the markets of the world to get our share."[25] Redfield was followed at the rostrum by a former member of the Anti-Imperialist League, Secretary of State William Jennings Bryan, who informed the businessmen that it was America's official policy to "open the doors of all the weaker countries to an invasion of American capital and enterprise." In case they were missing the point, he made it again: "My Department is your department; the ambassadors, the ministers, and the consuls are all yours. It is their business to look after your interests and to guard your rights."[26]

Bryan's stressing the doors of the *weaker* countries is significant. We had long imagined the poor world to be our oyster. Although we never for once abandoned our crucial and always increasing interests in Europe, control of the development of the vast, densely populated undeveloped countries was steadily seen as the key to our own fulfillment—in part because of their natural-resource wealth, in part because of their long-term market potential, and in part, too, no doubt, just because they were more available to our will than were the rich industrial states. When Wilson speaks of battering down closed doors, for example, or when he claims that "concessions obtained by financiers must be safeguarded by ministers of state, even if the sovereignty of unwilling nations be outraged in the process," he is of course not thinking of the door of a state like France or the sovereignty of a state like Germany. (We do not become effectively anti-colonialist about others' empires until after World War II.) It was Latin America, North Africa, and Asia that most fired America's expansionist imagination; and the archtype of the poor country was, of course, China. Julius Klein, Secretary of Commerce Hoover's top aide during the Coolidge Administration, gave our Oriental inclinations an almost mystical phraseology in a major policy statement called "The Tendency of the Frontier Is To Move Westward." He explained that the history of the United States no less than the history of the world itself was told in the steady westward movement of the frontier. He described how the world frontier had moved from China through central Asia, Greece, Rome, Europe, and finally America, where its progress copied on a continental scale its global pattern. The logical conclusion could hardly be missed:

Now the circle is complete, the last great frontier has been conquered, and we come to a new era of world history.

An era, perhaps, that would at long last see the end of frontiers and the conquest of "savages" by the "civilized"? Not at all:

America, with an economic and industrial organization which is the fruit of centuries of world progress, is facing across the Pacific what is at the same time the oldest and the newest trade area.[27]

So it turned out that the wheel was simply in for another go-round. There was naturally some debate about which new frontiersman was going to bring the good news to China, Japan exhibiting a persistent belief that history was in her hands, not ours; and even though some of our statesmen and businessmen tried to arrange a joint stewardship with her, a Pacific war finally had to be fought to clear up these ambiguities of Destiny. (Owing to the arrival of a third candidate, the Chinese themselves, this dispute remains unsettled. We shall explore it further in Chapter IV.)

Through it all, American leaders have retained their opinion about the importance of the backward. The following passage from Secretary of State Dean Rusk's 1962 speech to the National Business Advisory Council is typical of the less colorful bureaucratic style in which the traditional opinion is now expressed:

[American] business must expand its present important role in the world economy. The dynamism that has been central in the development of the United States must now be employed on a global scale. . . . There are strong incentives for American firms to stake their claim now in these great potential markets [of the developing countries]. As nations develop, business opportunities are being created. Future profits will go to the firms which are enterprising and foresighted today. An American firm whose managerial skill, political sophistication, and contribution to development win the confidence of a developing nation should be in an enviable position. The risks are there; the long-term opportunities are there. The developing nations represent a classic challenge to American private enterprise.[28]

The United States Department of Commerce publication *Commerce Business Daily* carries announcements of government contracts that are open for bids from the "private sector." It may be that there is absolutely no connection between the attitude exemplified by Rusk's statement and the attitude exemplified by the following announcement, which appeared in the *Business Daily* of April 29, 1965; but it is hard not to speculate:

> Services and materials as required to perform [for the Army] a research study entitled "Pax Americana" consisting of a phased study of the following: (*a*) elements of National Power; (*b*) ability of selected nations to apply the elements of National Power; (*c*) a variety of world power configurations to be used as a basis for the U.S. to maintain world hegemony in the future.

The contract, incidentally (in the amount of $89,000—cheap for world hegemony), was awarded to that famous historian, the Douglas Aircraft Company.

America's expansionism is not debatable. It is a dynamic condition which describes our national career better than any other single term. It is not concealed; it is celebrated. All those sermons on the need to spread the American Way of Life are not just jokes—they are real sermons, and they come from a culture which really thinks its survival requires more and more converts. Our business principles on the one side and on the other side those freedoms—the civil liberties and rights, the individualism of which we have been so proud—have been consistently seen as cross-justifying virtues which will remain somehow jeopardized until their practice is universal. We need to look into this.

The philosophers of democratic capitalism have more or less explicitly tried to show that personal freedom and economic freedom are interdependent. We can enjoy all our rights of person only because our free-enterprise system guarantees our rights of property—and thus our right to exploit property for commercial ends. This theory has produced the blandest social pieties which the world knows of, surpassing even youth-club Marxism in its ability to banalize the unreal. At the moment, it is running afoul of two connected developments: the corporate bureaucratizing of the entrepreneur and the virtual privatizing of the so-called public sector. Modern Americans, that is, are by no means a "propertied" people. But it still remains for us a major ceremonial theme that we have personal freedom because we have economic freedom, and that any decrease of economic freedom, *when it stems from public action*, results necessarily in a decrease of personal freedom. And this economic freedom, of course, is simply the freedom of American businessmen to expand their commercial operations. It is not to be cynical but merely to make the obvious translation, to observe that the formula about "making the world safe for democracy" really means making it safe for capitalism—and, to be more concrete about it, making it safe for our own corporate capitalists. When the world is safe for our corporate capitalists, we can sleep; for when the world is safe for our corporate capitalists, political democracy is also safe.

Very rarely does this kind of reasoning make an effort to account for decreases of economic freedom (or the losses of property) that stem from private action; that is, the ones that ensue from the monopolist-corporatist impulses of a capitalism that has long since slipped the old frail public fetters. But it is not very hard to understand this omission. Since economic freedom is the freedom to expand business activity, any achieved business expansion is simply the concrete embodiment of expanded economic freedom, and therefore of expanded personal freedom. If the two are really interdependent, then each grows as the other grows; and if some freedom is good, then more freedom is better. To ask the corporatist to imagine that his newly won monopoly actually *limits* economic freedom, or to ask him to submit to controls on the ground that they *increase* freedom, is to ask him to go mad. How can freedom be unfreedom? How can freedom come from slavery? A critic points to the collusion of big business and government; he can in fact point to their virtual *identity*. But the implication of that is lost on the big businessman, who (if he admits it) will only see this "collusion" as the victory of freedom. For when business has overcome government, the slave has overcome his master; when big businessmen are free, everyone is free; what's good for General Motors is good for America; what's good for America is good for the world.

Contemporary business intellectuals can supply endless justifications for our system's expansionary march: We democratize the world, we modernize the backward, cure the sick, teach the illiterate native to admire the works of Doris Day, covet the color-TV set, and hustle for the buck; expressways, skyscrapers, suburbs, and ghettos one day for Dar es Salaam, just like Chicago. But all these virtues seem incidental. All the arguments about culture, freedom, and the rights of man seem to be nothing but tactical positions which can always, if necessary, be exchanged for others (like stopping communism). To raise a doubt as to corporate capitalism's exclusive ability to make people freer and give them better lives is not to raise a doubt in the capitalist's mind as to his system's most primitive virtue—which is simply that it is *his* system, that it frees *him*, and that, from this point of view at least, it is stable.

Probably the best thing to be said about corporate capitalism is that it has contrived to relate itself in a not always destructive way to that quite independent, long-term technological revolution that underlies the current abundance of the North Atlantic world. In an important and possibly crushing respect, it has subverted and betrayed that revolution. That our spacemen look down *without despairing* on rat-infested tenements in every last one of our famous modern cities reflects a social derangement much too immense for the compass of the ordinary brain. Science has squandered itself in our time on space capsules, tail fins, and shaving-cream dispensers. Deformed and misspent as it is, however, it has arrived in the world; and since its intrinsic rationality may ultimately have some social pay-off, its arrival may be more portentous of change than certain free-enterprising investment houses now imagine.

The point is that the two most observed social defenses of modern Western capitalism are fishy. Does it produce personal freedom? For quite some time, it was rather famous for not even producing a setting in which personal freedom could have a meaning. Then has it at least produced economic freedom? Relative to others, the American worker is in fine financial shape; but relative to the abundance he produces, he works too many hours a day and too many years of his life for too little purchasing power. And on the other side of the picture, the crucial facts about the act of free-enterprise competition are that somebody wins it and somebody loses; that winners tend to keep winning and losers to keep losing; that financial (and therefore political) power unfailingly condenses around exclusionary elitist groups whose interests are increasingly coordinated; and (to generalize the foregoing) simply that capitalism has failed to conceive, must less institutionalize, the forms through which the basic, freely initiated competitive act can be continuously renewed within the market place. (Much "competition" now is intracorporate and a good deal of it is nonproductive.) After all these years of being reformed, the system of "modern" capitalism still proves as convincingly as ever those very old-timey observations that richness and poorness beget themselves, and that it takes it to make it.

But what of that other major claim, the one that praises capitalism as the modernizer of the world? There is no use being deceived about this. The growth of the capitalist state resulted from that scientific rain which we call the technological revolution. It was this technology which revolutionized labor, and it was revolutionized labor which produced abundance—an abundance, by the way, which labor had to battle ferociously to partake of. By a few Marxists and more neo-Smithians, I may now be told that capitalism made technological progress possible by luring science into the service of the finance bureaucracy. But that is misleading and beside the point. It is a purely historical statement pretending to be analytic. One might have raised as a sound surmise in 1917 what one can assert fifty years later as a demonstrated truth, namely, that the technological revolution will indiscriminately propagate itself through any sufficiently coherent system of social communications, raw wealth, and manpower. That this is now proved is apparently what the North Atlantic world finds so disgusting about the Russian and Chinese revolutions. Science produces and mobilizes wealth, not the other way around; and science is ideologically blind.

Beyond this, there is the embarrassing fact that capitalism does not seem to know even yet how to cope with this abundance which it supposedly invented. It seems that man and machine produced too much. The financial priesthood was accordingly obliged to invent the really astounding concept of the "surplus product." This surplus was, of course, nothing but a theft that threatened to destroy everyone, robbed and robber alike (a most important point to which we shall return later). For the moment, observe only that properly there should be no surplus until needs are satisfied, and that the problem of surplus production has in fact been most acute when needs have *least* been satisfied. When fruit rots on trees and unemployed men go hungry, something is wrong with the resource-allocation, wealth-distribution system. As we shall see, the solution of this domestic problem has become a primary task of American foreign policy.

Related to the surplus-product problem is the problem of the technological surplus: that increment of available wealth or material progress that is calculatedly withheld from the market through the patent system and such practices as planned obsolescence, designed-in failure rates, and "sales engineering"—practices that are evidently peculiar to the West and which the West needs to be ashamed of.

But in the teeth of these very contrary winds, it turns out to be a version of this same capitalism-for-progress argument that is currently being promoted in defense of the modern American (often multinational) corporation. The huge and growing corporation is apparently different from the Gay Nineties era monopolies at which the Sherman Act was aimed, and its apologists may be right in claiming that some of the original fears of bigness are now misplaced. The big corporation, formed through vertical, horizontal, and conglomerate mergers (there were 2100 in 1965), is certainly capable of committing the old ordinary sins of the trusts. The drug and electronics industries' scandals are famous. The old black arts of price-fixing, deceiving the consumer, limiting production, and conspiring to allocate markets have not been exactly forgotten. But it is not in order to commit such sins that the corporation comes into existence, and it might not be necessary to destroy it to ensure that such sins go uncommitted. The corporations exist because the rates of change in the affluent market put a premium on a flexibility, an ability to redirect resources, that small product-defined firms do not seem to be able to muster; they exist because the affluent market's promiscuity ("hyperelasticity of demand") can be stimulated and harnessed only through a technical diversity too expensive for small firms; they exist, most generally, simply because a more global management of resources is more *rational*—a point, by the way, which some socialists and more fascists have been making for a long time. What may be good about the big corporation is its ability to innovate, to generate or absorb change, and to inject change into the economy. Bigness may not be the same thing as badness.

But what is certainly bad about the big corporation is that its immense innovative power is curtailed by its very fundamental and very hopeless addiction to financial efficiency. GM's business is not cars but profits. Its profitability, measured in money, is the one basic criterion by which it evaluates its performance. *This is not socially rational. It is a kind of voodoo.* Robert Frost's observation about the two tramps comes to mind: "Except as a man could handle an ax, they had no way of knowing a fool." Besides handling axes and making profits, there are many other and much better measures of value. But since the corporation is the main repository of our national wealth, and because it is condemned to see its management of that wealth as good or bad depending on how much profit it makes, we have an industrial society which is as much troubled as enticed by the prospects of cybernation, and much more to be blamed for its inner cities than admired for its airports.

If this new creature of our capitalist system could *really* innovate, then our prodigious national wealth would long since have eradicated poverty and the numberless social evils that poverty spawns. If the management of our resources was really integrated and really rational, then the measure of our managerial performance would not be financial efficiency but the quality of social life. As it happens, we proceed to debase ourselves with this harum-scarum inventiveness whose achievements are graded mainly by accountants, recorded mainly by cash registers, and commemorated mainly in the nostalgia of salesmen. And all the time that we talk so boldly about our plans for developing the backward world, we overlook the fact that we have proved—put it kindly—unadept at developing the backward world that smoulders with distress and bitterness within our own boundaries.

This overview of American capitalism is not gratuitous. We know that our system is an expansionist one. We have wanted to know what promises we can expect this system to keep. We shall return to that in the following section. Now we want to ask: Why expansion? Sometimes—most notably in the period 1895 to 1905—we have explained our foreign expeditions, commercial and military alike, in terms of a nakedly imperialist ideology. More often, with an immodesty more or less concealed, we have considered our economic-political system to be the one best hope of the world. We have justified our world-wide presence by thinking of it as a favor to our hosts, even when those hosts are themselves not convinced. Our system, we have said, is a good one, and we have expanded over the world, like so many Christians, because others should have the opportunity to share in its goodness.

Our system may or may not be good. The foregoing may at least have indicated why it is healthy to entertain certain doubts: We expand to make men free? If a libertarian version of personal freedom is meant, the argument is baldly wrong (see Latin America). If a capitalist version of economic freedom is meant, the argument is circular and the question is begged. We expand to modernize the world? Our domestic record does not make the point that we can; other systems are at least as conductive of technological progress as ours is, and may be even better at giving that progress a more attractively social orientation.

We have expanded for none of these reasons, but because our businessmen have wanted to as consistently as our statesmen have believed that we had to.

Senator William Frye stated the problem with noble simplicity in 1895. "We must have the market of China," he said, "or we shall have revolution."[29]

This idea may seem amusing today, at least at first glance. But it could not have been laughed down at the time. For one thing, we already had a sizeable part of the China market, our exports were growing, and even as the desirability of further penetration impressed itself on our businessmen, troublesome sphere-of-influence competition with the European powers was brewing. But Frye expressed his point so brutally because in his view this trade was not merely good, it was mandatory for survival. The reasoning could not have been simpler. It was the nature of the American economic system that it produced more goods than could be sold to

Americans—it constantly produced a surplus. These surplus goods could hardly be allowed to rot in the warehouses. What was to be done? One obvious alternative was to cut back in production. But that was not only defeatist, it was suicidal: Cutbacks would lead to unemployment, unemployment to mass resentment, and mass resentment to class warfare, revolution. So said the bloody history of mid-century Europe.

More important, so also said the bloody history of nineteenth-century America—history which must have been very much in the Senator's mind as he set forth his gloomy prediction. Economic distress and class-conscious violence were never strangers in America. In the background of America's political consciousness were the use of troops in 1846 to suppress the striking New York Irish workers; the two depressions that bounded the massive violence of the Civil War; the Great Upheaval of 1877, which saw troops go over to the side of the railroad workers and the virtual fall to rebels of Martinsburg, Reading, Pittsburgh. And very much in the foreground were the Haymarket Riot of 1886, the Homestead Strike of 1892, the Panic of 1893 and the subsequent depression, and the massacre at Chicago that grew out of the Pullman Strike of 1894. It was not silly to think that more and greater violence could come. It was not naive to say that fundamental to the prospect of this violence was America's nagging inability to deal somehow with persistent economic and social dislocation: how to escape the boom-bust cycle, how to stabilize at a high level of employment and consumption, how to solve the problem of the concentration of power in the hands of a steadily smaller-growing cluster of men, the masters of the trusts—and how to do these things *without fundamentally changing the nature of the system itself*. An American free-enterpriser might have picked up Marx those days and fainted dead away from the shock of self-recognition.

The answer proposed by the socialist was popular control of the nation's wealth, with the artificial problem of the surplus being solved through the redistribution of economic power. Maybe that proposal was all right for some other cosmos. But here, it happened to confront its judges with a request that they condemn themselves: something no judge has ever done. Socialism was offensive in the nostrils of the gods, a heresy against those divine rights of owning and exploiting property upon which our republic was based. Besides, there was another solution: Sell more goods abroad.

By the 1890s, we had established ourselves as an exporting nation and had entered a troubled but genuine market economy. We had become the world's leading manufacturer. We were chipping away at the debt we had accumulated in Europe over the preceding century, during the first part of which we had borrowed and bought abroad more than we had sold. No one could foresee, of course, that we were not even a quarter-century away from the world war which would turn us at last (almost overnight, as the standard description has it) into a creditor nation. But it was already clear that creditorship was in the cards. Everything in the experience of those who were making the decisions pointed to the oceans as the outlet, the final solution. How could it be otherwise with an island people? An island people, in fact, whose origins lay mostly in *another* island, one which *also* shipped, *also* looked to the Continent, and which *also* tried to deport its social-economic problems through the export of its surplus industrial product.

But certain conditions would have to be met before this dream could come true. Every one of those conditions directly interlocked with and reinforced the others. We wanted to have high production, no revolution, and access to foreign markets. So we had to have high production and no revolution *in order* to have access; high production and access *in order* to have no revolution; and access and no revolution *in order* to have high production. Given our origins, our frontier experience, our business morality, this was an unbeatable formulation. It derived only an added charm from the facts, clear even then, that more maritime commerce would need a larger navy, and that the building of navies, whatever Jefferson thought, was good for business. The *Maine* had been launched in 1890, the *New York* in 1891, the *Olympia* in 1892, the *Oregon* in 1893. The populists never had a chance against that kind of firepower.

Indeed, it was odds-on for a very long time in our country as to whether or not even a nominally liberal-reformist answer would have a chance. At the century's turn, it could not have been unclear to anyone that the American people had good reason to be angry, and that their anger was socially explosive. But the slackening of labor's bondage *always* had to be forced; the most mildly progressive proposals were *always* attacked; the very elemental injustice of big capital's behavior was *always* protected or denied. Of course there were reformers, radicals, anarchists, liberals, revolutionaries, social middlemen—in the streets. It was in the streets that America's progressivism was born, bred, and given what force it has had. But upstairs and downtown where Power sat, the typical attitude was that of George Baer, president of the mine-owning Philadelphia and Reading Railroad, who expressed himself as follows on the 1902 mine workers strike:

> The rights and interests of the laboring man will be protected and cared for—not by the labor agitators, but by the Christian gentlemen to whom God has given control of the property rights of the country.[30]

Protected and cared for, one must suppose, much as that Christian gentleman George Pullman protected and cared for his workers who earned from four to sixteen cents an hour, and who, living in his "model" company town, paid him ten cents for the thousand gallons of water for which he paid four cents and $2.25 for the thousand feet of gas which he bought for thirty-three cents.[31]

Why rattle these old bones? Because these old bones are in our national flesh. If affairs are a bit different with us now, that is only because a good many men died in a very bitter fight to *make* them different. *This is a crucial political fact.* It has to be accepted, understood, remembered, and applied hard when we think about American policy, whether domestic or foreign: *The big American businessman and his associates in the Commerce and State departments do not characteristically refrain from exploiting what someone else's power does not prohibit them from exploiting.* Any other view of our "leaders" is a namby-pamby hallucination that pays too little respect to that "toughness" for which they so much esteem themselves.

We have to bear consistently in mind that it was such men, who had such ideas, who were out to spread abroad those "free institutions" that Senator Beveridge so proudly hailed in 1898. Like Beveridge, they always tried to give our expansionism a crusadingly humanitarian if not overtly Christian halo. But, also like Beveridge, they very well knew that there were arguments and arguments, reasons and reasons, and that some certitudes were more certain than others. Beveridge again:

There was not one reason for the land-lust of our statesmen from Jefferson to Grant, other than the prophet and the Saxon within them. But, to-day, we are raising more than we can consume, making more than we can use. Therefore we must find new markets for our produce. . . . The commercial supremacy of the Republic means that this Nation is to be the sovereign factor in the peace of the world. For the conflicts of the future are to be conflicts of trade—struggles for markets—commercial wars for existence. And the golden rule of peace is impregnability of position and invincibility of preparedness. . . . So Hawaii furnishes us a naval base in the heart of the Pacific; the Ladrones another, a voyage further on; Manila another, at the gates of Asia—Asia, to the trade of whose hundreds of millions American merchants, manufacturers, farmers, have as good right as those of Germany or France or Russia or England; . . . Asia, whose doors must not be shut against American trade. Within five decades the bulk of Oriental commerce will be ours.[32]*

The point had, of course, been made earlier and in terms of other Eldorados—or maybe we should say other Fountains of Youth. For example, S. O. Thacher testified as follows before a subcommittee of the Senate Foreign Relations Committee in April of 1886 (not more than a few days before the Haymarket Riot):

The industrial outlook of our land is not one of entire sunshine. There are more laborers than there is work for them to do. . . . In every department of industrial life there is production beyond consumption. . . . On the whole, as never before, our future growth, peace, and tranquility depend on finding more consumers for what we have to sell. . . . In vain do we turn our eyes to any other part of the world for a people who at once need and are willing to take from our farms, looms, forges, and wells of mineral oils that [which] we are able to produce and spare. The nations of Central and South America offer not alone the most alluring and most profitable markets whereby to relieve our excessive productions, but there is no other field.[33]

There is nothing more common in our economic mentality, nothing more constant in our foreign policy, than this con-

* In 1938, 51 percent of our raw-materials imports came from Asia.

viction that the basic problem of the American business system is domestically undistributable wealth, and that the basic solution to that problem, its essential and only anodyne, lies in our penetration of foreign markets—most especially, the markets of those lands which we now think of as the underdeveloped (or in the new State Department tact, the *less*-developed) countries. Only see how the same speech is made over and over again: in 1897 by Theodore C. Search, president of the National Association of Manufacturers: "Many of our manufacturers have outgrown their home markets, and the expansion of our foreign trade is their only promise of relief."[34] Woodrow Wilson during his campaign for the Presidency in 1912: "Our industries have expanded to such a point that they will burst their jackets if they cannot find a free outlet to the markets of the world. . . . Our domestic markets no longer suffice. We need foreign markets."[35] President Herbert Hoover in 1928: "We must find a profitable market for our surpluses."[36] In that same year, a top Washington lawyer and friend of the Far East, John Foster Dulles, sounded an important variation on the main theme: "We must finance our exports by loaning foreigners the wherewithal to pay for them."[37]

Perhaps in part because that advice was not taken, dark days came to America—and with them, Franklin D. Roosevelt. The New Deal seems to be thought of now as an attempt to apply internal stimulations to the economy, an attempt to invigorate it *from within*. But even for the New Deal, government-financed projects were *not* considered to be structural change, they were merely structural repair, stop-gap, marginal, or temporary—pending the revival of the country's dramatically depressed foreign trade. New Deal reconstruction pivoted around the liberalizing Trade Agreements Act of 1934 (and, of course, repeal of the protectionist Smoot-Hawley Tariffs) as a means of restoring Europe's ability to buy from us what we wanted to sell. American exports had fallen from over $5 billion in 1929 to $1.6 billion in 1933. In a March 1934 radio address, Assistant Secretary of State Francis B. Sayre ran down the gloomy meaning of this decline: "Remember this: Reduction in world trade means reduction in world production; and reduction in production means, inescapably, unemployment." Sayre's tone quite well reveals the intensity of the New Deal's feelings about foreign trade:

What does this decrease in American trade actually mean in the lives of our farmers and manufacturers? Although it is true that the United States normally exports only about one tenth of its total production, nevertheless, certain staples are dependent for their continued existence upon an export of very much more than one tenth. . . . The failure to sell these surpluses abroad would mean inevitable disaster to great agricultural sections of our country. Such destitution and economic disaster would not be confined to the producers themselves. It would be transmitted, through diminished purchasing power, into the business life of every town and village in the producing areas, and from these would spread injury throughout our country. Without the income from the sales of these surpluses, real estate values must fall sharply, tax revenues must be curtailed, banks threatened, and the cultural life of entire sections of the country stricken, if not permanently injured. . . . Cut off these foreign markets, and the inevitable result is unemployment, suffering, and human misery.[38]

The language could hardly have been more nightmarishly apocalyptic—all for the ears of people very well acquainted already with "unemployment, suffering, and human misery." No one could have agreed more that things were bad and that the only answer was more foreign trade than Roosevelt himself: In 1935 he said:

Foreign markets must be regained if America's producers are to rebuild a full and enduring domestic economy for our people. *There is no other way* if we would avoid painful economic dislocations, social readjustments, and unemployment. [Emphasis added.][39]

The war postponed and then intensified, it did not cancel out, the urgency of this need. As with World War I, the growth it stimulated in American business (industrial and agricultural expansion, technological take-off, creation of large pools of skilled and highly paid labor, the accumulation of immense capital reserves) only added more power and other dimensions to the already strong conviction, held everywhere, that America could not survive without what may as well be called commercial colonies. As early as 1940, Cordell Hull made it clear that our "primary object is both to reopen the old and seek new outlets for our surplus production."[40] Not only did we demand and get free access to the Axis colonies, but we also used our economic leverage against our needy British ally to pry open the door to her colonies as well. We have already noted Secretary of State Byrnes' declaration that a major postwar objective was "the maintenance of the open door in the Balkans." Later, as Truman's Secretary of State, Byrnes supplied the familiar argument for such an objective: "The United States cannot reach and maintain the high level of employment we have set as our goal unless the [foreign] outlets for our production are larger than they've ever been before in peacetime."[41]

There is a virtually unbroken universal consensus on this point. Even Secretary of Commerce Henry Wallace, who finally broke with Truman on the question of our postwar Russia policy, did not doubt that "private enterprise in the United States can survive only if it expands and grows." "The old frontiers must be rebuilt," he said, and claimed that our expansion into the poor countries represented our "unlimited new frontier of opportunities."[42] Assistant Secretary of State Dean Acheson, testifying in 1944 before the special Congressional Committee on Post-War Economic Policy and Planning, argued that if postwar America should fall back into the prewar depression, "it seems clear that we are in for a very bad time. . . . We cannot go through another ten years like the ten years at the end of the twenties and the beginning of the thirties without having the most far-reaching consequences upon our economic and social system." Acheson then elaborated:

> You don't have a problem of production. The United States has unlimited creative energy. The important thing is markets. . . . We could argue for quite a while that under a different system in this country you could use the entire production of the country in the United States. . . . I take it the Soviet Union could use its entire production internally. If you wish to control the entire life of the people, you could probably fix it so that everything produced here would be consumed here, but that would completely change our Constitution, our relations to property, human liberty, our very conceptions of law. And nobody contemplates that. Therefore, you find you must look to other markets and those markets are abroad. . . . If I am wrong about that, then all the argument falls by the wayside, but my contention is that we cannot have full employment and prosperity in the United States without the foreign markets.[43]

Let us reduce all this to its elements.

Our economic system functions in a state of sustained disequilibrium. The better it works, the greater its surplus. The greater its surplus, the greater its need for an external market.

The greater its external market, the better it works. So the machine puts its big steel head down, leans forward into the future, and runs, accelerates, is always just this side of being off balance. This is good. But it has to be adroitly done, and the suspense is terrific. (Capitalists are *supposed* to be anxious, anticipatory, ulcerated.) The theory is that properly controlled expansionary disequilibrium converts into a constantly rising standard of living.

There are, of course, some classical problems. For one, the export of this surplus has to be financed. So there ought to be an external, independently generated source of wealth to which our traders have access. That this external, independently generated wealth may have to be generated here and controlled by us is basically the story of the more than $110 billion in various categories of financial assistance which we disbursed abroad from 1945 through 1962.

Related to this, there is the very plain question, How is it that the imports by which foreign sale of the surplus is to be financed will not simply replace the domestic surplus and so recreate the original problem? At the meanest level, this is handled by our demand that others "multilateralize" their trade accounts. We scorn the European who wants a balanced import-export relation with us. He should not keep one book for each trading partner, we say, he should keep one for all; that is, we expect him to finance his purchase from us through favorable balances achieved with others. At a more civilized level, the theory of international specialization of labor is invoked: Demand bites into *things,* not dollar values. But most basically this problem is handled by what at bottom is simple confidence in the future: If the assembly-line auto worker believes GM can sell all the cars he finds himself bolting together, then he will count on having a job and an income next year, and he will therefore borrow money for, say, a Japanese camera, both he and the bank being confident that he will be able to meet the payments. The soul of capitalism is private debt.

Another problem, more "modern" and more difficult, stems from the fact that a full-tilt capitalist economy produces a different kind of export item—money itself. Over the long haul, one man's foreign-invested dollar makes money—as we shall see later, quite a lot. But aggregate outflow in any period of expansion will exceed aggregate inflow, and that difference amounts to a dollar deficit which, curiously enough, is both short-range and permanent. (The reason is that two perfectly good accounting systems can be used in reporting it.) Government people characteristically call it permanent; business people say it is short-range. Both know it exists: It was $2.8 billion in 1964. This was cut in 1965 to $1.4 billion through the Administration's "temporary" program of "voluntary" restraints, but it was on the way up again in the first quarter of 1966, a period during which our customary favorable trade balance was disappointingly low. (In fact, if U.S.-subsidized exports are subtracted from the total, the 1965 trade surplus falls to what *Fortune* calls "a puny rate of $1.5 billion, the lowest of the 1960s."[44]) If nothing is done to stop the expansionary outward flow of capital, the dollar deficit mounts; but if government wants to retard it and therefore raises taxes and the rent rates on money, continuing high demand will inflate the currency, and the foreign dollar holders react by cashing dollars in for gold. In 1964, when the boom had captured everyone's heart, only 5 percent of the deficit was converted into gold. In 1965, the year of the restrictions, more than 90 percent was converted.

These are tough, real problems, and their management requires great skill. But they are not finally the central preoccupation of American statecraft. They can always be solved, so it is believed, if the *prime* problem is solved. And that prime problem—the main nut and kernel of American foreign policy from its earliest days onwards—is to ensure the availability of fertile frontiers to American business. The economic doors must be opened; the survival of our system depends upon it.

The Cold War ideology which we manipulated in Chapter II had put quite another face on things. That ideology held that the peace American leaders pursued was of a plain, unvarnished kind, a simple peace in which good-neighbor nations let each other alone. This is incorrect. We want peace, to be sure. All nations want peace. But we want a certain kind of peace, one which seems to have very little to do with letting good neighbors alone or with democracy or progress. Put it roughly: For us, peace finally exists when the world is finally safe for American businessmen to carry on their business everywhere, on terms as favorable as they can be made, in settings managed preferably by native middle-class governments, but if need be by oligarchic and repressive ones, by the old foreign grads of Fort Bragg, or if the panic hits in a pivotal place, by our own Marines.

But such a formulation no doubt seems a thousand times too crude. This immensely violent struggle that divides the world must be about something much larger, much more important and epic than mortals' purses, must have more in it that this primitive, even shabby lust for profit at any price. It must surely not be for plunder alone that the West, under the imperial leadership of first this great state, then the other —Spain, France, England, America—has labored to make its dominion universal. This labor, which has galvanized our bravest hands, must have been undertaken in the name of Western civilization at its best, the highest known form of human culture—in the name, for example, of the Renaissance.

Such phrases make Cold War Man happier about himself. I would not begrudge him his happiness, but only wonder if he might not try to understand its basis a little better. What was the soul of this Renaissance? Was Florence the art of Leonardo the Great or the cash control of Lorenzo the Magnificent? Was Venice Titian or the merchants who ran it with such composure? Was Isabella's hero Bermejo or Columbus—or the Archbishop of Toledo? Who was closer to the soul of Elizabethan England, Shakespeare or Francis Drake? One can talk of cultures as one pleases. What our Western culture most plainly announces to the world is that things—people, land, oceans—are to be defined by their uses and the type of ownership to which they submit themselves. It is under the piercing gaze of Western man that the world turns into property. The denominating questions of our culture are: Who owns this? What is it good for? Who stands to profit from it? Culture philosophy does not transcend the profit motive. It merely reveals the profit motive's transcendency.

The West wants a world that is integrated and (in Max Weber's sense) rationalized in terms of the stability of resources, labor, production, distribution, and markets. As the leader of the West, America wants that integrated, rationalized world to run under the management of her own business people. Others do not. They have acquired powers of resistance in the East. Therefore there is an East–West struggle, in our time called the Cold War.

IV

Free World Empire

Even anti-Imperialists welcome an Imperial policy which contemplates no conquests but those of commerce.

—London *Times*, 1900[1]

We [Americans] shall run the world's business whether the world likes it or not. The world can't help it—and neither can we, I guess.

—Holroyd, in Conrad's *Nostromo*, 1904

Neither America nor the Western tradition which America has brought to maturity will be rightly understood until one understands that free enterprise is ultimately a political theory, that it bases itself upon an ethical premise of conflict, and that its virtue system appropriately confers esteem and privilege not upon the humane (although humanity is not precluded) but upon the willful and relentless—the powerful.

Applied to international politics, these virtues demand imperialism, imperialism being most basically the forcible (however indirect) management of one state's political economy by another state.

But imperialism has many operational modes. The American world businessman may very well think of himself as a liberal, a liberator, a hardened anti-imperialist *cum* anticommunist. He points out to us that he has no flag of commerce and arms, assures us that he wants only the chance to do business, and feels no contradiction when he at once repledges his support for the holding and extending of the Free World.

It is the word "free," of course, which is so misleading. One supposes off hand that the Free World must be that part of the earth in which men enjoy civil rights and liberties. That these rights and liberties are of the Western liberal tradition more than of any other, that they are both more practiced and more practical in the West than elsewhere, and that their existence is intimately connected to the development of Western capitalism are all historically indisputable truths. The Free World is freer in this sense than the non-Western world. But we also observe that this Free World is considered to include more than the Western democracies. It includes Spain and Portugal, Mozambique and South Africa, Paraguay and Argentina, Thailand and Formosa. So, whatever its connotation, the freedom denoted by this term "Free World" must be different. It can only mean freedom of capital access: The Free World is the world economic area in which the American businessman enjoys greatest freedom of commercial maneuver. Simply add to this the observation that America is the *leader* of the Free World, and one has grasped the essentials of America's Free World imperialism. The Free World, full of special situations, ununiform and continually in flux, is nevertheless at root the basically integrated zone of American economic hegemony. The Free World itself is the American Empire.

America's contribution to the steadily evolving art of Western empire is simple but profound. Almost haphazardly, America built an efficiency case against colonial imperialism. Colonies created a host of ugly and unnecessary problems—centrally, the problem of colonial nationalism, which always threatened to culminate in riot and rebellion and thus impaired the security of the economic control mechanisms. Much better than the idea of the imperial colony (defined by earth coordinates, rivers, mountain ranges, and racial and ethnic discontinuities) was the idea of the open market (defined by real and potential wealth, labor reserves, shipping and distribution networks, and so on). This idea relocates the center of imperial impulse (shutting off such fustian as "the white man's burden") and more sharply defines the dimensions of imperial victory. It sees cultures in terms of their systemic economic components and pays less attention to their political habits and geographical shapes. An imperfect example (imperfect because it finally worked itself out in nearly ritual militarism) is Japan's prewar doctrine of the Greater East Asia Coprosperity Sphere, in which China was seen not as a unitary geopolitical entity to be conquered whole, devoured by destiny, but rather as a specific uneven pattern of economic resources and potentials whose most strategic relationship was with other such systems. Economies were to be organized horizontally with other economies instead of vertically with their national cultural environment. Transnational economics replaces national politics.

In America's pragmatic and opportunistic revision of the forms of empire, the old-fashioned European colony or sphere of influence becomes a materials source and a market to be developed in concert with other sources and markets, often along the lines of a global specialization of labor. In an old and famous instance, China makes silk, Turkey opium; American traders monopolize Turkish opium, barter it for Chinese silk, and bring the silk to America.* Of the local political position of Turkey or China, it is important only that it not obstruct the orderly development of the systemized whole. The colony, an economic sphere whose boundaries are no longer seen as mainly territorial, becomes the site of an open, free-enterprise competition—which of course will be won by the leading economic power. For the idea of the nation, Free World imperialism substitutes the idea of the integrated global economic system. For the conqueror's idea of territorial boundaries, it substitutes the engineer's idea of interwoven economic components.†

America produced such a theory at least in part because she had come last to the table to find the bountiful places already occupied. Our half-century-old anticolonialism may have originated as a somewhat resentful demand for access to the imperial spheres already established (notably in China) by the European and Asian powers. The Open Door Policy affirmed the priority of our economics over their politics, a specific to American commercial requirements.‡

Free World imperialism responds to the problem of small-state nationalism by arguing in effect that collaborative native

* Comecon, the East European response to the Common Market, is a bloc attempt to "rationalize" an international economy along these lines, one country producing the food, another mining the ore, a third refining the steel. This departed from the more autarkic model employed up to about 1955, and that departure is one of the reasons for Romania's difficulties with the U.S.S.R.: Romania has voiced a basic preference for national self-sufficiency over bloc interdependency.[2]

† Thorstein Veblen's *The Engineers and the Price System* (Harbinger, 1963), first published in 1921, is an interesting and wieldy elaboration on the theme of economic systems engineering.

‡ And during World War II, as America continued to push for access to Europe's colonies, justifying this with the same open-

government is more stable than foreign overlordship, and that through the sophisticated use of economic pressure and inducement (sometimes called "education"), native governments can be persuaded to make all the correct decisions. The colonial governor and the Foreign Legion become simultaneously obsolete, there remaining no need to debase and infuriate native peoples with colonial status. That is, one of the saddest features of America's open-door, free-market, anticolonial, Wilsonian, Free World imperialism is that it preferred not to be imperialism. Like the wasp that masters but does not mutilate its prey with one well-placed paralyzing sting, America wanted the substance without the show, the riches without the act of overt plunder. Her wild anticommunism is some kind of evidence that she failed. The colonial governor is back, calling himself now an ambassador, and our Foreign Legionnaires wear green berets. But whether from naïveté or a very tall guile, we seem to have wanted a different outcome, an expansion confined to commerce, culturally unintrusive, even helpful to the host. That was a new idea. Compare it with the French attempt to Frenchify their colonies, to transplant French cultural forms at whatever expense to the native culture, with unsurprisingly disastrous results to the life of the colonized and the composure of the *colon*. As French Indochina's first civilian governor confessed in 1885, "We have destroyed the past and nothing has taken its place."[4] What France got for her trouble was a great deal of rubber at a very good price and a handful of superb Asian scholars; and transported back to that time, a modern American consultant might have pointed out that these prizes were available without the misguided effort to turn Hanoi into a kind of Paris.

But for all its pretenses of cultural and political nonintervention, American Free World imperialism has been fully as damaging and fully as predatory. The economic life of a culture cannot be changed without consequence to every other aspect of the culture. Money propagates. Western economic systems need Westernized economic infrastruc-

---

doorist rhetoric, Roosevelt policy-maker William L. Clayton said: "As a matter of fact, if we want to be honest with ourselves, we will find that many of the sins that we freely criticize other countries for practicing [i.e., colonial protectionism] have their counterparts in the United States."[3]

tures, a Westernized legal apparatus, a Westernized labor force, and ultimately a Western political bias. Commercial impact is total impact.

It is this same impact of West on East, so often a mauling of sophisticated but undynamic cultures, which the explainers of Free World imperialism represent as at root a healthy phenomenon. They explain over and again to the good American people, whom they apparently suspect of retaining a residual antipathy for injustice, that such social fissures as may agonize the "developing" countries are the entirely natural by-products of the "revolution of modernization" (or "rising expectations"), which is depicted as basically independent of external causes: a historical process which unwinds of itself as slumbering peoples come awake. It could hardly be clearer that this "modernization" is only a polite name for the rude, concussive impact of technological cultures upon the nontechnological. But official theories gloss over American responsibility for the dislocations induced by American expansion, and the idea that the nearly ubiquitous traumatizing of the Third World might have something to do with a specific American cash profit is rarely even entertained. A representative expression of this viewpoint, the following passages are from Walt Whitman Rostow's famous address to the 1961 graduating class of the Army's Fort Bragg Special Warfare School (Rostow is President Johnson's chief foreign-policy adviser and probably America's leading Cold War theoretician):

> What is happening throughout Latin America, Africa, the Middle East, and Asia is this: Old societies are changing their ways in order to create and maintain a national personality on the world scene and to bring to their peoples the benefits modern technology can offer. This process is truly revolutionary. . . .
>
> Like all revolutions, the revolution of modernization is disturbing. . . . Men and women in the villages and the cities, feeling that the old ways of life are shaken and that new possibilities are open to them, express old resentments and new hopes. . . .
>
> This is the grand arena of revolutionary change which the Communists are exploiting with such great energy. . . . We Americans are confident that, if the independence of this process can be maintained over the coming years and decades, these societies will choose their own version of what we would recognize as a democratic, open society. . . .
>
> Thus, our central task in the underdeveloped areas . . . is to

protect the independence of the revolutionary process now going forward. . . .

The diffusion of power is the basis for freedom within our own society, and we have no reason to fear it on the world scene. But this outcome would be a defeat for communism. . . . [Communists] are driven in the end, by the nature of their system, to violate the independence of nations. . . . We are struggling to maintain an environment on the world scene which will permit our open society to survive and to flourish.[5]

The key elements of Rostow's thoroughly mainline vision are the following:

1. Tacit disavowal of Western responsibility for that "turbulence" that is caused primarily by the Western intrusion—commercial, ideological, military—into the East and South.

2. The claim that America's purpose is the creation of free, independent, and (what is not so obvious) *technological* societies. This is, of course, an inherently contradictory claim.

3. Repudiation of the possibility that "communism" (which, for Rostow, probably stands for any oppositionist political violence) can also be a nationalism. That is, Rostow's language presents us with that old familiar image of the Communist as a man without a country, someone who has always appeared from some other place, and whose allegiance always lies elsewhere. (Communists, he says, are "scavengers," and communism is "a disease of transition.") What such a description has on its side is the theory of some Bolshevik ideologues, mostly the Trotskyists, that the proletarian revolution would be international (class above flag) and would have to result in the decomposition of the nation-state, a bourgeois institution. What it has going against it is about two hundred years of history. With the variously resolved American, French, Russian, Chinese, and Cuban revolutions behind us, we are obliged to conclude that popular revolutions, whatever their opening fusillade of rhetoric, are unfailingly nationalistic. The only genuinely internationalist (better, transnationalist) group in the modern world is what Marx called the ruling class; Veblen, the captains of finance; Mill, the power elite; and the organs of our popular culture, the jet set. Rostow pays attention to none of this. He is an inverted Trotskyist.*

* In his *Prospects for Communist China* (M.I.T. Press, Cambridge, 1954, pp. 27–28), Rostow takes on the problem, Why did

4. Virtually explicit declaration that America shall be the sole judge of the permissibility of social change everywhere, that America confers upon herself (as Free World leader) all rights of preemptory intervention in the change process, and that America requires the ultimate emergence of "independent, modern" societies. Both American practice and ideology require us to assume that this means open-door economies. Thus, America demands and will only tolerate such "revolutions" as widen the Free World empire.

5. Insistence (a traditional theme) that the final emergence of open-door societies *is required for America's survival.*

The Holy Roman arrogance of this will grow only more suffocating if one reflects upon the harrowing inability of this judge, jury, and executioner America to solve her own internal problems. Worsening American racism, poverty, Big Brotherhood, and militaristic oligarchism confer upon the world a right to wonder about us. How can an America which cannot develop east Kentucky or pacify Harlem develop India and pacify Vietnam?

But we should push the question harder. The Rostovian thesis can be boiled down to two large claims; namely, that what he calls our "protecting the independence of revolutionary modernization" and what I call our Free World imperialism

1. develops the underdeveloped; and
2. promotes their freedom, meaning
    a) that their governments are independent, and
    b) that their people enjoy basic civil rights and liberties.

---

the Chinese Communists prefer military coalition with Chiang's Nationalist forces against the Japanese invaders? Why did they not prefer continued civil war? With stroke after stroke, in an intellectual performance that strikes me as no less brilliant than bizarre, Rostow lays bare an immense Red dissimulation: They wanted coalition because Russia wanted Japan stopped, because they wanted Chiang to spend himself against the Japanese, because they wanted to seem patriotic to the people, because coalition offered propaganda channels, because it would allow them to extend their civil administration. For Rostow, it is not even a possibility to be named and dismissed that these Reds may also have been Chinese people who cared about China, and who for ordinary patriotic reasons wanted to hit the invaders with everything China could muster. For him, the Communist is a political Martian. Rostow is my favorite Cold Warrior.

These are concrete claims and they can be concretely examined. What follows is, first, a pointillistic statistical sketch of the American corporation whose impact, for good or bad, is being felt by the underdeveloped countries; next, looking at a few of the countries considered to lie in the domain of the rescued and protected, we shall ask: Are their economies developing? Are their governments independent of other governments? Does the freedom of their people prosper, and is its growth being stimulated?

The American supercorporation is no longer defined mainly by its product. It combines in itself the basic functions that once distinguished finance and industry as separate spheres. It pulls together and coordinates the economic acts of capital accumulation and dispersion (banking), technological innovation ("inventors"), production (plant construction and management), distribution (middleman enterprise), and demand management (the free market). By persuasion and purchase, it has won the cooperation of the labor bureaucracies, whose corporate responsibility is to guarantee the stability of the nation's labor force. Between management and organized labor, there are no fundamentally divisive questions of values or aims; they are unequal members of the same corporate entity. With the active or passive support of labor and government, management coordinates centrally all operations in the source-to-user product stream, vertical integration being crucial for efficiency. Decision-making is scientific and centralized.

The supercorporation's immensity and power may be suggested by the following passage from *In Few Hands* (Penguin, 1965), Estes Kefauver's posthumously published record of his Senate committee's antitrust investigations:

> In 1962 the 20 largest manufacturing corporations alone had $73.8 billion in assets, or about one quarter of the total assets of the United States manufacturing companies. In turn, the 50 largest companies held 36 per cent; the 100 largest, 46 per cent; the 200 largest, 56 per cent; and the 1000 largest, nearly 75 per cent.

Geared in directly or indirectly with the major financial and industrial centers of Europe, these giants inspired Development and Resources Corporation Chairman David E. Lilienthal (TVA director for Roosevelt, AEC director for Truman) to coin the now standard term "multinational corporation."[6] With the equally globalized big banks with which they are interlocked, the multinational corporations are the chief sources of American overseas investment capital.

The value of direct U.S. investment abroad, less than $25 billion in 1955, was about $50 billion a decade later and increasing at a rate of about $10 million a day.[7] Total U.S. foreign investment, direct and portfolio,* was about $130 billion in 1965, of which more than 30 percent was in oil.[8] Of the $50 billion total direct foreign investment, 60 percent is invested in Canada and Europe; of the 40 percent invested in the underdeveloped countries, half is in Latin America.[9]

The multinational corporation does not merely export its products and money; it transplants itself. In 1965 about 2000 American firms were doing business abroad, and of their net foreign sales of $110 billion, only one fifth of that amount came from sale of goods and products shipped from the United States. Extreme instances of transplant occur in the automobile industry. In 1965 General Motors built 20 percent of its cars outside the United States, Chrysler 30 percent, and Ford 40 percent.[10]

Europe is apprehensive. The aggregate sales of Volkswagen, Fiat, Daimler-Benz, British Motors, and Renault are only two thirds of Ford's sales, only one third of GM's. U.S. firms control almost the entire electronics industry of France, produce 90 percent of her synthetic rubber, distribute 65 percent of her petroleum, and manufacture 65 percent of her farm machinery.[11] Louis Armand has said, "Unless Europe reacts and gets organized, we are condemning ourselves to industrial colonization."[12] He is echoed by Gaston Defferre: "The economic invasion by the United States is a clear and present danger. American economic power, the dynamic power of its big businesses and the size of their investments in Europe . . . are the beginning of the colonization of our economy."[13] German officials of government and industry react by urging the merger of European firms, especially in steel and cars, both on a national and continental basis.

The direction of the growth of American corporate control abroad is no easier to predict than its inner process is to describe, but Richard J. Barber, special counsel for the Senate

* Direct investments give the investor a voice, sometimes controlling, in the management of the enterprise. Portfolio investments usually do not.

Subcommittee on Antitrust and Monopoly, offers an expert's guess:

> By functioning multinationally, American and other business corporations have effectively avoided the reach of the antitrust laws of any single country in which they produce or sell their wares. . . . Based on recent experience, 300 corporations will by 1975 control more than 75 per cent of all industrial assets.[14]

The overseas expansion of corporate America has the ardent support of the American government, if not of the French. The U.S. government cooperates in many different ways. For one, it operates the Agency for International Development, which *Forbes* calls "the principal agency through which the U.S. government finances business abroad. . . . AID distributes about $2 billion a year. Of this, 85 percent is spent in the U.S. for American products and raw materials."[15]* For another, the U.S. government helps capitalize and manage such Free World financial institutions as the International Bank for Reconstruction and Development (the World Bank), the International Finance Corporation, the Export-Import Bank, the Inter-American Development Bank, the Overseas Development Fund, and the International Development Association, all of which (but notably the World Bank and the Ex-Im Bank) exist to serve the international interest of the American-dominated multinational corporation either by the direct financing of certain ventures or, more importantly, by financing the development of that infrastructure—roads, railroads, docks, power plants—which private capital feels it cannot afford to build, cannot live without, and deserves to have.[18]

This expansionary corporation may or may not stimulate

* For a different but complementary view of AID, consider this statement by D. A. Fitzgerald, former deputy director of the United States International Cooperation Administration: "A lot of criticism of foreign aid is because the critic thought the objective was to get economic growth, and this wasn't the objective at all. . . . The objective may have been to buy a lease, or to get a favorable vote in the UN, or to keep a nation from falling apart, or to keep some country from giving the Russians airbase rights, or any one of many other reasons."[16] AID also uses the public money to ensure American companies' overseas operations. Toward the end of 1965, AID issued its biggest single policy, $179 million, to guarantee International Telephone & Telegraph's Chilean expansion against losses from inconvertible currency, expropriation, war, and revolution.[17]

the growth of material prosperity and the advance of democratic values in the host countries; we shall look into that shortly. But there is no question that this expansion is highly profitable to the corporations themselves. Chase Manhattan Bank Chairman David Rockefeller insists that U.S. profits in Latin America are not usually great: "The United States investment in Latin America has fortunately been moderately successful [he puts it at about 13 percent], but it can hardly be called 'exploitative.' "[19] This is not an entirely lame dissimulation. Figures can be produced to serve his point. It is not at all easy to determine the absolute profitability of our overseas operations. One reason for this is that a variety of concealing accounting techniques are available to the imperial clerk. For a simple and basic example, imagine a corporation in which the home-based production unit buys its materials from the foreign-based extractive unit. Corporate management may direct the latter to keep its prices low since low book profits will result in local tax advantages, and in any case will be recouped at the production end.

But it is still possible to get a good general sense of the immense cash value of our corporations' foreign adventures. "In industry after industry," said *Business Week* in 1963, "U.S. companies found that their overseas earnings were soaring, and that their return on investment abroad was frequently much higher than in the U.S. As earnings abroad began to rise, profit margins from domestic operations started to shrink. . . . This is the combination that forced development of the multinational company."[20] Department of Commerce figures show that in the period 1950–61 there was a direct American foreign investment outflow of $13.7 billion. In the same period, returned income was $23.2 billion, a profit of $9.5 billion.[21] A survey made by the First National City Bank concluded that "remitted income [i.e., repatriated profit] on private investment abroad is actually the largest single item of our international receipts apart from merchandise exports."[22] A British survey in 1961 showed that American companies doing business in England averaged a 17 percent return on their investment, twice as high as the average return in the United States.[23]

For profitability, the underdeveloped world is at least Europe's equal, more probably its superior. Standard Oil of New Jersey *reports* a 17.6 percent return on its Latin

American investment and a 15 percent return on Eastern Hemisphere investments for 1962, compared with a 7.4 percent return on domestic.[24] Commerce Department figures show Americans putting $516 million (new investment and unreturned earnings) into Europe in 1956 and taking home $280 million. By 1961 the nearly 2-to-1 investments–earnings ratio had dropped toward 3 to 1: $1.5 billion new investment, $525 million returned earnings. Compare the figures for Latin America, remembering that the stakes here are the real wealth and real labor of Latin American people, not just so many numbers in a book: In 1956 we invested $500 million and returned a profit almost half again as big, $770 million, for a net capital loss to Latin America of $270 million.[25]

That cold, still statistic of profit and loss is a statement about someone's happiness and someone else's pain, the uneven qualities of the lives of men and women. It needs to be worked, mined, laid open. With some general sense of what the multinational American corporation is doing for itself, we move now to examine the condition of its hosts. Does the global expansion of the American commercial state develop the underdeveloped? Does it democratize the public life of man? Does it make for nations which, in Rostow's words, "stand up straight" and are "strong, assertive, and independent"?

Some cases.

Brazil stands first among Latin American recipients of U.S. military aid ($206 million through 1963), third in U.S. economic assistance ($172.6 million plus $1.4 billion in World Bank and Ex-Im Bank loans), and is only second to Venezuela in direct U.S. investment (more than $1 billion).[26] It is the biggest, most populated, and potentially richest of all the South American countries; in any long-term sense, the key to the economic and political development of the continent. It deserves more than a glance.

Brazil's revolution has been fitfully pulsing since 1930, when Getulio D. Vargas of the Labor Party came to power, first as provisional president (1930–33), then as elected president (1933).[27] Attacked once from the left and three times from the right, he was finally overthrown in 1945 by a right-wing military junta which called itself democratic and revolutionary, reversed his moderate reformist policies, and brought on depressed wages, high joblessness, rising inflation—and more U.S. corporations. The 1950 elections returned Vargas to power, convinced more than ever of the need for national management of national resources, Brazilian ownership of Brazil. He created Petrobras (national oil) and Electrobras (power), and in August 1954, despairing of the struggle against what his farewell note called "the looting by international economic and finance groups," he killed himself.

After one year of routine dictatorship under Café Filho (more social decay, more foreign money) came the presidency of Juscelino Kubitschek, who founded the interior capital of Brasilia, a visionary's act, but who could not resist the further penetration of Brazil's economy by the strong northern interests. He was followed in 1961 by Janio Quadros, winner of the largest majority vote ever received by a Brazilian president. Quadros was a ramrod conservative. He put down hunger riots in the agony-rich northeast with the Fourth Army and student agitation with the police. But he was also a nationalist. He saw a Brazil which led the world in coffee exports, had more arable land than all of Europe, 15 percent of the world's forests, 35 percent of its iron deposits, and one of its highest hydroelectric potentials. That such a country was poor was a disgrace. That it should remain poor was a crime. Quadros moved to change Brazil. "Why should the United States trade with Russia and her satellites," he said, "but insist that Brazil trade only with the United States?"[28] He renewed relations with the U.S.S.R., made trade agreements with Communist countries, and treated Castro as that nationalist revolutionary whose motive was so easy to grasp from the vantage of the slums of Rio. The right-wing barons Adhemar de Barros and Carlos Lacerda were observed to cast dark intimate glances to the north.

In August 1961, Quadros went too far: a show of independence at the Punte del Este founding of the Alliance for Progress; the *Cruzeiro do Sul* for Che Guevara; vice president João Goulart in Peking on a trade mission; worst of all, a new tax proposal designed to strengthen the federal budget, stimulate investment in the northeast, and retain for Brazil's uses a larger share of the profits being removed from the country.

Within days the army held Quadros' "resignation" in its

hands. But the Barros-Lacerda plans for an old-fashioned junta rule were resisted by the people, who demanded that succession of office be maintained and that Goulart succeed to the presidency. Some now contend that at that moment the liberal millionaire Goulart might have broken the hold of the plutocrats once and for all. The army was divided and the people were behind him, peasants and workers, students and the middle class, leftists and nationalists together in the constitutionalist resistance called the *Legalidade*. But Goulart was indecisive. He chose to negotiate with the rightists and accept their demand for a weakened presidential office. After a year and a half of stagnation, a plebiscite restored full presidential power by a vote of 6 to 1. Goulart, however, ignored the mandate. His speeches blazed with the promise of social change, but not one of his reform proposals even reached the congress. The Bank of Brazil continued to print the watered money with which the monopolies financed their inefficiency; expensive coffee price supports were never touched. General Peri Belacuva used troops to break up popular demonstrations that called for nothing more than implementation of Goulart's own program; Belacuva was made chief of staff. More concessions were granted to American oil and mineral firms. Having tightened to 600 to the dollar at the time of the plebiscite, the cruzeiro fell to 1700 to 1.

Exasperated progressives and nationalists began to press harder for action, and perhaps Goulart was at last beginning to respond. Suddenly he was defying America on the Cuba question, disarmament, and trade. He spoke of suffrage for illiterates (half the people) and legal relief for the bedraggled and conservative Communist party. He revealed his socialist tendencies by expropriating some oil holdings (Brazilian, not American). On January 17, 1964, he committed again the most criminal crime of attacking American profits. "The new regulations," wrote Juan de Onis from Rio, "limit the legal remittance of profits abroad to 10 percent a year of the real foreign investment of a company in equipment and capital." "Regarded as hostile to foreign capital," the new profit-restriction rules were a response "to nationalist demands for higher controls on foreign investors." (*NYT*, January 18, 1964.)

This finally triggered a response from an intriguing São

Paulo group, which *Fortune*'s Philip Siekman ("When Executives Turned Revolutionaries," September 1964) says had been growing since the middle fifties. Known either as the Paulistas (after their city) or the Mesquitas (after their leader Júlio de Mesquita Filho, owner of São Paulo's conservative newspaper, *O Estado de São Paulo*), the group consisted of important São Paulo businessmen like Paulo Ayres Filho (its founder and one-time head of the Bank of Brazil), Flavio Galvão, Luis Warneck, and João-Adelino Prado Neto (editor of the Mesquita paper). By 1964 the group had won the support of Adhemar de Barros, governor of São Paulo and commander of that state's forty-thousand-man militia; Carlos Lacerda, governor of Guanabara; and the (World War II) Brazilian Expeditionary Force, which gave it access to important members of the military elite. Early in 1964, writes Siekman—perhaps spurred by Goulart's last-minute reformist vigor—the Mesquita group sent an emissary to ask U.S. Ambassador Lincoln Gordon what the U.S. position would be if civil war broke out. The emissary reported back that Gordon was cautious and diplomatic, but he left the impression that if the Paulistas could hold out for forty-eight hours they would get U.S. recognition and help.[29]

Event chased event. On March 14 the Brazilian right wing met to plan impeachment proceedings against Goulart (*NYT*, March 16, 1964). On March 15 Goulart called for new constitutional amendments to "free national energies crushed by the narrowness of an outdated economic structure that serves the interests of the privileged groups only" (*NYT*, March 16, 1964). On the same day, Latin delegates to the third-anniversary conference of the Alliance for Progress assembled in Washington. In the air were the still-unsettled Panama dispute, de Gaulle's triumphant trip to Mexico, rumblings of unrest in Colombia, new leftist electoral gains in Chile, China's about-to-be-announced major grain deal with Argentina, and, above all, what Tad Szulc called "the pre-revolutionary state" of Brazil (*NYT*, March 15, 1964)—pro-Goulart rioting in Brasilia, anti-Goulart demonstrations in São Paulo, and presidential candidate Kubitschek's promise to make the Alliance "wilt like a flower" (*NYT*, March 19, 1964). On March 16 President Johnson addressed the Alliance delegates: "But I now today assure you that the full power of the United States is ready to assist any country whose freedom is threatened by force dictated from beyond the shores of this [*sic!*] continent." On March 18 Assistant Secretary of State for Inter-American Affairs Thomas C. Mann conferred privately with U.S. Latin American diplomats, and Tad Szulc's front-page *Times* story the next day was headlined: "U.S. May Abandon Effort to Deter Latin Dictators." Szulc wrote, "Mr. Mann's views were considered as representing a radical modification of the policies of the Kennedy administration" (*NYT*, March 19, 1964). On March 19 State Department spokesman Richard I. Phillips came forward to deny a policy change, but seemed in fact to confirm it. Alluding to the Estrado Doctrine (diplomatic recognition based on control, not on politics), Phillips explained that "United States policy toward unconstitutional governments will, as in the past, be guided by the national interest and the circumstances peculiar to each situation as it arises"* (*NYT*, March 20, 1964).

It appears that all of Latin America immediately understood what it had heard. Brazilian Communists left for Mexico City; the idealistic governor of Rio Grande do Sul, Leonel Brizola (then a JFK admirer, today in exile), called on the people to prepare for a new *Legalidade*; and two weeks after the Johnson speech, on April 1, Goulart was almost ritualistically removed from office by the Barros-Lacerda-Mesquita combine. Less than twenty-four hours after the news of the *golpe* reached Washington, before it was even known that Goulart had left the capital, President Johnson wired "America's warmest good wishes" to the new government, which was shortly to consolidate around General Humberto Castelo Branco (elected president, April 11, 1964) and to proclaim its love of democracy and revolution.† On July 22 the Congress voted to extend Branco's term to March 15, 1967.

* In fact, this had not been United States policy "in the past." At various times and for varying durations, Kennedy had suspended aid to and broken diplomatically with undemocratic governments in Argentina, Haiti, Peru, Guatemala, Ecuador, the Dominican Republic, and Honduras (*NYT*, March 19, 1964). Nor was Brazil the first instance of the Johnson turnabout. *The New York Times* reported on March 21 that the United States had renewed aid to Haiti, which Kennedy had suspended in 1962 (see discussion of Haiti). The new loan had been approved on March 9. To avoid an open policy reversal, the loan had been placed through the Inter-American Bank.

† Castelo Branco plays an intriguing game with the generals of the so-called hard-line right. In this game, the generals demand

By November 1964, the United States had dramatized its enthusiasm for the new regime by a loan of $400 million over and above already programed Alliance for Progress funds.[30]* Castelo Branco was quick to reveal his understanding and gratitude. On November 25, 1964, the government imprisoned one hundred former aides of the governor of Goias on a vague charge of subversion. Four months later, a new law made possible the lengthy imprisonment of individuals without declaration of offense or pressing of charges. During the same period, the government announced a new tax proposal designed to finance a 35 percent increase in military salaries. On October 27, 1965, Institutional Act No. 2 was promulgated, banning all thirteen existing political parties and creating two new ones, one to serve as "loyal opposition."[31] Around the same time, government attempts to sanitize the faculty of the University of Brasilia provoked student-faculty protests, mass faculty resignations, and finally the virtual closing of the university. On January 27, 1966, all ports were declared national security zones, which automatically made all dock strikes and slowdowns military crimes.[32]

A month after that, speaking in Belo Horizonte, Branco defended his government against the charge that it was dictatorial. "Say what they will," he declared, "the adversaries of the revolution . . . cannot negate the fact that here in Brazil we have in full force the two greatest and most basic expressions of a real democracy: the National Congress and

---

fascism, Castelo Branco answers that they go too far, everyone is impressed with Castelo Branco's courageous stand, and Castelo Branco proceeds to do essentially what the hard-liners wanted in the first place. As this is written, the Brazilian people are showing a surprisingly solid resistance; the activist students are beginning to enjoy more and more popular support; and within this turbulence other surprises unfold: The formerly reactionary Catholic hierarchy takes an advanced antigovernment stand, and Carlos Lacerda, of all people, comes out for land reform, nationalizations, democracy, and so on. Perhaps the ecclesiastical elite has really been converted to Christianity and perhaps they have saved Lacerda. But perhaps the oligarchic fugue only adds a new variation, orchestrates itself with new brass. There is at the moment no reason to believe that hard-liner General Costa e Silva's "election" will not take place as planned. (Since the forgoing was written, he has been named to a four-year term.)

* For the way $400 million can be shrunk to $40 million and then advertised as a cool billion, see note, page 92.

freedom of the press."* Four months earlier, the day after the Second Institutional Act was decreed, Minister of Justice Juraci Magalhães is supposed to have met in Rio with a select group of Brazilian editors and publishers to explain the act's provisions and "complementary decrees." The meeting was private, if not secret, and certainly off the record; but a verbatim transcript was made and smuggled out, later to be printed in the organ of the Brazilian Christian underground movement, *Revolution.* Portions of the transcript follow.

Magalhães informed the press that the government would no longer permit:

(*a*) the publication of interviews with those who have had their mandates in office curtailed or their political rights annulled . . . ; (*b*) any threats to or provocations of the revolutionary government, such as referring to it as a dictatorship . . . ; (*c*) aid to subversion by any means or the publication of news that causes the people to oppose the government; (*d*) the publication of articles written by newsmen who have lost their political rights.

That last point provoked the following conversation:

DANTON JOBIM (of the *Última Hora*): Your excellency means that we cannot publish any pronouncements whatsoever made by people who have had their political rights suspended?

MAGALHÃES: That's exactly what I said. You are an old friend of mine, but you'll be punished if you disobey. Is that clear?

JOBIM: Very clear.

ROBERTO MARINHO (*Globo*): I do not agree that a newsman who has lost his political rights should be punished. I assume the responsibility—the full responsibility for everything that is published in my newspaper. And I shall vehemently protest if you try to make me fire some of the newsmen that work for me who have lost their political rights.

MAGALHÃES: The law will be enforced. You and the newsman will be punished. You are both responsible.

MARINHO: Even if the article is not signed?

MAGALHÃES: No. It is obvious that if he writes an unsigned article, we wouldn't know about it. The law means that these newsmen who have lost their political rights cannot use the press

* This quotation and the material that follows are from the English-language edition of *Revolution*, the newspaper (mimeo) of the Brazilian Christian underground. Verification of the Magalhães dialogue is impossible for the obvious reason that those supposedly taking part in it would condemn themselves by confirming that it took place.

to provoke or threaten the government or to spread subversion. It's simply that.

MARINHO: Oh! Okay.

NASCIMENTO BRITO (*Jornal do Brasil*): How can we know if we're threatening the government? Does this mean we cannot comment on the acts of the government?

MAGALHÃES: No. The government does not have the intention of restricting your liberty, but of preventing subversion. We have a criterion by which to decide what constitutes provocation, and we will adhere to it strictly.

JOÃO DANTAS (*Diario do Notícias*): How do you expect us to know if someone is the spokesman of someone who has lost his political rights? How are we supposed to guard against this?

MAGALHÃES: You will be able to know this by reading the material the spokesman gives you. In any case, the majority of these spokesmen are well known to all of us.

AN UNIDENTIFIED PERSON: I would like to take this opportunity to ask a few questions. Is there a new list of people who will lose their political rights?

MAGALHÃES: This is a good example of the kind of question we consider provocative. If you ask it again, you will be punished according to law.

SAME PERSON: Don't misunderstand me. I'm only asking a question.

MAGALHÃES: And if you ask it again, you will be punished.

So much for the promoting of Rostow's Free World democracy. What about developing the underdeveloped?

Within the year, the Mann-Gordon-Branco government had passed a set of bills cutting short the construction of new steel mills and authorizing Castelo Branco to sell a majority interest in any national industry. Consultec, the government's technical advisory board, announced that Brazil should abandon or indefinitely postpone its independent industrialization efforts and concentrate on the production of foodstuffs and the extraction of raw materials for export. Steel and iron works nationalized under Kubitschek were returned to their private owners.[33]

The most poignant of these success stories features Cleveland's Hanna Mining Company.[34] Back in 1935, Hanna had bought control of a British mining firm, St. John d'el Rey, and from that time forward had cultivated an epicure's interest in Brazil's immense iron deposits, situated principally in the state of Minas Gerais. In 1958, during the presidency of Juscelino Kubitschek, Minister of Mines Gabriel Passos canceled three of Hanna's concessions on reserves estimated at four billion tons of exceptionally high-assay (65 percent iron) hematite. Hanna pulled out the stops in an effort to reverse this cancellation and to acquire as well the rights to develop new rail and port facilities at Sepetiba Bay, a few miles south of Rio. Hanna's big guns were its president, former Secretary of the Treasury George Humphrey, Herbert Hoover, Jr. (like his father, a mining engineer), and John Dulles, son of the late Secretary of State (*NYT*, June 16, 1966). Kubitschek and Passos were unyielding, however, and Hanna's attempted recovery foundered in Brazil's courts. Into the early sixties, with most of its concessionary rights still enjoined, Hanna was shipping about 400,000 tons of iron ore a year through Rio and claiming that it was not making money.

The April 1964 *golpe* changed the picture. Step by step, with the deliberateness proper to momentous events, Hanna came back into its own. In June 1964, the Paulista-Mesquitas were in New York to explain the new Brazil's friendliness to foreign capital, and Robert Campos, the new finance minister, announced that the government was reconsidering its profit-repatriation regulations in light of the foreign businessmen's "realistic" needs (*NYT*, June 18, 1964). Moved by this realism, the Hague-Paris Club* was disbanding, creditor states were generously preparing to refinance Brazil's debt, and the World Bank was about to end its fourteen-year-long virtual boycott of Brazil by sending a twenty-man ("largest-ever") mission on a seven-week tour of the Redeemed Potential's interior (*NYT*, October 2, 1964). Most moving to the new realists perhaps was Brazil's willingness to discuss legislation under which the Brazilian government would guarantee foreign investments.

On November 6, 1964, President Castelo Branco received

* President Goulart had abruptly informed Brazil's foreign creditors that Brazil would be from $350 to $400 million short over the 1964–65 period in foreign-exchange needs. The United States, Britain, France, West Germany, Italy, and Japan had therefore met at the Hague (hence, "the Hague Club") apparently to determine on a collective policy toward their common debtor. Later meetings took place at Paris (hence, "the Hague-Paris club") and were attended also by Austria, Belgium, the Netherlands, Switzerland, the International Monetary Fund, and the World Bank. After the April *golpe*, evidently on the sound principle that Castelo Branco was no Goulart, the club members decided to treat individually with Brazil in refinancing her debt (*NYT*, July 2, 1964).

a call from two famous gentlemen. One was the U.S. Ambassador Lincoln Gordon. The other was John J. McCloy, former U.S. High Commissioner in Germany, but at this time employed as a representative of the Hanna Mining Company. They had come, reported *The New York Times* dispatch of November 7, "to discuss company plans to develop iron ore deposits totaling an estimated four billion tons" and Hanna's "long-standing proposal to build an iron-ore shipping port at Sepetiba Bay." "After presenting Mr. McCloy," said *The New York Times* story, "Ambassador Gordon paid President Castelo Branco a second visit, outlining the United States' financial and economic mission to Brazil."

Castelo Branco's position must not have been an easy one. Clearly, the United States was pressuring for release of Hanna's concessions (then under litigation in Brazil's Federal Court of Appeals, where Hanna's claim was about to be denied). But at the same time, Castelo Branco was being pressured domestically by at least two strongman Mesquitas *not* to accede to Hanna's demands. One was the fiery Governor Carlos Lacerda, who had plans to construct a state-owned steel mill in his state of Guanabara and who wanted all iron-ore shipping in the area to keep going through Rio, Guanabara's chief city. The other heavyweight opponent was Jose Magalhães Pinto, governor of Minas Gerais, where the disputed concessions lay. General Peri Bevilacqua, army commander of São Paulo, was also opposed to Hanna's proposition (*NYT*, December 24, 1964).

One does not know what Gordon told Castelo Branco on his second visit that day. But within two weeks, *The New York Times* (November 23, 1964) told of unconfirmed United States aid plans for $400 million "to rebuild the country's deteriorated economic position." The money would be used to support Brazil's monetary stabilization program and to finance imports (financing of American sales abroad, as noted above, is AID's basic function). A month later (*NYT*, December 15, 1964), the happy story broke: "U.S. Gives Brazil a Billion in Aid."* And little more than a week thereafter (*NYT*, December 24, 1964), Castelo Branco promulgated "a

* Here is how to invent a billion dollars: According to the cited *Times* story, AID "gives" $150 million in budgetary investments

Presidential decree [which] called . . . for private competitive development of Brazil's vast iron ore reserves and ordered discouragement of any monopoly by the state or other enterprises." Within two months (*NYT*, February 27, 1965) the World Bank had put up $80 million for the development of hydroelectric power in the south-central region—that is, the region which (a) is already most developed, and (b) is the site of Hanna's claims. Lacerda and Co., it seemed, were losing out.

But Hanna still faced the hurdle of Brazil's supreme court, which would have to decide its concessions claim and which was still dominated by "leftist" judges appointed by Goulart. By August 1965, Finance Minister Campos was complaining that U.S. investors were not exactly flying down to Rio. He had hoped for $150 million in U.S. investment and had seen less than $20 million (*NYT*, August 10, 1965). Senator William Fulbright, in Brazil with an American "fact-finding" mission, explained that American investors were waiting to see if Brazil would really become the democracy its officials

---

—that is, U.S. dollars are banked in Brazil (where they earn interest) in order to help harden the inflated cruzeiro. An unnamed source (probably the World Bank) "gives" $100 million to develop the economic infrastructure needed by business—a "gift" that is, of course, merely a loan that Brazil must repay with rent. The U.S. Treasury "gives" $50 million to meet exchange requirements—which amounts to a credit extension. Next, this breathless Brazil is "given" the right to buy $90 million worth of surplus U.S. commodities—the price is no doubt right, but it is still a price. The Export-Import Bank "gives" Brazil $30 million—in the form of rescheduled 1965 debt. The same sort of "gift" comes in the amount of $90 million from European countries and Japan—which may be amused to find their favors counted as American beneficence. Finally, the *Times* story itemizes a $25-million food donation and $15 million in grants earmarked for "agriculture and education." The real market value of the food donation is anyone's guess, but we may assume that the grants are good honest grants. Thus, we have here a total of $40 million in goods and services that may properly be termed "gifts." That puts us, with the other items named, at a paper level of $550 million. "The remaining $450 million," continues the *Times* story, "*estimated for next year* [ital. added]," will come from the World Bank (which only lends, does not give), the International Monetary Fund (ditto), the Inter-American Development Bank (ditto), and private investors (who tend to make big profits in poor countries). Look again at the *Times*' good gray headline: "U.S. Gives Brazil a Billion in Aid."

vowed they were making it; that is, would the elections scheduled for October really take place? But Thomas Mann, who was along on the same mission, seems to have suggested quite another, less frivolous, theory. Said *The New York Times* (*ibid.*), "The impression is that political uncertainty over the continuation of present policies by an elected Government is holding back potential investors."

American businessmen's fears of the Brazilian people proved generally well founded. The October election resulted in important victories for the left opposition. But their faith in the resourceful Castelo Branco should have been tougher. On October 27 he responded to the crisis of the "revolution" by issuing Institutional Act No. 2 (see page 88), which not only had the effect of nullifying the election but which also provided him with the (self-conferred, army-backed) right to pack the supreme court, which was proving such a nuisance to Hanna. On November 2 five new "revolutionaries" were admitted to the bench (*NYT*, November 3, 1965). Seven months later (the mills of the gods!), on June 15, 1966, the supreme court gave Hanna its four billion tons of iron ore back and the go-ahead for the Sepetiba Bay project (*NYT*, June 16, 1966).

Nationalist resentment over Hanna's privileged position was perhaps somewhat blurred by Hanna's agreement to go junior partners (49 percent of the stock) with Brazilian steel baron Auguste Antunes, who holds 51 percent of the stock in the new development company, United Brazilian Mining (*ibid.*).

Antunes is also a 51 percenter with Rockefeller's Bethlehem Steel, which owns 49 percent of the Industria e Comercio de Minerios (ICOMI). For more than fifteen years, ICOMI has been mining manganese in the Amapa Territory near the mouth of the Amazon and more recently has been taking niobium, a rich atomic ore, in the same area. This firm was godfathered in 1949 through railroad-building loans from the World Bank and the Ex-Im Bank. Since its first manganese shipments in 1957, it has been turning an annual profit of $12 to $15 million.*

* So says David Rockefeller of Chase Manhattan in his *Foreign Affairs* article of April 1966, "What Free Enterprise Means to Latin America." In this same piece he discusses the question: Are American profits too high in Latin America? His answer is in character, and he cites a study that showed North American profits

The production of fertilizers, formerly the preserved domain of Petrobras, has been penetrated by Gulf and Esso, which have been allowed to make a $250-million foray into the petrochemicals industry (*Time*, October 15, 1965, p. 104). According to the underground Brazilian newspaper *Revolution*, Petrobras was essentially squeezed out of refining and sales by mid-1966 and found itself limited to exploration and extraction, the least profitable operations in the oil industry.

Crucial to this "development" of Brazil's underdeveloped economy was the National Congress's rubber-stamp approval of the Guarantee of Investments Agreement, which certain cynical Brazilians claim was drafted in Washington, D.C. By this act, the Brazilian government committed itself (1) never to expropriate an American firm except with that firm's "full and complete agreement"; (2) to pay any damages caused to American enterprises by "war, revolution, insurrection, strikes, and sabotage"; and (3) to allow American firms to invest in Brazil under the regulations of American laws (*NYT*, February 13, 1965; December 28, 1965).

There is, of course, an argument for these democratic, revolutionary, and patriotic derangements of the Brazilian economy: Inflation had to be stopped. That indeed was the argument by which the April 1964 *golpe* announced and explained itself. Brazil's economy was paralyzed in chaos and extreme correctives were required, and (so it was explained) it was all for the sake of fiscal stability that strikes were outlawed, dissent crushed, national Brazilian industries decimated, northeastern reform abandoned, the army's pay increased, schools closed, courts packed, unemployment allowed to move past 15 percent, wages frozen, doors thrown wide to foreign capital. It is therefore only doubly poignant

---

in Latin America to be about 13 or 14 percent. High enough, one might think. But perhaps—who really knows?—they are even higher. In *Fortune*'s April 1966 profile on Antunes, this same ICOMI is named. *Fortune* says, "Since shipments started in 1957, the venture has grossed $235 million." Rockefeller's above-quoted figures are annual *net*. If we assume that both Rockefeller and *Fortune* had access to figures through most of 1965, then the time span is roughly eight years. If ICOMI has netted an average of $13.5 million per year for eight years, its total profit through 1965 is $108 million. Given *Fortune's* figure for an eight-year gross of $235 million, ICOMI's profit is thus not a merely robust 14 percent, but a towering—and perhaps "exploitative"?—46 percent.

that inflation is worse than ever. The government, having predicted a cost-of-living increase of 25 percent for 1965, confessed to an actual increase of more than 45 percent.* But it is not dismayed; indeed, it pursues its democratic revolution with unbewildered confidence.

A final Brazilian-American story. It is about two coastal villages in Brazil's northeast, a region notorious for its poverty even in impoverished Latin America. One village is Ponta de Carvelhos; the other, Pontezinha. Near them flow two rivers, the Pirapanga and the Vaboatão, which are connected by the high tides. Both villages, mostly Negro, at one time could barely subsist on the two rivers' sweetwater fish and crabs. Then one day not long ago, in Castelo Branco's time, America's Union Carbide Company came to the banks of the Pirapanga and built for itself a gleaming chemicals plant. It was explained to the people that this plant represented "development" and "progress."

But what American chemical plants do in America to American rivers, they do doubly in Brazil to Brazilian rivers; so the plant's pollutions very soon killed the fish and the crabs of the Pirapanga and the Vaboatão.

Since the villagers now faced death straight ahead, they felt they should do something. They sent spokesmen to appeal to the authorities. The authorities commiserated with them, but explained that they had no authority. Then the villagers decided they would have to make a demonstration. The police would not hear of it. But desperation makes ingenuity, and two priests asked, What about a religious procession? That was different, said the police.

No one knew whether or not the procession would be understood and joined, there never having been such a thing in either of these two obscure fishing villages in the backward northeast. But on August 16, 1965, more than 2000 fishermen and their wives and children marched twenty miles over the blistering highway in equatorial summer heat, all the way

* *NYT*, February 3, 1966. This figure compares favorably, of course, with the 80 percent increase in 1964. But it is probably a low estimate. *Business Week* of March 13, 1965 ("When Cruzeiros Spiral, Think Dollars") reports that many Brazilian businesses were automatically boosting their prices by 7 percent every month. From January to June of 1966, the cost of living had already increased 25 percent (*NYT*, July 11, 1966), and *The New York Times* of October 4, 1966, was heading its Brazil story, "prices soar, imports decline."

down to the softly gleaming fenced-in aluminum tanks and pipes, giant retorts and vials, of the Union Carbide Company's Pirapanga River chemical plant. Marching in the lead was a man who carried a large wooden cross. Over the cross was draped a fishing net. Behind him, the people carried signs whose slogans told their story very well. *O rio é vosso pão.* (The river is our bread.) *Homens é peixes vivem é morrem juntos.* (Men and fish live and die together.) *O desenvolvimento é a favor ou contra nos?* (Development: Is it for us or against us?) *Progresso que traez miseria não presta.* (Progress that brings misery is not worth a damn.) *Eis a horo em que viemos pedir a solução.* (Behold the hour in which we demand a solution.)

They came to the plant, gathered together, and some made speeches, priests and fishermen, each hearing the others say what each knew each one already knew. Besides the police who had come to guard against trouble, there were no onlookers. The Union Carbide Company's Pirapanga River chemical plant quietly continued making chemicals for someone, heaving back to the river poisoned what it had taken unpoisoned from the earth, for it was automated.

This plant is not alone in its quietude. The people of the two villages are dying quietly, or quietly joining the revolutionary priest Padre Alepio de Freitas, who is working quietly in the country, a fugitive from Castelo Branco's unquiet, other-directed revolution.

Or consider South Africa, where some twelve million black people are the culture slaves of the growing Afrikaaner fascism of some three and a half million whites. Said J. G. Strijdom, the second Prime Minister of South Africa, "If we reject the *Herenvolk* [i.e., master-race] idea and . . . if the franchise is to be extended to non-Europeans . . . and the non-Europeans are developed on the same basis as the Europeans, how can the European remain *Baas* [master]?"[35] Said the late H. F. Verwoerd, his successor: "There is no place for him [the African] in the European community above the level of certain forms of labor."[36]

American statesmen affirm their concern for the material advance of all men and the prosperity of democratic values. There is no clearer case of the blockade of that advance and the spoilation of those values than the case of South Africa, where whites have the fourth highest standard of living in the world but where every third black child dies of undernourishment before it is a year old and 60 percent of all blacks live below the bread line.[37] American statesmen periodically make strong speeches—in the UN, on commencement days at great universities—against this apartheid South Africa. But everyone understands that speeches are not actions. So we ask: In this least ambiguous of all cases, what is the material nature of the American response?

The Sharpeville massacre occured on March 21, 1960. Fears were at once aroused among some foreign investors that a South African rebellion might be brewing; and when the government subsequently declared itself a republic and abandoned the sterling standard, European capital became sufficiently nervous to threaten the regime's economic stability. At that time about eighty American firms had substantial investments in South Africa.[38] They had to decide to pull out or push in. Some meetings were apparently held in certain financial centers, because when action came in 1961 it was concerted and direct. American firms increased their investments by $23 million (to about $442 million in 1962[39]), and an *ad hoc* financial consortium advanced a $150 million loan to the government, the First National City Bank putting up $5 million, the Chase Manhattan Bank $10 million, the International Monetary Fund $38 million, the World Bank $28 million, and "U.S. lenders not publicly identified" $70 million.[40] The situation was saved. Since that crisis, the number of American companies investing in South Africa's future has nearly tripled.

The giants are there, the Babe Ruths, the Horsemen of the Dollar Apocalypse. One is the investment banking firm of Dillon, Read & Co., whose chairman until 1953, C. Douglas Dillon, was Secretary of the Treasury under Kennedy and Johnson and who has since moved to the board of the Chase Manhattan.[41] Another is American Metal Climax, which owns the largest mine in South West Africa (which South Africa regards as its "fifth province"). A huge consumer of South Africa's uranium (which accounted for close to 40 percent of our South African imports in 1961), AMC supplies about 10 percent of the total U.S. production. (Former AMC vice president and current board member Arthur H. Dean is a leading figure in the shaping of American nuclear-weapons control policy.[42]) Another is the Atomic Energy Commission itself, which is collaborating with Allis-Chalmers to bring the boon of nuclear power to South Africa.[43] Another is the formal consortium of American banks which has made available to South Africa a revolving credit fund (principal automatically replenished upon rent payment) which stands now at about $50 million. The participants in this consortium include the powerhouses of corporatized American finance: Chase Manhattan, First National City, Morgan Guaranty Trust, Bank of America, Bankers Trust, Chemical Bank, New York Trust, Manufacturers Hanover Trust, First National of Chicago, Irving Trust, and Continental Bank and Trust.[44]

The supergiants are Harry Oppenheimer's twin empires, Consolidated Gold Fields of South Africa Ltd. and the Anglo American Corporation, entities so immense as to scale, global as to extent, intricate as to operations, and absolute as to power as to humble the imagination of a Dante. Paradise for hundreds, Purgatory for thousands, Inferno for millions, these two corporations wholly dominate the economic life of sub-Saharan Africa. Now and then, a fragment of this cosmos may be forced to yield to some impious African.* But in the long term, it is simply not subject to the whims, bright ideas, or anger of any tribe or nation, because it transcends all peoples and all leagues. There is not one legislative or judicial body that can confront it. By itself and in Africa alone, Anglo American is 8 diamond mines, 17 coal mines, 5 copper mines, 15 gold mines, 11 "other" mines, 11 prospecting operations, 22 industrial firms, 7 land and estate centers, and 31 finance and investment houses.[46]

America's ambassador to Oppenheimerdom is Charles Englehard of Englehard Industries and the domestic Anglo American, whose 1965 stockholders' report devotes one sentence to African operations. Involved also in Canadian, Australian, and Colombian mining industries, and with distributing houses in Paris, Rome, and London, Englehard holds directorships in 23 South African companies, is a director of the government's Witwatersrand Native Labour

* Until 1955, for example, one element of Anglo American, Sierre Leone Selection Trust, had exclusive diamond rights throughout Sierre Leone. In that year, a nationalist protest led the government to reduce SLST's concession area to the 209 square miles then being worked (including the rich Konor area). The victory was, of course, not complete, SLST retaining unlimited rights on deep deposits and collecting $4 million from Sierre Leone as compensation for its "lost opportunities." Again, in 1963, Sierre Leone required a service fee from Consolidated

Association and the Native Recruiting Corporation (which import black labor for mine work), a director of the Chamber of Mines (which sets standards for mine wages and working conditions), and is a member of the even more exclusive United States Foreign Policy Association.[47]

The claim of the liberal imperialist—Englehard, a close friend of Hubert Humphrey, is a good specimen[48]—is that the expansion of industry and the resulting transformation of society which this expansion accelerates are in the long haul liberating forces. If he means that these forces induce revolutionary violence, the liberal imperialist seems to be horribly correct. If he means that the imperialist process is itself progressive, he is baldly wrong. The stronger Afrikaaner fascism grows, the more uninhibited grow its racial mutilations. In 1953, 47.3 percent of Africans taking the college entrance examination passed it. In that year, the hyper-segregationist Bantu Education Act went into effect. In 1960, the figure having steadily declined over the intervening years, the test was passed by only 17.9 percent. In 1954, one of the apartheid "bush colleges," Fort Hare, had an enrollment of 374 students. Ten years later enrollment had dropped by a hundred, and the previous yearly average of 60 B.A. degrees had fallen to 13. In 1965, out of 3.4 million whites, 33,000 attended universities; out of 12 million blacks, 946. In 1935, the average annual income of a white mineworker was $2,264. By 1964, this had increased to $3,214. The average African miner made $203 in 1935, $196 in 1960.[50] Mining profits were close to $400 million.

At the end of 1964, direct American investments in South Africa were $467 million, concentrated in manufacturing ($192 million) and mining ($68 million). Net earnings on this investment were $87 million, $41 million in manuufacturing and $20 million in mining. The rate of return was thus 20 percent over all, 24 percent in manufacturing, and 31 percent in mining.[51]

Publicly, our government deplores Afrikaaner racism. It imposed an arms embargo at the beginning of 1964 (under

---

African Selection Trust Ltd., SLST's parent organization. (CAST itself is only a fourth-tier body in the Anglo American hierarchy.) CAST paid under protest, but in spite of the tax still returned a 70 percent dividend for that year, not one point under the previous year's return.[45]

pressure to do so from the independent African countries) and is no doubt appalled to know that the poison gases soman, sarin, and tabun are being manufactured in large quantities in South Africa.[52] But embargo or not, the South African armed forces fly in 36 F-86 Sabrejet interceptors (to intercept whom?), C-47 and C-130B transports (to supply what front?), and about 30 Sikorsky helicopters (to leap to the scene of whose insurgency?). This is not only an American game, however; it is a Free World game. France, whose policy is not to supply arms "which can be used in defense of apartheid," supplied 16 Mirage IIIC (Mach 2) jet fighters with AS-30 air-to-surface missiles, about 30 Aloutte helicopters, and license for the production of Panhard armored cars. Britain, whose policy is "not to export arms to South Africa which would enable the policy of apartheid to be enforced," has supplied 16 Buccaneer light bombers, 16 Canberra B-12 light bombers, seven Shackleton long-range reconnaissance bombers, 30 subsonic Vampire jets, and about 500 Harvard light aircraft with a per-plane payload of eight 19-pound antipersonnel fragmentation bombs.[53]

But maintaining the peace and quiet, no matter at whose expense or what the cause of anger, may very well be worth a few scruples in a country which absorbs an extremely profitable $4 billion in U.S., British, French, and German direct investment, which offers nearly twice the world average investment return rate,[54] and which produces 70 percent of the Free World's gold.[55]

Consider the Free World's Paraguay, where the per capita income is $95 and 25 families own land equal in area to Denmark, Belgium, and Holland combined.[56] Alfredo Stroessner has held absolute dictatorial power since 1954, and probably the best single symbol of his regime's evolving democracy is Peña Hermosa, the Chaco Island prison camp where his unluckier political opponents are being permanently rehabilitated. Has this totalitarianism at least been materially efficient? In 1940, Paraguay had over 2500 industrial firms; there were 700 in 1965. In 1955, the agricultural index was 113.5; in 1965, only one percent of the land was cultivated and the index was 77.6. Three quarters of the land is timber forest, and wood exports in 1956 were 229,000 tons; in 1961, although demand had increased, exports were little more than half that.[57] The Liberal party's President Carlos Pastore, a wealthy pro-American self-exiled in Uruguay, told John Gerassi: "If all United States aid to Stroessner stopped today, democracy might still be salvageable tomorrow." Gerassi writes:

> When I repeated this to United States Embassy officials in Asunción, they answered, "But Stroessner is anti-Communist." The argument that anti-Communist butchers accelerate Communist takeovers seemed to carry no weight. "In the last analysis," I was told, "our policy is one of survival. Thus, a sure anti-Communist, no matter how despicable, is better than a reformer, no matter how honest, who might turn against us."[58]

Or Free World Haiti. Duvalier has received more than $57 million in AID support and nearly as much in loans from the likes of the World Bank and the Ex-Im Bank;[59] a very few Haitians are very rich, Duvalier is bodily secured by a 20,000-man palace guard trained by the U.S. Marines, and for their part the Haitian people have the lowest school attendance in the hemisphere (5.7 percent, the next lowest, Bolivia's, being 20.9 percent), the fewest hospital beds and doctors per inhabitant, and the lowest per capita income ($70) in Latin America.[60] Democratic Americans might prefer their financial support to show better social results than tyrant Duvalier seems able to produce; but American Cold Warriors, on the other hand, might fear that a Haiti without its dollar would be a Haiti without its Duvalier; and without its Duvalier, yet another segment of the Greater Antilles archipelago that shields the strategic Panama Canal Zone might go the way of Cuba.

Jamaica ought to be for Jamaicans that island paradise which the travel advertisements claim it is for others. It has fewer than two million people on 4500 square miles; it is a major exporter of sugar; it does a strong tourist business; and, most importantly, it is the world's leading supplier of bauxite, from which all aluminum blessings flow. How is it that on the base of such wealth this country is in debt to outsiders, with 93 percent of its people earning less than $480 a year? Jamaica should be the Switzerland of the Caribbean—at least. But it is not, nor is it moving in that direction. It is moving in the direction of deeper debt to outsiders. And as Jamaica's poverty gets worse, Alcan, Alcoa, Kaiser, and Reynolds continue to ship to the north the Jamaican bauxite which is owned not by Jamaica but by Alcan, Alcoa, Kaiser, and Reynolds.[61]

Venezuela belongs to the same camp. Venezuelan oil and iron have an annual average dockside value of about $4 billion —a solid economic base, it might seem, for a country of some eight million people (three percent of whom, however, own 90 percent of the land). But Venezuela's annual income on the $3 billion in oil she ships each year is only $800 million —revenues collected from the outsiders who control the oil. Rockefeller's Creole Petroleum Corporation accounts for more than 40 percent of the total production and sales volume, Mellon's Mene Grande Oil for 15 percent, Mobil for 5 percent, and Royal-Dutch Shell for most of the remainder[62]. The government-owned Venezuelan group has "concessionary rights" on less than one percent of the oil reserve and is too underfinanced for profitable operations.

If the claim that American free enterprise collaborates with the revolution of rising expectations is ever going to be valid, then it ought to be valid for Venezuela, which has absorbed well over $3 billion in direct U.S. investment (behind only Canada, Britain, and Germany), and which has been a favorite territory of the Rockefeller modernizers since the turn of the century. It is indeed true that Venezuela's per capita income is the highest in Latin America; but it is unfortunately also true that it is only $800, that per capita figures by no means represent real national wealth or its distribution,* and that of the gross national product figure upon which this is calculated, well over one third is in exports, more than 90 percent of that third is in oil alone, and that oil income is effectively monopolized by American and European interests.[64]

Moreover, Venezuela's long-term prospects seem still darker: known oil reserves will be exhausted in about fifteen years. Especially since the world oil market is in a protracted glut, it would seem prudent for Venezuela to slow down oil extraction and concentrate now on developing a diversified, balanced, and essentially self-sufficient urban-rural economy. But oil extractions are far from being curtailed. Of the five

* From per capita income figures, for example, one could conclude that the second loveliest place in the world to live is Kuwait, whose per capita income is $1800—ahead of Canada

major oil exporters among the underdeveloped countries (the others are Kuwait, Saudi Arabia, Iran, and Iraq), Venezuela has both the smallest reserves and the highest annual production rate. Kuwait, with reserves of 62 billion barrels in 1960, produced 601 million barrels; Venezuela, with reserves of 17 billion barrels, produced one billion.[65] The fact is that the decision is not Venezuela's to make. Production rates are determined by the outside firms holding the concessionary rights—*rights which are scheduled to expire in 1984.* One may certainly say that Venezuela is being "developed." One then asks: By whom? And to serve whose needs?

The roll is long. We might as well have looked at Iran, where in 1953 the CIA and British intelligence conspired to overthrow Premier Mohammed Mossadeq because he advocated Cold War neutralism for Iran and threatened to nationalize foreign oil-holdings. We might have pursued the career of the James Bond of that operation, the CIA's Kermit Roosevelt, through the time of the coup itself, the subsequent reallocation of Iranian oil rights to the advantage of American companies (Standard and Gulf), on up through 1958 when Gulf made him its "government relations" man and to 1960 when he became a vice president.[66]

Or we might have looked at Guatemala of 1954, where the CIA helped overthrow democratically elected President Arbenz because his modest agrarian reform program threatened unused United Fruit Company plantation land. We might have combed for the implications of the facts that then-Secretary of State John Foster Dulles' law office had written the United Fruit Company's 1930 and 1936 agreements with Guatemala; that then-Assistant Secretary of State for Inter-American Affairs John Moors Cabot was a major United Fruit Company shareholder; that then-CIA Director Allan Dulles had been president of the United Fruit Company; that Dulles' predecessor in the CIA directorship, General Walter Beddell Smith, was to become a United Fruit Company vice president in 1955.[67]

($1600), Switzerland ($1400), Sweden ($1300), and Britain ($1100), and not very far behind the United States ($2300).[63] The more revealing figure, much harder to calculate for any country and close to impossible for the underdeveloped, would be the distribution of income, the mean. A huge part of most underdeveloped-country populations is not even in the money economy.

Or we might have looked at our Dominican Republic intervention of 1965 and probed the facts that its chief architect, Organization of American States Ambassador Ellsworth Bunker, Jr., is a board member of the National Sugar Refining Company, which depends upon privileged access to Dominican sugar; that roving ambassador Averell Harriman's private investment house (Brown Bros. Harriman) owns about 10 percent of National Sugar; that President Johnson's close friend Supreme Court Justice Abe Fortas and a leading rhetorician of corporate liberalism, Adolf Berle, Jr., have sat since 1946 on the board of the Sucrest Company, which imports black-strap molasses from the Dominican Republic; and that former ambassador to the Dominican Republic Joseph Farland is on the board of the South Puerto Rico Sugar Company, which owns 275,000 acres of the best plantation land in the Dominion Republic and is the largest employer on the island (average wage to Dominicans, about a dollar a day).[68]

Or we might have looked at the Philippines, favored child of American anticolonialism, whose "national" constitution's U.S.-drafted "parity amendment" prohibits Filipinos from protecting their internal markets and resources against American commercial penetration—that is, effectively obstructs the development of an independent Filipino entrepreneurial class.[69]

Or at Liberia, another child of American humanism, whose rubber plantations have netted Firestone an average net profit three times the amount of the entire Liberian national revenue, and whose rich iron deposits in the Nimba range have been conceded to private European and American (Bethlehem Steel) interests.[70]

Or at hapless Ghana, whose anti-Nkrumah coup of February 1966 appears to have had CIA support, and which in any case led at once to the explicit opening of the Ghanaian door to U.S. business and the collapse of Ghanaian efforts to achieve diversified self-sufficiency. As E. N. Omaboe, the new regime's chief economic official, told a New York meeting of the African-American Chamber of Commerce on May 20, 1966: "We want New England and Californian fishermen to fish our coasts and set up canneries." As enticements, Omaboe offered ten-year tax exemption, duty-free import of materials, and a guarantee that on the outside chance of an expropriation the settlement would be arbitrated by the World Bank.[71]

Or at India, two thirds of whose currency is controlled by

the United States government, which used this leverage to help persuade Madam Gandhi that fertilizer plants run by expensive Rockefeller oil were better for India than fertilizer plants run by cheap Iranian gas.[72]

Or at Indonesia, where history's most appalling bloodbath and the new government's return or "purchase" of formerly nationalized American rubber and oil holdings led directly to the resumption of U.S. aid.[73]

But the list is endless. We should attempt a generalization.

The United States has shown in Europe that it knows how to reconstruct bombed-out capitalist economies. But it has not shown in the Third World that it can develop Western-style political economies: in preindustrial countries where there is no capitalist class structure, no entrepreneurial tradition, no skilled urbanized work force, and no internalized commitment to capitalist life-styles, the arrival of the American corporatist is in fact a disaster. Preoccupied with the extraction of resources for export and the immediate exploitation of all opportunities without regard to the damage this does to others, our business statesmanship may justly claim to have excited the underdeveloped world's growing revolutionary demands. But it is nothing but double talk for this same statesmanship to pretend that it assents to those demands—the demands for unobstructed opportunity to develop the natural wealth of the nation, for time and freedom to cultivate a national economic style, for exemption from the Cold War, for political independence.

America is not baby-simple, and her imperialism has other moods. There is, for example, the apparently genuine effort of some AID (and even some CIA) people to foster social reform under frustrating and often dangerous conditions; there is the Peace Corps, which, as badly as it has been abused, no doubt embodies a popular American willingness to be of help to other people; there is the Asian Rice Institute in the Philippines, a joint effort of the Rockefeller and Ford foundations which may prove very valuable to the people of Asia. If these represented the behavioral core, the main driving force of American foreign policy, a political humanist could throw his efforts behind that policy without much hesitation. But all imperialisms have produced their mercy angels; and one has to conclude that the good people of AID, the Peace Corps, the Rice Institute, are performing only marginal and auxiliary roles. The America which the rising world most deeply experiences is the America of United Fruit and the U.S. Marines, cool plunder, and the napalm fist. One may wish that the Peace Corps were the State Department. It is not even a match for the CIA's third string. America is not the friend but the enemy of that deformed, uneven, frustrated, and frightening revolution whose fundamental motives seem so compelling and whose fundamental claims seem so just.

It is hard to see how it could be otherwise with the corporate state. Adolf Berle, Jr., who has been a sympathetically insightful analyst of American corporatism, has himself recognized that "preachments about the value of private enterprise and investment and the usefulness of foreign capital [in the underdeveloped countries] were . . . a little silly. . . . Foreign and/or private investment may industrialize, may even increase production, and still leave the masses in as bad a shape as ever."[74] It may seem strange to hear as much from Berle. But worried corporate capitalists are not at all hard to find. It is often from them, in fact, that we get the most perceptive and realistic descriptions of Free World imperialism's effects on the backward. Gerassi quotes the 1958 statement of J. P. Grace, Jr., President of Grace & Co., whose Latin American profits are immense: "Chile, Peru, Mexico and Bolivia," said Grace, "have seen the export prices of their metals drop from 40 percent to 50 percent during the last several years. At the same time, since 1951, the average price that Latin America pays for its imports from the United States has risen about 11 percent."[75]

The editors of *Fortune* have pointed out that the long-term debt of the underdeveloped countries, some $40 billion in 1966, costs $4.5 billion annually in interest charges and consumes one eighth of all their foreign-trade earnings. "To get enough foreign exchange for what they import, [underdeveloped countries] have to borrow more, which in turn means they will have to meet greater servicing costs."[76] Sanz de Santamaria, chairman of the Inter-American Committee of the Alliance for Progress, has made the same point: "[Latin American] debt amortization alone will require $1.7 billion this year [1966], thus pre-empting 16 percent of all export earnings."[77] Josué de Castro, one of Brazil's foremost economists and a former president of the United Nations Food and Agriculture Organization, has written of the Alliance for Progress that it "is nothing but pure colonialism. . . . Colonialism is the only cause of hunger in Latin America."[78]

That might seem a bitter exaggeration. But there is only a difference of tone, not of substance, between that statement and the following passages from the editorial page of the *Wall Street Journal*:

The industrial nations have added nearly $2 billion to their reserves, which now total $52 billion. At the same time, the reserves of the less-developed group not only have stopped rising, but have declined some $200 million. To analysts such as Britain's [Barbara] Ward, the significance of such statistics is clear: the economic gap is rapidly widening "between a white, complacent, highly bourgeois, very wealthy, very small North Atlantic elite and everybody else, and this is not a very comfortable heritage to leave to one's children." "Everybody else" includes approximately two thirds of the population of the earth, spread through about 100 nations. . . . Many diplomats and economists view the implications as overwhelmingly—and dangerously—political. Unless the present decline can be reversed, these analysts fear, the United States and other wealthy industrial powers of the West face the distinct possibility, in the words of Miss Ward, "of a sort of international class war."[79]

But there is rarely any indication that this problem is *caused* by someone, that it is in preponderant part caused by American corporations, that this problem (instead of communism) is what lies behind Third-World revolution. Indeed, there is always an implicit suggestion that the man who can solve this problem best is none other than the Free World capitalist himself. It seems to be certainly true that many aspects of the development problem could be solved by that figure—if he would just remove himself from the picture. But how will he be persuaded to do that? To surrender in someone else's name the immense profits which he considers it his main business to make? Further, how is his disengagement to be achieved by a government which has always considered his foreign successes to be America's domestic successes, and which is unalterably committed to the political ideology of free enterprise?

Consider that the capitalist's commitment to capitalism does not entail a commitment to other capitalists. The ideology obliges him only to *compete*, and the interwoven morality obliges him to win *as much as he can.* If his dominance is to be restricted, his victories contained, that will only happen through the independent competitive action of other capitalists. In theory, this is indeed how the system is supposed to operate: New entrepreneurs, new capitalists, steadily emerge to create and wield new power, and thus continuously reconstitute the dynamics of the open, free market. But we have noticed a problem: Even in our own supposedly model economy, there is an accelerating breakout from this theoretically internalized and permanent system of competition-based limits. The competition is won, and the winner gets stronger; lost, and the loser gets weaker. Power condenses in the hands of steadily smaller, steadily more integrated and collaborative victor groups. And the federal government, not so very long ago the American businessman's arch enemy, now becomes his delighted and delightful partner. Without the federal government's Special Forces and Marines, United Fruit could not dominate Guatemala. Without AID and the World Bank and the supportive hands of the Commerce and State Departments, the corporations could not multinationalize themselves. Without the federal government's sugar subsidies, the sugar companies could not maintain their lethal grip on the economies of small states from the Caribbean to the Central Pacific. Without the State Department's Cold War sales campaign and the active support of the Defense Department's weapon hucksters, General Dynamics could not continue to fatten on arms sales to Europe. Without big government, big business would be lost.

One sees in America the emergence (maybe it is too late for such a word) of what we can only describe as a somewhat permissive, domestically benign fascist state. *Fascism*—an extravagant term? *Webster's* definition: "a centralized autocratic national regime with severely nationalistic policies, exercising regimentation of industry, commerce, and finance, rigid censorship, and forcible suppression of opposition." On the last two counts, I hope not too hopefully, I defer judgment. And in any case, there is no need to suppress an already harmless dissent. But centralization of the basic economic and political decisions, the sophisticated nationalism of our foreign policy, the *de facto* top-down "regimentation" (our word for it is "rationalization") of industry, commerce, and finance—

these are very clearly the dominant features of our system. Big government and big business are essentially one and the same. And the normative act of competition that now takes place does not occur between independent entrepreneurial groups and is apparently not fought out in terms of the superiority of one man's product over another's (product "superiority" now being purchasable, all but prepackaged, from any advertising agency). Rather, the crucial competition takes place on the inside of a homogeneous, informal, but very real and very bureaucratic commercial monolith, and the paramount issue of that competition is the internal succession of power and authority: not where power will be moved to, but who will win occupancy of power's present seats; not the rearrangement of power in the market place, but the acquisition of power within the closed system that commands it.

Will someone claim that the appetite for dominance which stimulated the growth of this corporate state will restrain itself when it goes on foreign cruises? David Rockefeller may very well exhort his fellow businessmen to "demonstrate [to Latin Americans] that a new brand of capitalism has evolved, based on the concept of a fair profit for free enterprise combined with social responsibility to the community as a whole."[80] And he may very well hope that someone takes his advice, for the businessman who does so, this same Rockefeller will crush. The idea of capitalism is that the "fair profit" will not have to be determined by a Christian capitalist alone with his morality. It will be set through his act of competing with *other* capitalists. Then where are the competitive capitalists of the Third World? And how are they to be produced? And who is to produce them?

Nothing the American businessman can see in past, present, or future will persuade him to forgo whatever commercial advantages may come to hand. *And for him, the Third World is a commercial advantage*. The Third World is that exposed, unprotected gold mine where his investment dollars fare better than anywhere else. Why should he want to change that? The United Fruit Company may be "enlightened," may (sometimes does, sometimes does not) build roads, houses, schools, and hospitals in model company towns on its plantations in the "banana republics." But why should it want to surrender its privileged position there, all in the name of some fuzzy humanitarian ideal? Or why should it rejoice to see the emergence of local capitalists who may some day get strong enough to give it some competition? Since when is the capitalist his colleague's keeper?

As ordinary, intelligent men giving the rest of the world a look, the American corporatists can see the truth as well as anyone else. They can even be concerned about the bloody implications of what they see, and they might even have an ideological, impersonal preference for a Third World, in the best sense, Americanized. But to build that "American" Vietnam, that dynamic, free-enterprising Brazil, that middle-class Guatemala—if that indeed is what these countries want—that is the job of independent, unharassed, unmanipulated Vietnamese, Brazilians, and Guatemalans; it can no more be the job of American capitalists than the building of the American nation could have been the job of British mercantilists. For matters to stand otherwise, the Yankee free-enterpriser would for the first time in his life have to work for his competition. He would have to recognize a difference of interest, a dual economic good, and take sides against himself. He would have to supplant his money ethic with a social ethic. He would have to change entirely his style of thought and action. In a word, he would have to become a revolutionary socialist whose aim was the destruction of the present American hegemony. I see no reason to suppose that such a metamorphosis is about to transfigure this Yankee.

The agents of change in this world are today, as they have always been, those whose battered lives stand most in need of change. The entrepreneurs of social progress are those whose condition requires it. And at bottom, this revolution is nothing but the emergence of competitors who employ the only means of competition available to them. Revolution is the collective free enterprise of the collectively dispossessed.

V

The Vietnam Case

The commercial supremacy of the Republic means that this nation is to be the sovereign factor in the peace of the world. For the struggles of the future are to be conflicts of trade—struggles for markets—commercial wars for existence. And the golden rule of peace is impregnability of position and invincibility of preparedness.
—SENATOR ALBERT J. BEVERIDGE, 1898

IF COLD WAR anticommunism is most basically an ideological mask for Free World imperialism, then one should be able to show somehow that the issue of the Vietnam war is not Western freedom versus Eastern slavery but foreign versus local control of Vietnam—to show, that is, that the war is being fought to determine how and by whom the Vietnamese political economy is going to be developed. And since the United States has committed itself so unreservedly to Vietnam's Free World salvation, this line of analysis is also obliged to show that Vietnam is somehow crucial for the security and growth of the American commercial state.

It is precisely on this point that the imperialism theory confronts a simple, serious objection: Are American commercial interests in that very poor, very backward part of the world so substantial as to justify so dangerous and unlimited a war? The war is now costing Americans upward of $20 billion a year. How many years will it take for a "saved" Vietnam to start paying dividends on that kind of military investment? The accountant will observe that saving Vietnam is costing us a great deal more than any resulting "colonial" advantage will ever be worth. This entirely common-sensical observation, on its face quite persuasive, directs us to dismiss the imperialist theory (at least for *this* war) and return to a more purely "political," noncommercial explanation.

But probe the case more curiously. We shall find that America's Vietnam policy does not merely illustrate American imperialism, it is a paradigm instance of it; and that in its fusion of imperialist motive and anticommunist ideology, the war is not only exemplary, it is also climactic.

There are four important points, argued below in ascending order of importance.

First, a direct American commercial interest in Vietnam exists. For the most part it is potential. That makes it no less real.

In its issue of January 1, 1966, *Newsweek* ran an essay called "Saigon: A Boomtown for U.S. Businessmen." A similar piece by Edmund K. Faltermayer appeared in the March 1966 issue of *Fortune* under the title "The Surprising Assets of South Viet-Nam's Economy." There is the possibility that both pieces may have been a bit contrived or calculated. Perhaps they were brought forth to bolster the business community's enthusiasm for a war which creates a few domestic nuisances (e.g., inflation, labor scarcities in key-skill areas, higher taxes, tighter credit). But whatever the motive, these pieces—and Faltermayer's especially—must have convinced many that South Vietnam is a plum quite delectable enough to be saved. "A South Viet-Nam preserved from Communism," Faltermayer wrote, "has the potential to become one of the richest nations in Southeast Asia." He notes that the country could become an exporter of sugar and cotton, both of which it now imports; that it exported a record 83,000 tons of rubber in 1961, and could easily surpass that record under normal conditions; that the Mekong Delta, the "rice bowl" which now produces about four million tons of rice annually, could produce 12 to 15 million tons. It is not by magic that the rice, the rubber, the sugar, the cotton—and the promising industrial crops, jute, ramie, and kenaf—will come leaping from the ground into the holds of cargo ships. That will require capital, whether the socialist or the capitalist kind.

The capitalist pioneers are already staking their claims. Chase Manhattan and the Bank of America have opened branch offices in Saigon. The New York firm of Parsons & Whittemore holds 18 percent interest in a $5-million American-managed paper mill at Bien Hoa. Foremost Dairies of California has controlling interest in a new condensed-milk plant and half-interest in a new textile mill. Another textile mill has been partly financed by the Johnson International Corporation. The American Trading Co. and Brownell Lane Engineering Co. are selling and servicing heavy equipment—bulldozers, tractors, trucks, and railroad locomotives—and averaging 20 to 30 percent returns on their investments.[1]

The giant is RMK-BRJ, a construction combine formed by Raymond International, Morrison-Knudsen, Brown & Root, and J. A. Jones Construction. RMK-BRJ is the major contractor for the enormous military construction program in airbases, ports, and roads (economic "infrastructure"), and its contracts may eventually reach $700 million. As of March 1966, it was already the biggest private employer in the country, with 25,000 workers on its payroll and plans for an increase up to 75,000.

"Never before," said *Newsweek*, "have U.S. businessmen followed their [*sic!*] troops to war on such a scale." Faltermayer is careful not to exaggerate the size of the present stake. He emphasizes that our total direct investment in Vietnam is at the moment no more than $6 million. But the niggardliness of that amount is itself a clear enticement: There is a new wide-open frontier's-worth of opportunity in Vietnam. The situation, he says,

> could change radically in the next few years. Esso and Caltex . . . are studying proposals to build a $16-million oil refinery, the country's first. Shell Oil and the South Vietnamese Government would participate in the venture, and the refinery might be included in the proposed Cam Ranh Bay industrial complex.

(It is surprising, however, that Faltermayer represents this "venture" as something new. The same $16-million refinery plans were already "under study" as early as April 1962, according to Indochina scholar Bernard B. Fall, who adds to the story a touching note: "There is strong evidence that the American Government 'urgently invited' the oil companies to proceed with the contract in order to show American confidence in the future of Viet-Nam."[2])

An important aspect of the commercial picture is, of course, the donation of American dollars to finance the Vietnamese import of American goods. We have already quoted *Forbes* (which calls itself a "capitalist tool") on the Agency for International Development: It "is the principal agency through which the U.S. Government finances business abroad. . . .

AID distributes about $2 billion a year. Of this, 85 percent is spent in the U.S. for American products and raw materials." In 1966, AID allocations to Vietnam were about a sixth of the $2 billion total. In 1967, this goes to a fourth: $550 million. If 85 percent of that is spent on American exports, South Vietnam will rank among our ten top buyers.

All new frontiers need their Paul Bunyans. Faltermayer offers a strong candidate in a New York entrepreneur named Herbert Fuller, head of an investor group which since 1958 has been promoting a $10-million sugar mill for the coastal city of Tuy Hoa:

> When the troops arrive to clear the area, as they sooner or later must, this American capitalist will literally be one step behind them. "I am in it for the money," Fuller says. "We could get back our investment in two years." Like all entrepreneurs, Fuller once again is pushing ahead with his plans because he assumes the U.S. is now committed to saving Viet-Nam.

But so what? Why is it so wrong for our businessmen to be right behind "their" troops? There is nothing strange about the pursuit of profit and opportunity; and that the businessmen should at once occupy, settle on, and begin to develop the ground just cleared by our troops does not mean that it is for them that the troops are there. Does it?

We encounter a problem of vision. It is hard to see these particular businessmen as being in any way crucial to the Vietnam drama. Their appearance in it seems incidental—important perhaps, but not especially significant. The war would be the same with or without them. It is being fought for freedom or to hold back the Communists. It is not being fought for this Herbert Fuller, "American capitalist."

No doubt. If Fuller decided the Tuy Hoa project was a bad bet and went back to New York, another coastal city, no one thinks the Marines would forgo the conquest of Tuy Hoa. But what do we suppose "freedom" means? And what is the real purpose of keeping the Communists back? Our functional definition of a free country is clear from our behavior. The definition says that a country is free when Americans like Fuller are free to do business in it if they have the skill and the drive to do so. It is free when there are native counterparts of Fuller. It is free when there is free enterprise. When there is *no* free enterprise, the country is Communist. It cannot be doubted that Vietnam's importance lies far more basically in its geographic and *historical* position than in its inherent commercial potentials, whether immediate or long-term. But, as we shall see, that is only because Vietnam is imagined to be the key to larger areas—areas whose commercial accessibility *is* important to us, and which will or will not themselves be "free," depending on the possibility of our doing business in them. Thus, when Faltermayer talks of "saving Vietnam," he is at one and the same time talking about saving both it and the region for Fuller, free enterprise, and Western-style freedom—for the last two are considered to define each other, and the first is an instance of their realization. "After the war," says Arthur Tunnell, of Investors Overseas Services' Saigon office, "there is going to be a big future for American businessmen here."[3] Analyze to the surface the vision which that statement makes concrete, and one will approach an exhaustive ideological description of the Vietnam war.

Second, the militarized economy demands a militarized politics; a militarized politics demands a militarized economy. Vietnam, as conflict colony, helps turn this wheel.

Consider that since 1946 the federal government has laid out about 60 percent of its budget for support of the military-industrial complex, a 20-year total of better than $850 billion. This is a *political* fact.

In 1959, when Khrushchev came to Camp David and the Cold War seemed up for reappraisal, the stock market took its sharpest downturn in nearly four years. This was called "peace jitters." In 1960, when Eisenhower came back from Paris via that broken U-2 (a Lockheed novelty), *The New York Times'* financial page headlined: "Summit Failure a Market Tonic."[4]

During the summer of 1965, as is very well known, certain informed people were again fretful about the national economy. Having cantilevered themselves out into the future on act of faith after vote of confidence, the lenders and the borrowers and their analysts began to make uneasy murmurs. News of an important inner-sanctum debate about the national metabolism drifted out in bits and pieces. The Administration seemed to favor confidence. But then the Federal Reserve Board's chairman, William McChesney Martin, Jr., began to say aloud in public places that he was not convinced things were as right as they ought to be. He even confessed that the economy was putting him in mind of 1929. No one knew quite how to react to this crack in the expert consensus. Was it deep? Was there any real danger? There was a ripple of discreet uncertainty.

In this subdued Perils-of-Pauline atmosphere, there all of a sudden appeared an unexpected hero whom no one was really surprised to see. The hero was the war: It would not get smaller, much less come to a quick end, and it became common knowledge that its direct costs would go to at least $21 billion a year. However nervous it might remain, the bull market had won its reprieve.

Those who argue that the Vietnam war *must* have been forced upon us since it is so uneconomical do not grasp the economics of state capitalism. The economic effects of the war are anything but unambiguous. The war generates very real fiscal management problems and disturbing anomalies in the pattern of foreign exchange. But over all, the war is good for the economy because the economy is addicted to federal subsidy in general and to military subsidy in particular. It appears that we *have* to spend, because what a high-employment economy produces has to be vended. Whether it goes into the sweet life or the limbo of government silos, the product has to go some place and it has to be paid for. Consider, then, a key economic fact about the defense product: *It is not produced at the expense of recognized domestic necessities.* It is not as if Americans are standing in queues to purchase automobiles, which, for the sake of tanks, are going unbuilt. The opposite comes closer to being the case: If it were not for the tanks, the planes, the submarines, the missiles—where would the economy be? Which is very much like asking: If it were not for the heroin, where would the junkies be? Obviously: in hospitals undergoing very painful therapy. Perhaps even of a revolutionary nature.

One does not claim that the Vietnam war was escalated only to cheer up an overblown, dour economy with that "external" and "expanded" market which it could not otherwise procure. But what if the Vietnam war ended and China said, Have it your way? What if the Cold War faded and faded until one day someone noticed that it had disappeared? What would become of this gargantuan Lockheed with its

$500 million in research and development contracts alone? What would become of the intensively specialized scientists, engineers, technicians, administrators, and line workers it employs? Or of the tens of thousands of shopkeepers, middlemen, lenders, and suppliers their salaries keep in business? Where are the concrete plans, the great Congressional debates, the enabling legislation on the management of defense-to-civilian industrial conversion? Who is hammering out the answers?

We have a scatterfire from assorted blue-ribbon commissions of scientists, economists, and businessmen whom everyone very well knows to be nonserious. They are a step wiser than Sisyphus, for they only circle their rock, staring at it soberly, poking at it now and then. What else? Are they foolish, these men of science, economics, and business? But it really seems not to matter. Not so deep down inside at all, quite on the surface of intuition, we are all privy to the main secret of state, which is that we are in no real danger of being abandoned by this "threat" that keeps the corporate state in its fighting trim.

Look at Europe, where there is no claim that the "threat" is increasing. The reverse is true: more trade with East Europe and the U.S.S.R., moves on both sides of the Curtain (of which de Gaulle's in the West and Ceausecu's in the East are only the most dramatic) to bring Europe toward accord and integration. Yet in this atmosphere of calm and confidence, after several years of the preaching and the apparent practice of coexistence, what is America's policy on European militarization? Over the past fifteen years we have given or sold to other countries some $35 billion worth of military equipment. Since mid-1961, military export sales have run to more than $9 billion, and the profit to American defense suppliers totals about $1 billion—nicely concentrated in the hands of three big and highly influential firms, General Dynamics, Lockheed, and McDonnell. Overseas military sales for 1965 were about $2 billion and, let the Cold War thaw as it pleases, they will run on at that high rate into the foreseeable future.[5] Why does this happen, if the threat is diminishing? It happens because our military sales abroad represent one of our major handles on our chronic balance-of-payments deficit. These sales are actively promoted by the Pentagon, which seems to care little more about the buyers' need and ability to pay for guns than any ordinary used-car salesman: The goodness of the guns is a good enough need, and if the price seems high, never mind, another part of our government will put up an easy-term loan. The number-one salesman—the Pentagon calls him a "negotiator"—is Henry J. Kuss, Jr., Deputy Assistant Secretary of Defense for International Logistics Negotiations. In May 1965, in recognition of his section's "intensive sales effort," Kuss was awarded the Meritorious Civilian Service Medal.[6]

Here is a prime instance: Germany earns about $675 million a year from the American troops who are stationed there. To offset these U.S. payments, Germany "has been encouraged" to purchase $1.3 billion worth of American military goods over the 1966–67 period. Very convenient, that Germany's military equipment "needs" so closely match our expenses. But Germany seems reluctant to buy what we insist she cannot do without. Foreign military sales in the first quarter of 1966 were the lowest since 1964, and the big reason was Germany's tardiness in making the agreed-upon purchases. That tardiness might have something to do with Germany's recession and budget problems. But that is small concern of ours. We have to move these goods.

It is argued that these weapons stabilize the world and make peace, as if the financial benefit which accrues to us from their sale were only a happy incidental. But the most elementary survey of what is now happening in European politics will make it clear that armaments—on both sides—are increasingly irrelevant to peace and stability, and that if they have any effect at all on the larger pattern of European reintegration, it is a negative and obstructing one. Outside Europe, realities counter the arms-for-stability thesis even more ominously. Former Ambassador to India John Kenneth Galbraith testified before the Foreign Relations Committee on April 25, 1966, that "the arms we supplied . . . caused the war between India and Pakistan. . . . If we had not supplied arms, Pakistan would not have sought a military solution [to the Kashmir dispute]."[7]

As bad as it was—and may yet be again—the India-Pakistan encounter will be nothing compared to what may at any moment erupt in the Near and Middle East. Neither the Arabian war with Israel nor Nasser's vendetta with Saudi Arabia has anything at all to do with the Cold War;

no one thinks the Russians are about to come howling down the Caspian or across the Kopet Mountains, and once upon a time it was American policy (as Rusk put it as recently as January 1966) "not to stimulate and promote the arms race in the Near East and not to encourage it by our direct participation."[8] Little more than two months after that statement, the State Department announced an agreement to sell Jordan (which already had American tanks) "a limited number" of advanced fighter-bomber aircraft, reportedly Lockheed F-104s. Senator Eugene McCarthy commented: "It is not clear how Jordan, which has an annual per capita GNP of $233 and which has been dependent on U.S. military grants and economic aid, will pay for these planes, which cost $2,000,000 apiece. *The availability of U.S. credit for arms purchases is undoubtedly an important factor.*"[9] [Emphasis added.]

Selling arms to both Israel and the Arab world at the same time is an embarrassing business, so we do it behind the barn as much as we can—but do it nevertheless because we suppose we have to. One interesting sequence begins with our demand that Britain purchase American fighter planes. Having complied, Britain now has need of sales to "offset" *her* imbalance. Britain is therefore allowed to bid on American munitions contracts. But should she win such bids, *that would result in a market loss for American munitions-makers.* So the Pentagon arranges to find British bids not quite up to standard. American sellers are content. But Britain still has her deficit. Enter Saudi Arabia, convinced that she will be unsafe so long as she does not have a big fleet of fighters. She would like to have American ones, the best. But against the background of American policy on Israel, this is a "need" which it would be politically ticklish for us to service—at least openly. So we persuade Saudi Arabia that ours are not the only aircraft in the world worth flying and she will be just as happy with a British mark. Britain thereupon sells Saudi Arabia what she wants—$400 million worth of supersonic fighters. And we, having lost no market which we might gracefully have entered, *count this British aircraft sale to Saudi Arabia as the quid-pro-quo balancer of our original aircraft sales to Britain.*[10]

So it goes. Apparently we are not really proud of this sort of thing, but what can we do? There stand the bright weapons in a row. Behind them stand their engineers. Behind the engineers, the executives, who serve on presidential committees and travel often to the capital. Behind the executives, the booming system for which they work, for which they speak, in which they have their being. The system must boom, the executives must have their being, the military engineers must design, the riveters must rivet, and the shining bright weapons must therefore be *marketed*. And that marketing is easier if there is a certain uneasiness in the world, a little tension and anxiety. Who could market aspirin if there were no headaches? Yet what is more antiheadache than aspirin? Preventive aspirin, these sleek fighter aircraft. But the world should not forget what a headache is. So to go with that conceptual beauty called "preventive war," we have preventive *threats*, just big enough to put an edge on things and keep the system from coming unstuck.

Harvard economist Summer Slichter explained the system very movingly in a 1949 address to a group of bankers. The Cold War, he said, "increases the demand for goods, helps sustain a high level of employment, accelerates technological progress and thus helps the country to raise its standard of living. . . . So we may thank the Russians for helping make capitalism in the United States work better than ever."[11]

Sad to say, we have had to watch Russia's glory fade, her power to inspire our capitalism decline. Besides, when we have put 7000 long-range nuclear rockets in West Europe alone, [12] we have perhaps begun to saturate a good market. But we are in luck, for new Russias keep entering the Cold War market. Today we have China—and therefore Vietnam. And in the wings, tomorrow's starlets—Guatemala? the Philippines? Iran?—are even now trying on their black-pajama *campesino* costumes and rehearsing their most splenetic Marxist curses. And the Third World is crawling with CIA and Special Forces talent scouts.

Third, the strategic heart of the matter.

Increasingly from the turn of the century, American policy has been preoccupied with the problem of pacifying the global commercial environment. As early as the mid-1890s we had already become the world's leading manufacturer and therefore internationalist in spite of ourselves. It had become critical to us that our foreign markets should not be disturbed. How were the required stability and freedom of access to be won? A distinctly minority opinion was that they could not be: The old nations were too bent on conquering one another. America should therefore be neutral and trade with all who would trade on proper terms. (This is one of the so-called isolationist positions. It is not isolationist, it is neutralist. Neutralism *might* be isolationist, but it need not be and usually is not. Neutralist Switzerland, for example, is anything but isolationist. For an example closer home, there is the prewar period of the New Deal, during which time we were internationalist, politically partisan, and economically neutralist all at once: our trade with Germany, Italy, and Japan remained basically solid in the years 1933–40.[13])

But what came to be the dominant belief was that the problems of advanced-power aggression and backward-state revolution *had* to be solved, *could* be solved, and *would* be solved through some combination of the advanced powers. The world needed a concert of industrial giants whose collective strength, will, and prestige would restrain aggressions and suppress revolutions. The question for statesmanship was which powers should make up the club. The question for diplomacy was how to get them into it.

Before World War I, the general belief was that the proper combination would consist of the United States, Britain, and France. After that war, Wilson explicitly revised this outlook, holding that Germany and Japan would now have to be integrated into the Atlantic concert. In this way, revolutionary Russia could be isolated and the Big Powers acting coordinately could protect the security of the world's increasingly integrated political economy. So in the 1920s the United States underwrote the reconstruction of Germany's prewar industrial structure, and in 1922 (the Nine-Power Treaty) brought Japan by the ears into a modern open-doorist agreement on hapless China. When trouble began to brew in the 1930s, Chamberlain struggled with all the considerable anxiety at his command to establish Four-Power hegemony in Europe (i.e., Britain, France, Germany, and Italy). The New Deal, not much more instructed by Japan's invasion of Manchuria than was Britain by Germany's Rhineland remilitarization, maneuvered with carrots and sticks through most of that period to secure a China accommodation with Japan.

We were steadily trying, that is, with a really remarkable constancy, to establish that political integration of the Big Powers which finally *was* established—at least temporarily—as one of the chief results of World War II. De Gaulle's France portends change today, and perhaps (it is debatable) Gaullism represents genuinely different ideas about how European power should be arranged and what its fundamental goals should be. But at least well into the mid-sixties, the postwar world was dominated by explicit or implicit alliances that linked the United States, Britain, France, Germany, and Japan into one another's economies, all our partners sharing our belief in a democratic-liberal political philosophy, and all of them more or less willing to accept and support our views on the Communist threat.

This system has two separate but integrated domains, the Atlantic and the Pacific. As Germany is the pivotal state of the Atlantic domain, Japan is the pivot of the Pacific. It is the situation of this Japan which we shall now examine more closely.

The first point is that Japan is a traditionally vigorous trader, one which has long been important to the commerce of the United States. From 1929 through 1940, our total volume of trade with Japan was surpassed only by our trade with Canada and Britain. The much-lusted-after China trade was not even half as heavy (over that period, about $3.5 billion total volume with Japan as opposed to about $1.5 billion with China). Our view of Japan's distinction is reflected in the fact that besides the quite special cases of Vietnam, Korea, and Formosa, no country outside Europe has received as much assistance from the United States (some $4 billion over the 1945–63 period). Her comeback in the postwar period was rapid and strong. Her 1965 volume of trade was close to $17 billion (more than double her 1960 volume), placing her ahead of Italy among the world's business-doers behind the United States, West Germany, England, France, and Canada. By 1961, she had taken over second place among our trade partners, with only Canada ahead. In 1965 she sold us $2.5 billion and bought from us $2.4 billion, achieving for the first time a favorable balance of trade both with the United States and the world ($8.5 billion exports vs. $8.3 billion imports).[14]

The second point is that a healthy, westward-looking Japan

is just as crucial to the containing of China as containing China is to the health and Western-orientation of Japan. To understand the essentials of this dynamic, we have to unpack the meaning of this concept "containment."

It can, of course, mean several things. For a pathetically brief period, Czechoslovakia's Beneš "contained" Hitler by answering the German troop concentration at his border with a military mobilization of his own. Thus, there is a type of containment that is distinctively military. The United States "contained" the growth of domestic communism by a program of systematic legislative, judicial, and propaganda harassment. Containment, then, can be political and legalistic. We could go through a set of such differing situations and define for each a differing form of containment. The common characteristic would be that in each case a perception of an active threat elicits a countermeasure that is specifically pitched to the threat's nature, and that does not commit itself to the direct and final liquidation of the threat.

What is the nature of the Chinese Communist threat? As should be perfectly clear, the threat is not basically military. No real threat ever is. China's power to aggress against her neighbors is not to be doubted. But two other things are also not to be doubted. One is that she would be all but defenseless against the kind of strategic nuclear attack which a clear act of aggression would surely provoke. The other is that she has never attacked for spoils, nor without provocation. (The Korean "invasion" came only after repeated U.S. bombings of Manchuria, the Tibetan "invasion" only after a clear mutiny of the theocracy, the Indian "invasion" as a result of a very plain border dispute in which she had by no means the worst of the argument.)

The threat is political. And as with any political threat, the guts of it are economic. It has long been a statesmanly wisdom in the West that any China which could organize herself would be a China indeed. Only recall Napoleon's words about the slumbering giant who will awaken to shake the world, Lenin's observation that "for world communism the road to Paris lies through Peking and Calcutta." She has the people, the resources, the energy, and the ingenuity to be—what? Given equity in what time can purchase, what time will inevitably bring, China could become the peer of America, Europe, and the U.S.S.R. What she lacked for centuries was order, a sense of national unity, and positive control over her inherent resources. The people—industrious—and the land—rich—have been there all along, waiting for some iron-minded Johnny Appleseed.

China's rate of growth in the first ten years following Chiang's flight to Formosa was anywhere from 15 to 30 percent, depending on which of several experts one believes. Apart from the problem of insufficient data, none seems to be really sure how to measure the performance of an immature planned economy. But there is general agreement that growth was strong, even allowing for the very abysmal state of the initial conditions. Assessments of the Great Leap experience vary even more widely, some scholars arguing a "catastrophe" interpretation, others claiming that the failure, now mostly recouped, was chiefly agricultural and that basic industrial growth remained healthy. To dare to say anything conclusive about China's economy one would have to base it on a lengthy analysis, and a major reason for its lengthiness would be the need to explain why nothing exactly conclusive could be said. But we need not be so technical here. What is important is that no one denies that for the first time in centuries there *is* such a thing as a Chinese nation, that it *has* an economy, and that this economy has established contact with the intrinsic potential of the land and the people. That potential, plagued as it is with natural and political difficulties, is as great as it needs to be. Reflect then, as our statesmen surely must, on the China of a hundred or even fifty years from now. Imagine a world in which creative action—economic, political, cultural—is no longer so densely and disproportionately concentrated in the North Atlantic global core—a world, that is, in which an independent and dynamic Asia *exists*.

Our response to the mammoth fact of Chinese revolution—something which has nothing at all to do with communism, but rather with the independent organization of China and her acquisition of modern fire—has not been exactly pragmatic. First we chose to believe that it was not happening. We exhausted ourselves in mirthful tales of the new China's blunders, sorrows, and epidemic pain, and poised ourselves for the next news dispatch, for it would tell us of the end of this extravagant mistake. The news was different. Then we adopted the view that its own inner evil would in time surely destroy this most total of totalitarianisms. Merely to give its self-destruction a little nudge, a little momentum, we set up an embargo. And it did not die. But then surely the Chinese people would rise against the "yellow peril" internalized, demanding capitalism and Chiang Kai-shek. Merely to give them pluck, we ostentatiously armed their real and true hero, that leashed whirling dervish of Formosa. And the people did not rise up. Strange ways of the Orient! Our recriminations meanwhile were endless. Clearly, this was all the work of Joe Stalin and certain State Department infidels. Reputations were garroted. China was still there, however, coming on like a freight train.

And there sits Japan in the very beam of the Manchurian industrial headlamp, *quite powerless to move.* (A roughly comparable situation would be one in which England found herself politically misallied against a Europe united to the Urals, a battering ram.) What are Japan's options? Isolationism vis-à-vis China was never even thinkable. Whether coerced by future political apprehensions or lured by present commercial opportunities, Japan is already China's foremost trade partner,* surpassing even the Soviet Union (with which, adroitly enough, Japan's businessmen are also arranging increased commerce). It is not as if Japan could pretend that China is just not there. It would be strange economics, politics, and history if she tried to. The only questions that are at all open are how much, when, and on what terms. Most specifically: Will Japan contrive to maintain her present pro-American political bias? Will she submit to world history's commonest law that the Higher Economics determines the Lower Politics and so cast in with Peking? Or will she try instead the Greek way of golden-meansmanship and make of herself a bridge between the two supergiants, well knowing (as one Japanese has remarked) that bridges get walked on?

It will be clear what the United States expects Japan to do. But how much pressure do we ask that nation to bear in our name whose principal cities we atomized? Japan understands that she bombed Pearl Harbor with no very great moral

* Japan's sales to China, $245 million in 1965, are rising annually at a rate matched only by her purchases from China. Exports (and imports) in her China trade from 1960 through 1965 are as follows (in millions of U.S. dollars): 2.7 (20.7); 16.0 (30.9); 38.5 (46.0); 62.4 (74.6); 152.8 (157.8); 245.3 (224.7).[15]

finesse. Japan understands that her new economy was built by us. But there is something especially memorable about that Bomb, callous about our nuclear appearances at her ports of call, humiliating about the 1960 Mutual Security Treaty for which the Kishi government had to pay with its life, infuriating about our overt colonization of Okinawa and the Ryukyu chain, frightening about our Vietnam war, which three quarters of her people oppose: the elements of Japanese anti-Americanism subsist. Japan, the keystone of our Asian containment perimeter, may do what she can to remain our long-haul affiliate. She will not do what she cannot do. If America has certain expectations, it is up to America to make their possibility concrete.

We now ask: Does Vietnam bear materially on this drama? The key facts would seem to be the following: (1) Two of China's principal import needs are rubber and rice, improved access to which will in some measure accelerate her rate of development and thus her over-all power. (2) The two principal export commodities of a normalized South Vietnam will be rubber and rice. (3) Japan's unemployment figure is an irreducible one percent. Increased industrialization will draw more workers from the farm to the factory. Urbanization of labor will reduce yield of unmechanized farms at the same time that the resultant higher purchasing power will raise demand. (4) Japan is traditionally a food importer, and she is becoming a greater one, her food imports being on the rise both proportionately and absolutely. Of 1962's total $5.6 billion imports, $700 million (12 percent) went for food; of 1963's $6.7 billion total, $1 billion (16 percent) went for food; of 1964's $7.9 billion total, $1.3 billion (17 percent) went for food.[16] (5) Japanese are the world's foremost shipbuilders and among its strongest steelmakers and textilers. They need markets. China needs ships, steel, and textiles. A developing Vietnam will want steel certainly and probably ships, but may be inclined to protect her textile industry.

Let us join a final fact with a professional observation. The fact is reported by the Indochina scholar Bernard B. Fall:

> DRVN [North Vietnamese] trade with Japan, after a period of coolness when Japan decided to pay war reparations to South Viet-Nam only, has reached important proportions that might well provoke concern in the United States. Trade rose from about $10 million in 1959 to more than $40 million in 1961–62 and in-

volves such items as chemicals, machinery of all kinds, and four seagoing 5,000-ton cargo ships and one of 2,000 tons; for these, North Viet-Nam pays in raw materials, notably coal.[17]

The observation was made by President Eisenhower at his press conference of April 7, 1954, almost exactly one month before the French collapse at Dien Bien Phu and the opening of the Geneva Conference on Indochina. The stenographic report reads:

In its economic aspects, the President added, [loss of Indochina] would take away that region that Japan must have as a trading area, or it would force Japan to turn toward China and Manchuria, or toward the Communist areas in order to live. The possible consequences of the loss [of Japan] to the free world are just incalculable, Mr. Eisenhower said.[18]

All the foregoing would appear to support the following propositions:

1. Japan's economic strength is the crucial element in America's policy of containing China and maintaining the peace in Asia. Japan is the bastion.

2. Behind only Canada among our trade partners, Japan is of major commercial importance to us. In fact, a primary direct purpose of containing China is the safeguarding of our commercial interest in Japan. Japan is thus both the bastion of the containment-expansion struggle and the prize of victory.

3. South Vietnam is an important prospective trade area for both Japanese sellers and Chinese buyers.

4. But China is also an important Japanese trade partner and cannot fail to become increasingly magnetic. The authoritative *Finance* (June 1966) said: "Some trade experts in Washington expect the Communist Bloc to supersede the U.S. as Japan's biggest trading partner during the next decade." (West Germany's sale of a steel plant to China further disarms the ideological argument against mainland trade and can only sharpen the commercial appetite of the Japanese businessman.)

5. If Japan and China develop economic interdependency —and as things now stand only shattering disturbances can even postpone that—then the brute mathematics of the relationship will doom Japan to juniority (much as Britain would be junior to an economically integrated European continent). If Japan has no long-term alternative to massive China trade,

she will be left without an alternative to a progressively more pro-Chinese orientation. The bastion and the prize, one and the same, hear the same clock ticking.

6. Japan's only remote chance (it *is* remote) for a long-term alternative to the developing market of China lies with the more slowly developing and less organizable markets of the South Pacific, South Asia, and Southeast Asia. In the first, America's position is traditionally privileged, especially in the crucial Philippines (where economic nationalism is growing) and in Australia (where direct U.S. investments, at about $1.5 billion, are greater than in all other countries but Canada, Britain, Venezuela, and Germany). In the second, India proves all but inert under the most exasperated Western proddings. In the third, South Vietnam's position is central owing to her coasts, harbors, resources wealth, and the fact that the war has *made* it central. South Vietnam's now buried treasures mean that her markets, once developed, will exert a great pull on Japan the Trader *regardless of who develops them.*

We can simplify this.

What the West faces in the Pacific is the formation of a regional economic system (*a*) whose potential and power are inherent in the Pacific situation itself, (*b*) which must include Japan, and (*c*) which would quite naturally be dominated by China. This is the "threat." America feels it most keenly because among the Western powers she now enjoys the dominant economic position in the Pacific, because her postwar Asian investment in blood and treasure is steep, and because she is by any measure the most international of the international states. Our purpose, then, is to frustrate the drawing together of this geoeconomic system by imposing political and military barricades between its elements and by holding out the alternative of other economic configurations. Thus, the struggle to hold South Vietnam. Thus, the United States-promoted Northeast Asia Treaty Organization (NEATO), which died a-borning. And thus, for more recent and more sensible approaches, the Asian Bank and the new, tentatively titled Asian and Pacific Cooperation Council (so it can be called ASPAC—"an attractive name with a masculine sound," said Thailand's Foreign Minister Thanat Khoman[19]). *New York Times* reporter Robert Trumbull, reporting the manly ASPAC's birth at Seoul in June 1966, quoted the chief of one delegation as saying that "although the organization initially will be purely for economic cooperation [e.g., a regional bank to handle development of rice and other commodities, and an international technician pool], it cannot avoid strengthening the policies of these non-Communist and anti-Communist countries."[20] The nine members are South Korea, Thailand, Malaysia, the Philippines, Australia, New Zealand, Nationalist China, South Vietnam, and Japan.

We lead from this into a final reduction:

The aim of the North Atlantic political economy is to frustrate the independent organization of the Pacific political economy.

Such has been Europe's traditional policy in Africa. Such has been the United States' traditional policy in Latin America. Such has been the traditional Asian policy of the Atlantic powers together. Nor does it very much matter that such a policy may or may not have been made explicit and consciously acted upon. An eloquent two and a half centuries of Western mucking about in Asia tell the story quite clearly enough. Everywhere in the poor world, in fact, the inveterate habit of the Western powers has been to absorb and integrate what they could command and to scatter and harass what they could not.

The most elemental meaning of the hit-and-miss, chaotic, and in many respects chronically malformed poor-world revolution is that to the traditional alternatives of subservient integration and harassment there shall now be added a third course: a South American South America, an African Africa, an Asian Asia—the very straightforward argument of it being that there can be no equable integration of the several global spheres (that's where peace is) until there is an approximate economic and political equity among them. Whether we happen to like it or not, and however we conceal the roots of our antagonism to it with panegyrics on democracy and equally irrelevent diatribes against Communism, this is the testament of revolution and this is what we are struggling to resist with our isolation of China, quarantining of Cuba, and pacifying in Vietnam.

The *fourth* point—for its powers of commentary on our culture, it seems to me, much the most important—is coiled up in a not very puzzling puzzle.

Saving Vietnam at the price of deploying some 600 Special Forces guerrilla experts, or even 16,000 Marine "advisers," whatever one thinks of the political motive, seems at least to be a proportionate act, cost-conditional and controllable. But half a million men? Who will apparently have to become a million? And a hundred billion dollars? Moreover, this "military solution" has long since proved to be no solution at all. Everyone can see that the air raids on North Vietnam, officially described as the best way to stop infiltration, have led only to stepped-up infiltration. In the south, the B-52s kill more monkeys, tigers, and civilians than Vietcong. The napalm destroys more villages than fighting forces. Sophisticated reports on our ground war argue most persuasively (if sometimes unintentionally) that it is fought without relevant pattern and without significant effect, our mechanized forces being unable to engage in any sustained and decisive way the guerrillas, whose mobility is not of the machine but of the culture itself.* And besides being militarily ineffectual, this destruction exacts a steadily higher toll in that political good will in which Johnson's America is in such miserably short supply. It means decades, if not centuries, of recrudescent anti-Americanism in Vietnam, the rest of Indochina, all of Asia; even West Europe begins to gag. One might suppose that a rational imperialist could invent other, more sensible ways to shore up the quivering dominoes of the Pacific—indeed, that he could see problems there that make Vietnam's "salvation" seem a small item. Without a wholly new order of concentrated Western will and wisdom, India will be communist within two decades. Every day, South Korea slips further behind North Korea in economic development and political independence. The political economy of the

* See, for example, Special Forces veteran Donald Duncan's "I Quit!" in the February 1966 *Ramparts*. Or a piece from the hand of a protagonist of the war, S. L. A. Marshall's "The Death of a Platoon" in the September 1966 *Harper's*, an essay of disaster whose between-the-lines message is distinct and harrowing. Or one of the few really powerful psychological studies of the ground war, John Sack's "M, An Account of One Company of American Soldiers in Fort Dix, New Jersey, Who Trained for War and Who Found It in South Viet-Nam Fifty Days Later" in the October 1966 *Esquire*. Or Marshall Sahlins' close-in study of Special Forces operations, "The Destruction of Conscience in Viet-Nam," *Dissent*, Jan.–Feb. 1966.

Philippines is stagnant and the Huks are again on the rise. Thailand's northeast remains as vulnerable as ever to those "outside agitators" whose main crime is pointing out the emperor's nakedness. Above all, there is what Stillman and Pfaff have strikingly called "the furious material energy and the eerie political passivity of contemporary Japan,"[21] an energy which we have seen to be in fact freighted with political meanings of the most momentous sort.

In sum: The military solution to the problem of Vietnam is not working; the attempt to achieve such a solution worsens and may begin to cripple our political position in Asia; and the really important and defensible eastern salients of the Western world—India, Thailand, the Philippines, Korea, Japan—drift every day a bit closer to that distinctively Oriental future which our policy-makers can hardly fail to see.

The government's computers have been no guard against a loss of control which may very well be unparalleled. Why does this happen?

This happens because the ideology that demanded and vindicated this "necessary" act of war continues to demand and vindicate the act even after it has overreached its necessity and become, on its own terms, *irrational.* What Western power opposes is the anti-imperialist social revolution of the poor. But in a time in which Western liberals have oversold themselves on their own slick humanism-*cum*-realpolitics, that position is not easy to sloganize. We have ourselves lately cursed imperialism—the more primitive imperialism of others; have ourselves once glorified revolution—our own. Perhaps because of this, America's leaders seem to have doubted that their subjects had the stomach for a repressive counterrevolutionary and imperialist war. Such a war, since it had to be fought, would have to be sweetened with a different name. Imperialism is thus rechristened as anticommunism, and our foe is instantly transformed from a human being into a pawn, a dupe, or an outright hard-core agent of that International Communist Conspiracy whose ultimate objective (so we are guaranteed) is the conquest of America.

This theory of the International Communist Conspiracy is not the hysterical old maid that many leftists seem to think it is. It has had an intimate affair with reality and it has some history on its mind when it speaks. There *is* a revolution which *is* international—one only has to count the perturbations and look at a map to see as much. In some less than technical sense, this revolution *is* "communistic," if by that we mean that it will probably not produce capitalist economies, that it will probably create autarkic and controlled economies, authoritarian central governments, programs of forced-march wealth accumulation, and the forcible dismantling of rich elites. And if not by any means melodramatically conspiratorial, the several national liberation movements, in their early stages especially, *do* make an effort to coordinate themselves; they do so, pathetically unadept, because they consider their enemy to be internationally coordinated himself—a view which is entirely correct. And to the extent to which this revolution aims at terminating the masterdom of the rich, an aim which automatically implicates America, the revolution *does* aim itself at America—it aims itself, rather, at an America which most Americans have forgotten about: Rockefeller, Englehard, U.S.A. There is just no use being deluded about that. But what is added on for pure political effect is that ugly edge of clandestinity, pointless and merciless ambition, that cloud of diabolism which has nothing to do with the sustaining force of the revolution itself. And what is *subtracted* from the reality—much more important—is the *source* of the ferment, the *cause* of the anger, the supreme question of the *justice* of rebellion. What this theory gives us is a portrait whose outlines are not unreal, but whose colors have been changed from human blacks and browns and yellows into devil's red, and whose background has been entirely erased. Thus, the theory wildly disorganizes and mismanages the very real history that allows it to survive. And if it lies within the power of an idea to pervert a nation's generosity and curse its children, then the widespread American acceptance of this view of revolution may forecast a bitter future for us all.

It is through the ideology of Cold War anticommunism (a cynic might abbreviate it to CWAC and call it "cwackery") that the masters of American power have rationalized and quite successfully dissembled their opposition to the Third World's diffuse and uneven movement for independence. This ideology is the root-and-branch descendant of that ideology by which the fathers of these same masters once sought to break the American labor movement. It has the sort of truth in it now, and the same sort of lies, that it had in the long bitter period between the Civil War and World War II. After years of perfection, and applied now to a remote world familiar to Americans only as the well-controlled mass media see fit to make it so, one has to say of this ideology that it is more effective now than ever. It entirely rearranges the moral terms of the encounter between the rich and the poor, and in one stroke deprives the revolutionary of the very right to name and explain himself. He stands already named—a criminal; already explained—an enemy. He is *not* the revolutionary which he pretends to be. The *real* social revolutionaries, it seems, are ourselves. This other one is a fraud, whether willfully so or not; and, whether or not *he* knows it, *we* happen to know that he is an imposter, an intruder on the scene of social change whose real hope, real demand—is the destruction of our country. Whatever he may think, we know that he will never be satisfied with Moscow or Peking, Havana or Algiers, Caracas or Saigon. He is out to get *us*—Kansas City, Birmingham, Washington, D.C. So it follows that the inner, central, driving theme of the drama being acted out in Vietnam's jungles is nothing less than the question of our own national survival. This is the theory by which the war has been explained to us.

If it is a good theory, then it is good *absolutely*. If it is correct to say that our national well-being requires the defeat of the NLF, then the NLF will have to be defeated. The explanation will remain correct regardless of how hard it might be to carry out its implicit commands. Preserving the well-being of the nation is an overriding and transcendent objective. It is not possible to imagine that such an objective can be qualified or repealed *even for one moment* by any other objective. It is an imperative. The awesome consequence of this is that *any struggle that is rationalized in its name is one from which we cannot withdraw.*

Everyone knows that some people in this country, some of them strong, consistently demand that we use all needed force to bring this war to a "speedy and favorable conclusion." If their view of history is not backward, then their moral system is; but to characterize them as ultraconservatives, to try to erase their argument by calling them names like warmonger, is to miss entirely the good, clear point which they make. The main thing wrong with this "ultraconservative warhawk" may in fact have nothing at all to do with conservatism or bellicosity, but rather with his unreserved acceptance of a theory which liberal American administrations have been drumming into his head for at least a quarter of a century—namely, the theory that there is an International Communist Conspiracy that threatens to capture the world, including *us*; that plans to impose upon that imprisoned world, including *us*, the bleakest tyranny that history ever saw; and that aims to achieve all this through the piecemeal conquest of increasingly less marginal states.

Let it be remembered that the government speaks to its people with a measure of authority. People do not expect it to lie, distort, or deceive. People trust it. When this selfsame trustworthy government informs the people that the war takes place because agents of the world-hungry tyranny came to a happy land from outside and proceeded to agitate, propagandize, subvert, terrorize, and spread chaos, hatred, and ammunition, then the people have every right to demand, Why not go after such a threat *at its source*? When our trusted government explains to us that the Red takeover of Vietnam (Laos, Cuba, Hispaniola, the Congo) is merely secondary, nothing but a conquistadorial way station on the road to this Xanadu of ours, then the people have every right to demand, *Why not act now?* Looked at *in itself*, as a problem of national survival, it does not seem to me that this has anything very much to do with conservatism. There is a murder going on out there in the street: A man with a knife is killing Kitty Genovese; after he finishes her off, he aims to invade the apartment house itself and kill one by one the empty-headed, empty-hearted cowards who gape at the atrocity from their windows. So *of course* the right thing to do is to leap now to her defense. First, because she is an innocent victim and not to defend her is dishonorable. Second, because her murder will not appease but only whet the killer's appetite, and we have before us an official American fact that unless someone stops him he will soon be putting his fangs into us. What is "conservative" about wanting to fight in that situation? What kind of whimpering lunatic thinks it is "warmongering" to intervene under such circumstances? The bravest case to be made against these reactionaries of ours is that they are so overeager to believe what the liberals have been feeding them. On terms of that belief, what nonsense it is to talk about a "limited" war with "limited" objectives.

"We are at total war right now," say the right-wingers—only making more succinct what Truman told them, what Eisenhower and Kennedy allowed them to believe, what Johnson's homilies have convinced them of all over again.

An ideology which originates in a distortion of history acquires an intrinsic power to sustain and add to historical distortions. It achieves an independent authority in the explanation of events and therefore in the forcing of national policy. We go to Vietnam to maintain a segment of the Western, North Atlantic community's sphere of influence—an objective which on its own terms is practical, concrete, definite, and perhaps not at all without limits; one which is subject to a cost accounting and for which there may be an excessive price to pay. But because they have rationalized this venture in terms of the ideology of anticommunism, our leaders are obliged to insist that we are in Vietnam to protect our vital organs of national increase—an objective that is not practical and cost-conditional but absolute and sacred. To ask what is the value of holding Vietnam becomes, in the grip of this ideology, as pointless as asking the value of the king in a game of chess. The war escapes the political relativity to become transcendent and sublime.

This is an affliction of the people. We might assume (although Johnson, Rusk, and Rostow make us shaky about it) that the political technicians of the State and Defense Departments only purvey, but themselves do not use, the quasi-religious doctrine of the Great Conspiracy. That will not help those whom they have made true-believer addicts to it. A big minority of Americans is one day going to be *betrayed.* The ideological bridgework between the fact and the fancy is coming unstuck today as perhaps never before for America. And when it crumbles, a great many good, strong people are going to find themselves marooned in the unreal. Their anger will shake the nation. To them, the conduct of the war already seems an act of madness if not perfidy. Here we are in a death duel with a most relentless foe, and look at us pulling our punches! The two basic criticisms of the war, which correlate with the leftist and the rightist dissents, aim at resolving the tension that exists between the war's most common political and military descriptions. The rightist accepts the political description and therefore wants the war to be more fiercely waged. The leftist repudiates that political description and therefore wants the war to be broken off. Both aim at a more rational position. Both have a much more solid line of argument than the center, which is only confused and trapped by its own dissembling gobbledygook. In a way, this warhawk is even more humane than the slow-death advocates, for he may at least lay claim to the stark compassion of Macbeth: "If it were done when 'tis done, then 'twere well it were done quickly." If we must destroy Vietnam, then let us have the mercy to do it with dispatch and put those poor people, broken-legged horses, out of their misery.

And the very sad fact is that when the time comes to pay the piper, it will not be to these "moderates" of ours that the deepest, most spirit-tearing agony will come. The example of the French experience in Algeria is all too instructive.

France fought to maintain her colonial control of Algeria for many of the same reasons that mobilize America in Vietnam today. Like America, France rationalized the colonial war in terms of transcendent national imperatives. When it became clear to the leaders of France that disengagement was required, important elements in the French army were outraged. The Secret Army Organization (OAS) was formed to resist what its members felt was the betrayal of the nation. The OAS aimed at nothing less than a *coup d'état*, and its existence created for France the most punishing internal torment. How did this happen in France, the heartland of European humanism? Western liberals have a theory about that which restores their confidence: The OAS happened because there were fascists in the French army who wanted it to happen. The OAS was only the last gasp of the old Nazi collaborationists. There is nothing like that in America.

But look again—not at America to find fascists, but beyond the fascist label itself, which has merely substituted a curse where an explanation is required.

On the first of August 1962, Captain Estoup, a lawyer of the First Foreign Legion Paratroop Regiment, arguing before a high French military tribunal, summed up his defense of one of the OAS conspirators: "How can it happen," he asked, "that a brilliant young St.-Cyr cadet, one of the outstanding young men . . . at the military academy . . . today stands accused [of treason] before a military court . . . ?"[22]

Let us fix our eye on the American counterpart of this "brilliant young cadet" before we go on. Let us imagine a good blond and upright young man, square-shouldered with a heart full of bravery, a West Point graduate from some very American place like Colorado Springs or Trenton or Seattle—in E. E. Cummings' phrase, "a yearning nation's blue-eyed pride." We must imagine the ballgames he has played, the cotton candy and the sweet spring nights and the sweetheart he has left behind him; the strong old clapboard houses, the gracious elms, the broad green lawns of the quiet streets from which he came. All that. He is not monocled or mustached. There is no *Mein Kampf* hidden in his footlocker. His voice is well modulated, his demeanor perhaps a bit retiring. He is proud but not arrogant about his Green Beret. He is not happy to be in Vietnam. He would prefer to be home. There is, however, a job to be done. Such is the villain of the peace: the traitor.

Estoup proceeds to explain that it was to the members of the elite forces—men like our young St.-Cyr cadet from Wyoming—that the most odious and dangerous of assignments fell. It was the cadet's duty to procure vital information about the enemy—"by all means available." That is, he was instructed to use torture. "I do not know," says Estoup,

> what sort of mental turmoil someone who gives an order like this must go through; but I do know the sense of shock and revulsion suffered by those who have to carry it out. All the fine ideas and the illusions of the young St.-Cyr cadet crumble. . . . But you will say, "Then why did not the young St.-Cyr cadet refuse to carry out the order?" Because the ultimate end had been so described to him that it appeared to justify the means. It had been proved to him that the outcome of the battle depended on the information he obtained, that the victory of France was at stake. . . . If the means are justified only by the end, there is no justification at all unless the end is achieved. If it is not, nothing is left but a senseless pattern of dirty indelible stains. . . . It is my testimony that for the most part the true motive for [the actions of the conspirators] was a secret, silent, inward, gnawing determination not to have committed crimes that achieved no object. In the final analysis, these are the actions of the damned souls making their last desperate effort to wreak vengeance on the devil who has lured them into hell. The people of France, in whose name justice is now being done, should know that it was in their name and for their sake that the accused were pushed, by those in authority, over the edge of this pit of destruction.[23]

No one knows better than the torturer himself what torture means. No one understands bombing better than the bomber, guns than the gunner, death than he who kills. You need not inform this Wyoming lad that his hands are bloody. He is the expert about that. But the blood will wash away, will it not? The dirty indelible stains will one day be removed? The cleansing water is victory. The sacrifice is redeemed by the rebirth for which it prepares the conquered land. But if the water is not brought, that deferred innocence in whose name the present guilt is borne vanishes from the future. And what becomes of this strange savage blood? It fuses permanently with the skin of the hands that shed it.

We ought to be able to understand a very simple thing: From now on in America it shall be with such hands that children are soothed, office memoranda signed, cocktails stirred, friends greeted, poems written, love made, the Host laid on the tongue and wreaths on graves, the nose pinched in meditation. In the forthcoming gestures of these hands—this is really very simple—we shall behold an aspect of Vietnam's revenge.

VI

The Revolted

Killing is evil. . . . All countries are different and progress should be achieved by peaceful means whenever possible.
—Che Guevara[1]

The young men joining them [the NLF] have been attracted by the excitement of the guerrilla life. —Robert S. McNamara[2]

Everyone in the rich world has heard that there is another world out there, almost out of sight, where two thirds of all of us are living, where misery and violence are routine, where Mozart has not been widely heard nor Plato and Shakespeare much studied.

There is a world, that is, which, according to the mainstream intuitions of mainstream middle-class America, must be somebody's exaggeration, a world which is fundamentally implausible. For the most part, we really believe in it, this poor world, only to the extent that we have it to blame for certain of our troubles. It is the "breeding ground," we say (a favorite term, packed with connotations of the plague), of those discontents which harass us. Most ordinary rich-world people would much prefer never even to have heard of Vietnam or Mozambique, not to mention the nearly thirty other states of the world where long-term insurgencies are under way.

The main fact about the revolutionary is that he demands total change. The corresponding fact about most Americans is that they are insulted by that demand. But what of that demand's moral force? When the statistics of world poverty reach us, as they now and then do, we can respond in several characteristic ways. Sometimes we cluck our tongues, shake our heads, and send a check off to CARE. Sometimes we tell tales about brave missionaries of either the Baptist or the AID persuasion. Someone might name the Alliance for Progress. And someone else might cough. When the statistics are voiced by the poor man's machine-gun fire, we are more decisive. While waiting for our bombers to warm up, we develop our poor-devils theory, according to which the wretched have been duped by Communist con men. It is a bad thing to be hungry; we can see that. But it is better to be hungry and patient than hungry and Red, for to be Red proves to us that all this hunger was really just a trick. It is probably the case that a Communist *has* no hunger.

In the land of remote-controlled adventure, the office-dwelling frontiersman, the automated pioneer—how can matters be seen otherwise?

Middle-class America is the nation to which the forthcoming obsolescence of the moral choice has been revealed.

Middle-class America is the condition of mind which supposes that a new, plastic Eden has been descried upon a calm sea, off our bow. A point here and there, a firm rudder, a smart following breeze, a bit of pluck, and we shall make port any time now in this "American Century."

Middle-class America regards itself as the Final Solution. Its most intense desire is not to be bothered by fools who disagree about that.

What must be difficult for any nation seems out of the question for us: to imagine that we may from time to time be the enemies of men who are just, smart, honest, courageous, and *correct*—who could think such a thing? Since we love rose arbors and pretty girls, our enemies must be unjust, stupid, dishonest, craven, and *wrong*.

Such conceptions are sometimes shaken. After the 1965 battle of Plei Me, Special Forces Major Charles Beckwith described NLF guerrilla fighters as "the finest soldiers I have ever seen in the world except Americans. I wish we could recruit them." After the same battle, another American said of a captured Viet Cong, "We ought to put this guy on the north wall and throw out these Government troops. He could probably hold it alone. If we could get two more, we would have all the walls [of the triangular camp] taken care of." Major Beckwith was intrigued with the "high motivation" and "high dedication" of this enemy force and suggested an explanation: "I wish I knew what they were drugging them with to make them fight like that."[3]

That curiosity, at least, is good. Why do men rebel? Let us try to find out what could possibly be so wrong with so many of the world's men and women that they should fight so hard to stay outside the Eden we think we are offering them.

I make three assumptions. First, everyone who is now a rebel *became* a rebel; he was once upon a time a child who spoke no politics. The rebel is someone who has changed.

Second, men do not imperil their own and others' lives for unimpressive reasons. They are sharp accountants on the subject of staying alive. When they do something dangerous, they have been convinced that not to do it was more dangerous. There are always a few who can evidently be persuaded by some combination of statistics and principles to put their lives on the line. Lenin, for example, did not materially *need* the Russian Revolution. His commitment was principled and it originated from a basic detachment. But I am not trying to describe the Lenins. I am after those nameless ones but for whom the Lenins would have remained only philosophers, those who (as Brecht put it) grasp revolution first in the hand and only later in the mind.

Third, I assume that the rebel is much like myself, someone whom I can understand. He is politically extraordinary. That does not mean that he is psychologically so. My assumption is that what would not move me to the act of rebellion would not move another man.

It is safe to say first that revolutionary potential exists only in societies where material human misery is the denominating term in most social relationships. No one thinks that bankers are going to make disturbances in the streets. Less obviously, this also implies that privation can be political only if it is not universal. The peasant who compares his poverty to someone else's richness is able to conceive that his poverty is special, a social identity. To say that hunger does not become a rebellious sensation until it coexists with food is to say that rebellion has less to do with scarcity than with maldistribution. This states a central theme: revolutionary anger is not produced by privation, but by understood injustice.

But the self-recognized victim is not at once his own avenger. He is first of all a man who simply wants to reject his humiliation. He will therefore recreate his world via social pantomimes which transfigure or otherwise discharge that humiliation. "They whipped Him up the hill," sang the black slave, "and He never said a mumbling word." That divine reticence is clearly supposed to set an example. But it also does much more. In such a song, the slave plays the role of himself and thus avoids himself, puts his realities at the distance of a pretense which differs from the realities only to the extent that it *is* a pretense. The slave creates for the master's inspection an exact replica of himself, of that slave which he is; and even as the master looks, the slave escapes behind the image. It is not that he pretends to be other than a slave. Such an act would be quickly punished. He instead pretends to be what he knows himself to be, acts out the role of the suffering and humiliated, in order to place a psychic foil between himself and the eyes of others. The American Negro's older Steppinfetchit disguise, or the acutely ritualized violence of ghetto gangs: these are intentional lies which intentionally tell the truth. The victim-liar's inner reality, his demand for freedom, precludes telling the truth. His outer reality, his victimhood, precludes telling a lie. Therefore he *pretends* the truth, pretends to hold the truth in his hand and to pass judgment on it. And by choosing to enact what he *is* he disguises from himself the fact that he had no choice.

A crucial moment comes when something ruptures this thin membrane of pretense. What can do that? A glimpse of weakness in his master sometimes; sometimes the accidental discovery of some unsuspected strength in himself. More often it will be the master's heightened violence that confronts the slave with the incorrigible authenticity of his slave act. A black man sings blues about his powerlessness, his loneliness; he has taken refuge behind that perfect image of himself. The white master, for no reason, in mid-song, takes the guitar away, breaks it, awaits the slave's reaction. The slave is at that moment forced into his self-image space, is psychologically fused with this truth-telling pretense of his: He *is* powerless; he *is* lonely. He cannot now enact himself; he must *be* that man of whom he had tried to sing. This encounter strips life of its formality and returns it to pure, primitive substance. For the victim, there is no longer even the fragile, rare escape of the simultaneous re-enactment of reality. He lives wholly now in his victim space, without manners, not even allowed to mimic the horror of victimhood in the same gesture that expresses it. He is nothing now but the locus of injustice.

Grown less random, injustice becomes more coherent. Confronted at every instant by that coherence, the victim may find that it is no longer so easy to avoid the truth that his suffering is *caused,* that it is not just an accident that there are so many differences between his life and the life of the round, white-suited man in the big hillside house. He begins to feel singled out. He rediscovers the idea of the system of power.

And at that same moment he discovers that he also may accuse. When the victim sees that what had seemed universal is local, that what had seemed God-given is man-made, that what had seemed quality is mere condition—his permanent immobility permanently disappears. Being for the first time in possession of the stark idea that his life could be different were it not for others, he is for the first time someone who might move. His vision of change will at this point be narrow and mundane, his politics naive: Maybe he only wants a different landlord, a different mayor, a different sheriff. The important element is not the scope or complexity of his vision but the sheer existence of the idea that change can happen.

Then who is to be the agent of this change? Surely not the victim himself. He has already seen enough proof of his impotence, and knows better than anyone else that he is an unimportant person. What compels him to hope nevertheless is the vague notion that his tormentor is answerable to a higher and fairer authority. This sheriff's outrageous conduct, that is, belongs strictly to this particular sheriff, not to sheriffness. Further, this sheriff represents only a local derangement within a system which the victim barely perceives and certainly does not yet accuse, a hardship which High Authority did not intend to inflict, does not need, and will not allow. (Once Robin Hood meets King Richard, the Sheriff of Nottingham is done for.)

We meet in this the politics of the appeal to higher power, which has led to some poignant moments in history. It is the same thing as prayer. Its prayerfulness remains basic even as it is elaborated into the seemingly more politically aggressive mass petition to the king, a main assumption of which is that the king is not bad, only uninformed. This way of thinking brought the peasants and priests to their massacre at Kremlin Square in 1905. It prompted the so-called Manifesto of the Eighteen which leading Vietnamese intellectuals published in 1960. It rationalized the 1963 March on Washington for Jobs and Freedom. The Freedom Rides, the nonviolent sit-ins, and the various Deep South marches were rooted in the same belief: that there was indeed a higher power which was responsive and decent.*

Sometimes mass-based secular prayer has resulted in change. But more often it has only shown the victim-petitioners that the problem is graver and change harder to get than they had imagined. The bad sheriffs turn out to be everywhere; indeed, there seems to be no other kind. It turns out that the king is on their side, that the state's administrative and coercive-punitive machinery exists precisely to serve the landlords. It turns out that the powerful know perfectly well who their victims are and why there should be victims, and that they have no intention of changing anything. This recognition is momentous, no doubt the spiritual low point of the emergent revolutionary's education. He finds that the enemy is not a few men but a whole system whose agents saturate the society, occupying and fiercely protecting its control centers. He is diverted by a most realistic despair.

But this despair contains within itself the omen of that final shattering reconstitution of the spirit which will prepare the malcontent, the fighter, the wino, the criminal for the shift to insurgency, rebellion, revolution. He had entertained certain hopes about the powerful: They can tell justice from injustice, they support the first, they are open to change. He is now instructed that these hopes are whimsical. At the heart of his despair lies the new certainty that there will be no change which he does not produce by himself.

The man who believes that change can only come from his

* What was new was the way these forms enlarged the concept of petition. Instead of merely writing down the tale of grievance, they reproduced the grievance itself in settings that forced everyone to behold it, tzar included, and to respond. The Vietnam war protest demonstrations are no different. The speeches they occasion may sometimes seem especially pugnacious. But inasmuch as the antiwar movement has never been able to dream up a threat which it might really make good, this fiercer face-making has remained basically a kind of entertainment. The main idea has always been to persuade higher authority—Congress, the UN, Bobby Kennedy—to do something. Far from calling higher authority into question, these wildly militant demonstrations actually dramatize and even exaggerate its power.

own initiative will be disinclined to believe that change can be less than total. Before he could see matters otherwise, he would have to accept on some terms, however revised, the power which he now opposes. The compromises which will actually be made will be arranged by his quietly "realistic" leaders and will be presented to him as a total victory. He himself is immoderate and unconciliatory. But the more important, more elusive feature of this immoderation is that he may be powerless to change it. He could only compromise with rebelled-against authority if he were in possession of specific "solutions" to those "problems" that finally drove him to revolt. Otherwise there is nothing to discuss. But the leap into revolution has left these "solutions" behind because it has collapsed and wholly redefined the "problems" to which they referred. The rebel is an incorrigible absolutist who has replaced all "problems" with the one grand claim that the entire system is an error, all "solutions" with the single irreducible demand that change shall be total, all diagnoses of disease with one final certificate of death. To him, total change means only that those who now have all power shall no longer have any, and that those who now have none—the people, the victimized—shall have all. Then what can it mean to speak of compromise? Compromise is whatever absolves and reprieves an enemy who has already been sentenced. It explicitly restores the legitimacy of the very authority which the rebel defines himself by repudiating. This repudiation being total, it leaves exactly no motive—again, not even the *motive*—for creating that fund of specific proposals, that *conversation*, without which a compromise is not even *technically* possible.

"What do you want?" asks the worried, perhaps intimidated master. "What can I give you?" he inquires, hoping to have found in this rebel a responsible, realistic person, a man of the world like himself. But the rebel does not fail to see the real meaning of this word *give*. Therefore he answers, "I cannot be purchased." The answer is meant mainly to break off the conference. But at one level, it is a completely substantive comment, not at all just a bolt of pride. It informs the master that he no longer exists, not even in part.

At another level, however, this answer is nothing but an evasion. The master seems to have solicited the rebel's views on the revolutionized, good society. The rebel would be embarrassed to confess the truth: that he has no such views. Industry? Agriculture? Foreign trade? It is not such matters that drive and preoccupy him. The victorious future is at the moment any society in which certain individuals no longer have power, no longer exist. The rebel fights for something that will not be like *this*. He cannot answer the question about the future because that is not his question. It is not the future that is victimizing him. It is the present. It is not an anticipated Utopia which moves him to risk his life. It is pain. "Turn it over!" he cries, because he can no longer bear it as it is. The revolutionary is not *by type* a Lenin, a Mao, a Castro, least of all a Brezhnev. He is neither an economist nor a politician nor a social philosopher. He may become these; ultimately he must. But his motivating vision of change is at root a vision of something absent—not of something that *will* be there, but of something that will be there *no longer*. His good future world is elementally described by its empty spaces: a missing landlord, a missing mine owner, a missing sheriff. Who or what will replace landlord, owner, sheriff? Never mind, says the revolutionary, glancing over his shoulder. Something better. If he is thereupon warned that this undefined "something" may turn out to make things worse than ever, his response is a plain one: "Then we should have to continue the revolution."

The fundamental revolutionary motive is not to construct a Paradise but to destroy an Inferno. In time, Utopian ideas will appear. Because the world now has a revolutionary past, it may seem that they appear at the same moment as destructive anger, or even that they precede and activate or even cause it. This is always an illusion produced by the predictive social analytic which revolutionist intellectuals claim to have borrowed from history. We may be sure that the people have not said: Here is a plan for a better life—socialism, Montes called it. He has proved to us that it is good. In its behalf, we shall throw everything to the wind and risk our necks. Rather, they have said: What we have here in the way of life cannot be put up with anymore. Therefore, we must defend ourselves.

It happens that at least the spirit of socialism will be implied by the inner dynamics of mass revolt: What was collectively won should be collectively owned. But it cannot be too much emphasized that the interest in developing other social forms, however acute it will become, follows, *does not precede*, the soul-basic explosion against injustice which is the one redemption of the damned. When Turcios takes his rebel band to a Guatemalan village for "armed propaganda," there is no need to talk of classless societies. Someone kneels in the center of the circle and begins to speak of his life, the few cents pay for a hard day's labor, the high prices, the arrogance of the *patrón*, the coffins of the children. It is this talk—very old talk, unfortunately always new—which finally sets the circle ringing with the defiant cry, "*Si, es cierto!*" Yes, it is true. Something will have to be done.

Revolutionary consciousness exists for the first time when the victim elaborates his experience of injustice into an inclusive definition of the society in which he lives. *The rebel is someone for whom injustice and society are only different words for the same thing.* Nothing in the social world of the master is spared the contempt of this definition, which, as soon as it exists, absorbs everything in sight. No public door is marked overnight with a device that permits its survival. The loanshark's corner office and the Chase Manhattan Bank, Coney Island and Lincoln Center, look very much the same from 137th Street. They are all owned by someone else.

Everywhere he looks, the man-who-is-being-revolted sees something which is not his. The good land which the *campesino* works belongs to the *hacienda.* That belongs to the *patrón.* As often as not, the *patrón* belongs to the United Fruit Company. And that prime mover unmoved belongs to nothing. It can only be for a brief moment that the *campesino* gazes with unashamed wonder at these skyscrapers. For all the justice they promise him, they might as well be so many rocks. He is soon unimpressed and grows apathetic toward Western grandeur. *The rebel is someone who has no stakes.* He is an unnecessary number, a drifter into a life that will be memorable chiefly for its humiliations. No use talking to him about the need to sustain traditions and preserve institutions or to help society evolve in an orderly way toward something better bit by bit. He very well knows that it is not in his name that the virtue of this orderliness is being proved. *The rebel is an irresponsible man whose irresponsibility has been decreed by others.* It is no doing of his own that his fantasy is now filled with explosions and burning Spanish lace.

But this new consciousness, this radical alienation from past and present authority, does not lead straightway to political action. A commitment to violence has only just become possible at this point. We have a man who certainly will not intervene in a streetcorner incident in behalf of the "law and order" of which he considers himself the main victim. He will even betray a government troop movement or shelter an "outlaw." But he may also find a tactical rationale for joining a "moderate" march or applauding a "reasonable" speech or doing nothing at all. At odd moments, he will abide talk of reform. Maybe things left to themselves will get better. He will keep the conversation open and the switchblade closed.

What is wrong with this man who thinks things can change without being changed? Who knows everything and does nothing?

Nothing is wrong with him but the fact that he is a human being. All these excuses, these cautions and carefully rationalized delays, add up to one thing: *He wants to be free.* He therefore temporizes with freedom. His desire for an independent private life has been intensified everywhere by the conditions that prohibit it. He has understood his situation and the demands it makes. He knows he is being asked to become a historical object. But he seems to recognize in this demand an old familiar presence. He has been drafted before by this history, has he not? Is the new allurement of rebellion really so different at bottom from the old coercion of slavery? Are his privacy and freedom not pre-empted equally by both? Is the rebel anything more than the same unfree object in a different costume, playing a new role? When the slave kills the master, argues Sartre, two men die. He meant that the slave dies too and the free man materializes in his place. Very well, the image is nearly overwhelming. But where is the freedom of this ex-slave who, instead of cutting cane, is now sharpening knives? That he has removed himself from one discipline to another does not hide the fact that he remains under discipline. It will be said that he at least chose the new one. But that does not diminish the servitude. When the slave conceives rebellion and remains a slave, one may say that he has chosen his slavery. That makes him no less a slave, no more a free man. In fact, the free man was glimpsed only in the moment at which he said: *I can! I may!* At that moment, the whole world shook with his exhilaration. Everywhere, he saw commotion and uncertainty where there had been only stillness and routine before. He stops at the window of a firearms dealer. He does not go in. He proceeds to the window of an agency of escape. This is not irresolution; it is freedom, the liquidity of choice. When he changes *I may* into *I will*, when he has taken the rifle and changed *I will* into *I am*, this man who was for one moment a profuse blur of possibilities, a fleeting freedom, has disappeared into another pose, has transformed himself into another image: that of the rebel.

Of all people, Sartre should have been distant enough from his partisanship to see that in this case freedom was only the possibility of transition from one binding contract to another—*and therefore not freedom.* As the slave found himself isolated from freedom by the master's power, so the rebel finds himself isolated from it by the decision which his life has forced upon him not merely to be a slave no longer, but *to be this rebel.* Once again, he is not his own man. Once again his future, which was for one moment molten, has hardened into a specific object.

Do not be deceived by the high-mindedness of these concepts. Freedom is not an ecstasy reserved for enlightened Europeans. It is not as if its subleties confine their influence to the bourgeois radicals who anatomize and name them. The psychiatric appendices to Fanon's *The Wretched of the Earth* often read like case-study illustrations for Sartre's *Being and Nothingness.* Drop-outs on Lexington Avenue are jangling and illumined with this torment. Freedom is not something which only certain men will discover only under certain conditions, and its goodness is not limited by the well-known fact that there are better and worse, nobler and baser ways in which it can be lost. We must not get it into our heads that the rebel *wants* to be a rebel. We must not think that he hurls his Molotov cocktails with a howl of glee, much less with a smirk on his face. We have to catch the wince, the flinch, those moments when he unaccountably turns aside. For the slave, there is simply no way to put an end to his current servitude except to exchange it for another. He is not at liberty to be just a nonslave. He is only free to choose between two hard masters. He will struggle to escape this fork, to liberate himself from these titles, to balance on the peak between them. But always he is about to be blown off on one side or the other. For him, it is a clear case of either/or.

I think Camus misses this. I cannot otherwise understand how he could believe himself to be making a useful, relevant moral point when he affirms that men should be "neither victims nor executioners." This is excellent advice for the executioner. It is less illuminating for the victim, perhaps even beyond his depth. The victim does not belong to that category of men for whom action can be regulated by such advice. This does *not* mean that he will recognize himself as the object of Camus's brilliant epithet, "privileged executioner," much less that he somehow prefers to be such a thing. What is so poignant about the victim, in fact, is the desperation with which he seeks to *enter* that category, to become *available* to Camus, for that is the category of free men. It is ruthless to assume that not ourselves but others are so appallingly strange as to choose shattered lives—as if pursuit, revenge, estrangement made up a career.

On the contrary. The rebel will have resisted his rebellion fiercely. The same inner agility that guarded his spirit from his body's subjugation, the same good guile that kept him from becoming for himself that slave which he could not help being for others—this talent for inner survival now stands up to ward off the new version of the old threat. At the moment at which he is most accelerated by his revulsion, he may also be most alarmed to see that he is about to be *reduced* to that revulsion, that he is in danger of becoming it—of becoming a revolted one, a revolutionary. He will for a long time affect a kind of reserve; he will not permit the loss of what Harlem has named his "cool," a word which could only be translated into the languages of oppressed people—"native tongues." To be cool is to float upon one's decisions, to remain positioned just barely beyond the reach of one's commitments. To be cool is to act freedom out without quite denying that there is a hoax involved. It is to tantalize oneself with the possibility that one may do *nothing*, at the same time never letting anyone forget the *fatefulness* of one's situation. Since he wants to be free, the slave cannot renounce rebellion. Since he cannot renounce rebellion, he craves freedom all the more hungrily. That tension can only be controlled by irony: The slave-rebel evades both captivities by refusing to destroy either.

But the evasion is only a more precarious form of the older

ritualized self-enacting, and it dooms itself. As soon as the slave defines himself as *other* than the slave, he has already defined himself as the rebel, since the slave is precisely that person who cannot otherwise define himself without committing the act of rebellion.

How can he be said to make a choice when to choose anything at all is already to stand in rebellion?

This man's predicament can almost be touched with the hands. He wants nothing but freedom. That simple demand pits him against the injustice of being defined by the master. It also pits him against the internal and external forces that pressure him to define himself. The choice seems to lie between submitting to murder and committing suicide. Freedom is always escaping him in the direction of his anger or his fatigue. Desiring only that his objective life can have some of the variousness and elasticity of his subjective life, he is always rediscovering that this will be possible only if he forgoes variousness for concentration, elasticity for discipline. *The revolutionary is someone who is nothing else in order to be everything else.*

"We have come to the point," writes someone from the Brazilian underground, "of making a rigorous distinction between being leftist—even radically leftist—and being revolutionary. In the critical situation through which we are now living, there is all the difference in the world between the two. We are in dead earnest. At stake is the humanity of man."

Anyone who wants to know where revolution's strange capacity for terror and innocence comes from will find the answer vibrating between these last two sentences. How can ordinary men be at once warm enough to want what revolutionaries say they want (humanity), cold enough to do without remorse what they are capable of doing (cutting throats), and poised enough in the turbulence of their lives to keep the aspiration and the act both integrated and distinct? How is it that one of these passions does not invade and devour the other? How is it that the knife that is still wet from a second person's blood and a third person's tears can be raised in an intimate salute to "humanity"?

Thus the rebel's picture of himself: a dead-earnest soldier for the humanity of man. If we join him in accepting that picture, if we take the rebel's *machismo* as offered, then we shall probably convince ourselves that he is trapped in a deadly moral contradiction which can be resolved in only one of two ways. Most sympathetically, stressing his aspirations, we should then decide that he is *tragic,* someone driven to disfigure what he most highly prizes. Least sympathetically, stressing his actions, we should find in him the hypocrite *criminal* who cynically pretends that death is only relatively evil.

Both views are wrong. When the "criminal" affirms that he is "in dead earnest," his tone of voice attributes to himself a decision that has originated elsewhere. "In dead earnest" is a euphemism for "desperate." When the "tragic" figure affirms that his cause is "the humanity of man," he has either forgotten the way he came or he has failed to see that negating one thing is not the same as affirming its opposite. "The humanity of man" is a euphemism for "survival."

This abstract man has come through a good many changes. From one whose reaction to his own victimhood was resignation and ritual flight, he has become a self-conscious victim who understands that no one will change things for him, that he may himself take action, and that there is such a thing as revolution. Wretched man has come to the edge of violence. But he is not yet revolutionary man. He may very well piece together an entire habit of life out of hesitation, ambiguity, reserve. He is oblique, ironic, elegant, and cool, someone whose detachment tries not to become treachery, whose sympathy tries not to become irreversible involvement.

What drives him over the divide? What is the difference between the Guatemalan, Mozambiquan, Brazilian farmers who have joined Turcios, Mondlane, Alepio in the mountains, and those likeminded ones who have remained onlookers in the villages? What is the difference between the "revolutionary" and the "radical leftist" which the Brazilian informs us is so critical?

If I am correct in assuming that men resist danger and want freedom from *all* servitudes, then it follows that rebellion does not take place until it has become compulsory. The rebel is someone who is no longer free to chose even his own docile servitude. He has been driven to the wall. Somebody is even trying to pound him through it. He has been reduced from the slave to the prisoner, from the prisoner to the condemned. It is no longer a matter of standing before two objects and choosing which he shall be. Totally possessed by his predicament, and therefore in its command, he is no longer able to make even a subjective distinction between that predicament and himself. His anger, like his previous humiliation, was for awhile still something which he could set beside himself and contemplate or enact: his *situation*, not his *person*. But this changes. In spite of himself, he is pushed into the same space which he formerly quarantined off for his anger. He is fused with it—with the poverty, estrangement, futurelessness which gave it its murderous content. He is turned into the venom from which he has tried to stand apart. Except for rebellion, there is nothing. The strange apparent freedom of the rebel, and hence that pride of his which is so enormous when it arrives as to dwarf everything else, a psychic flood which sweeps everything before it, lie in his having finally affirmed the only life that is available to him: *The rebel is someone who has accepted death*.

It is this deprivation of choice that makes the difference between the "revolutionary," who may not be at all "radical," and the "radical," who may never become "revolutionary."

Who determined that this most severe and absolute of reductions should have taken place? We contented Westerners prefer to think that it was the rebel himself. This gives us the right to treat him as though he were a criminal. This is what allows us to single out for pity those "innocent women and children" whom our bombs also destroy, as if there is nothing wrong in killing adult male rebels. But this distinction, because it presupposes that the rebel has had a choice, obliges us to concoct a whole new second definition of man, a definition to place beside the one which we reserve for ourselves. The rebel will in that case be for us the very astounding slave who found it in his power to walk away from his slavery.

There is a more mundane explanation.

Here is someone who was lucky. He was *educated*. It was systematically driven into his head that justice is such and such, truth this, honor that. One day he surfaced from his education. Powerless not to do so, he observed his world. Having no measures other than those that had been nailed into his brain, and unable to detach them, he found himself possessed by certain conclusions: There is no justice here.

Innocently, meaning no harm, he spoke the names of the guilty. No doubt he vaguely expected to be thanked for this, congratulated for having entered the camp of Socrates and Bruno. Matters were otherwise and now he is in prison making plans. This happened.

Here is another, a humbler person. Belly rumbling but hat in hand, he goes before the mighty; does not accuse them of being mighty, far from it; points out politely that there is unused grain in the silos and untilled land; makes a modest suggestion. His son is dragged from bed the following dawn to see someone whipped for having dangerous ideas. This happened.

A third spoke of a union. He survived the bomb that destroyed his family, but it appears that no one will accept his apologies.

Another who joined a freedom march believing that men were good; he saw an old black man fall in the heat, where he was at once surrounded by white men who said, "Watch him wiggle. Let him die." This is memorable.

A quiet one who spoke for peace between the city and the countryside. It is whispered to him that he must hide; the police have his name; he has committed the crime of neutralism. Where shall this quiet one go now that he is a criminal?

A scholar speculates in a public article that aspects of his nation's foreign-trade system are disadvantageous to development. A week later he hears that his name has been linked with the names of certain enemies of society. Another week, and he finds that he may no longer teach.

One day someone's telephone develops a peculiar click.

Two bombs go off in San Francisco. No clues are found. Two pacifists are shot in Richmond. The police are baffled. Gang beatings of a political nature occur in New York. There are no arrests. The murder toll in Dixie mounts year by year. There are no convictions. One group proposes to rethink the idea of nonviolence. Its supporters are alarmed. Another group arms itself. It supporters disaffiliate.

Stability, after all, must be ensured. The *peace* must be kept.

But the master seems to grow less and less confident with each of his victories. Now he requires the slave to affirm his happiness. Suspicion of unhappiness in the slave becomes ground for his detention; proved unhappiness constitutes a criminal assault upon the peace. The master is unsure of something. He wants to see the slave embracing his chains.

Trying only to reduce his pain for a moment, the slave forces his body to fade away. The backward faction acquires hard proof from this that its assessment of the situation has been correct. "See this docility? After all, the whip is the best pacifier."

Exasperated, the slave spits out a curse. Shocked to discover that a slave can have learned to curse, the advanced faction hastens forward with a principled rebuke: "Bad tactics! No way to change the hearts of men!"

It is almost comic. As though he were really trying to produce the angry backlash, the master grinds the slave's face deeper and deeper into the realities of his situation. Yet the master must be blameless, for he is only trying to satisfy his now insatiable appetite for security, an appetite which has actually become an addiction. He only wants to know that he is still respected, if not loved, that matters stand as matters should, and that no threat to the peace is being incubated here. "I love you, master," whispers the slave, squinting up between the two huge boots, thinking to steal a moment's relief. To no one's real surprise, he is promptly shot. The master's explanation rings true: "He was a liar. He *must* have been. Liars are untrustworthy and dangerous."

The rebel is the man for whom it has been decreed that there is only one way out.

The rebel is also the man whom America has called "the Communist" and taken as her enemy. The man whom America now claims the right to kill.

VII

Two Issues Revised

We may trace the contest between the capitalist and the democratic pioneer from the earliest colonial days.

—FREDERICK JACKSON TURNER[1]

IF WARS FOUGHT for the acquisition of empire are politically the same as wars fought for the protection of empires already acquired, then there is no radical difference between the politics that takes the United States to Vietnam and the politics that took Spain to Mexico, England to North America, France to Africa, and the whole awesome armada of European powers together to old Asia.

From the time of the decay of the Islamic empire and the waning of the Middle Ages, from the onset of the great northern commercial Renaissance, the expansionary dynamic of Western commercial culture has been the root, the denominating constant, of modern history.

The grandeur of Western liberalism, its material abundance, the flourishing of its arts and sciences, its painful construction of constitutional democracy—these interconnected achievements have been financed by the sustained theft called imperialism.

America's frontier epic copied on a continental scale the larger, overarching story of the transoceanic imperialisms. Having filled the North American continent and gathered up and centralized its might, the United States unhesitatingly embarked upon its own course of empire-building, south to the Caribbean, east to the Philippines, to Japan and the mainland of Asia.

The same imperial plunder continues, Gargantuan now, justified as usual by some combination of the three traditional elements of orthodox imperialist ideology: keeping the peace, now called "Free World responsibility"; conquest of the wilderness, now called "developing the underdeveloped"; and defeating the Heathen (Pagan, Barbarian, Savage), a figure who is now brought up to date and secularized as the Red Menace—same as the redskin, this Red, except more ferocious, wilder, more resistant and cunning.

First issue revised: Instead of a choice between freedom and tyranny, Americans will have to make a choice between continuing the theft and breaking it off. If we decide to continue the theft, Vietnamese-type wars will be as typical of our worsening future as they have been of our lamentable past.

And if history is cumulative instead of repetitive, then there is a second issue to be revised, this one even more personal, more intimate for Americans than the first.

Toward the end of the nineteenth century, in his inaugural address at the University of Freiburg, Max Weber, one of the modern West's great social economists, made a rare prophecy:

> Together with the machine, the bureaucratic organization is engaged in building the houses of bondage of the future, in which perhaps man will one day be like peasants in the ancient Egyptian State, acquiescent and powerless, while a purely technical good—that is, rational official administration and provision—becomes the sole, final value, which sovereignly decides the direction of their affairs.[2]

The drive for the "rationalization" of the state is not the product of one political philosophy or another. It springs, rather, from the development of techniques that make such a rationalization possible, from the consolidation around those techniques of professional, bureaucratized elitist groups whose special interest becomes the extension of the use of their techniques, and from the coordination of such groups within larger, corporated, institutional power structures. It does not much matter whether these power structures call themselves "public" or "private." They strive in either case to perpetuate themselves and to extend the social territory in which their influence is dominant.

Look again at Weber's prophecy. See if the system he predicts from a "capitalist" viewpoint is so very different from the one demanded by Thorstein Veblen from a "technocratic-socialist" viewpoint:

> [The] technological specialists whose constant supervision is indispensable to the due working of the industrial system con-

stitute the general staff of industry, whose work it is to control the strategy of production at large and to keep an oversight of the tactics of production in detail. . . . It is essential that that corps of technological specialists who by training, insight, and interest make up the general staff of industry must have a free hand in the disposal of its available resources, in materials, equipment, and man power, regardless of any national pretensions or any vested interests.[3]

Or see if the same kind of cultural spirit does not animate the following passage from a recent *Fortune* polemic against antitrust.

As for conglomerate mergers, public policy ought to welcome them. The trend to conglomerates allows corporate capital or managerial skill to be applied in new markets that might otherwise languish for lack of these ingredients. . . . The real "social and moral" danger to this society is that we will continue to pursue our present line of economic development while keeping alive in antitrust policy a set of ideals, derived from the Bryan-Brandeis form of conservativism [*sic*], which denigrate the business system we have. . . . Every year the business system cries out more loudly for men of independence and character to take on the massive new burdens of decision making in an innovating society.[4]

In the light of the foregoing quoted passages, reflect on the following from Charles Francis Adams' biography of his grandfather, John Quincy Adams.

Among the federalists . . . were to be found a large body of the patriots of the Revolution, almost all the general officers who survived the war, and a great number of the substantial citizens along the line of the seaboard towns and populous regions. . . . But these could never have succeeded in effecting the establishment of the Constitution [i.e., of a strong central government] had they not received the active and steady cooperation of all that was left in America of attachment to the mother country, as well as of the moneyed interest, which ever points to strong government as surely as the needle to the pole.[5]

The single pattern unfolds again and again from itself, the dimensions steadily enlarging, the forms retaining their identity. As in 1789, against the evident will of the American people, big business demanded and acquired a strong central government to protect it against the unruly states of the former Confederation, so in our time it demands a federal government for protection against the unruly states of the world. The scope of American commerce now being global, the scope of the federal government must also be global. Without the federal interventionary forces on continuous alert, American fruit interests could not plunder the "banana republics," and the Brazilian oligarchy could not fearlessly ignore the Brazilian people's most elemental economic and social needs. Imperialism is the national public concomitant of private commercial expansionism; big business makes big government, and multinational business globalizes it. And as business and government cooperate to rationalize and dominate the world political economy, chanting "peace, law, order" just as the old Romans did, so they cooperate to rationalize and dominate the domestic political economy. The ultimate demand is for nothing short of total order, total control—the total state of the total world. As clearly as we can now see that the Inquisition was only the Crusades turned inward, we should also be able to see that the totalitarian society is the logical interior of the imperialist state.

A totalitarian society need not be an outright police state. Whether or not it becomes one will depend on its traditions and on the character of the resistance which the people are able to conceive and express. There is a possibility that the total American state will more resemble Huxley's *Brave New World* than Orwell's *1984*. Small solace. But we can hardly forget that the impulse for police-statism has been with us at least from the time of the Alien and Sedition Act, the forerunner of our time's McCarran Act and the phenomenon of McCarthyism. If our society has for the most part resisted this impulse, that says neither that it has shown itself proof against it nor that it will continue to resist it in the future. Once the foundation of the total state is laid, whether or not that state is benevolently administered in the beginning, the probability of ultimate totalitarian malevolence exists.

What seems especially ominous about the current situation with America is that a number of interlocked forces seem bent on cooperatively stimulating the drive toward the totalizing of economic and political society.

First, the Vietnam crisis is unparalleled. By no means the first of its kind (Mexico, Cuba, the Philippines), it is still the first of its kind to be so protracted, to require so much American effort to achieve even an ambiguous standoff; the first to be fought under slogans so transparently hypocritical;

the first which an entire world has watched close up in the intimacy of its living rooms; the first in which the reputation of the state has been unconditionally, repeatedly, and publicly laid on the line. At the crest of her relative power, modern America experiences for the first time a frustration that begins to seem impenetrable. This initiation to limits is infuriating and her composure shakes.

Second, the historical situation of this war may make it climactic, may mean that the culture will not be able easily to tolerate another of its kind. Who has a clear imagination of "victory" which is not also absurd? At best, the third administration from now may find itself in the possession of a corpse—a forecast which assumes, precariously, that succeeding administrations will maintain the obstinacy of the present one and that history will in other respects stand still. At the same time, "defeat" is also inconceivable without an immense upheaval in the American consciousness and conscience, two markedly unlikely events. Even a superbly skillful political maneuver probably could not represent a "compromise" as a "victory" (as with Korea); and on the terms by which the war has been explained to the American people, and given the suffering which no doubt still awaits them, nothing short of victory can sustain the present legitimacy of the state. If victory cannot be achieved and defeat cannot be dissembled, there is no resolution that will not in some way traumatize at least a large segment of the polity. In this case, the only escape for those whom power has made responsible lies in suppression of the terminal event, either by concealing or overriding it with a large event (as war with China), or by forcibly expunging it from current history via the silencing of historical criticism.

Third, the economics of the war has the effect of raising to still greater power both the warfare generalists and those individual-interest groups which have most to gain from warfare expenditures. Relatedly, the war deepens and intensifies the economy's already advanced addiction to federal defense subsidies, which directly and through the multiplier effect may account for as much as a quarter of the nation's gross national product. Thus, at the very moment in which the economy stands in clearest "need" of war—or contrariwise, is least able to withstand the deceleration of defense spending—power gathers in the hands of those whose special interests bias them toward greater bellicosity abroad and toward more direct forms of political suppression at home. Those who administer these interests, along with multinational corporatists generally, constitute the American political oligarchy, the prestigious, decision-making class; and their power has never been less subject to popular review or veto than it is now. Thus, if the classical decision between war and depression must again be made, it will once more be made by the group which has most to gain from war and most to lose from depression.

Finally, the agonies of the war intermesh psychologically with the agonies of urban decay and racial turbulence. There is a clear mechanical connection between the war and the problems of the American ghettos, the welfare state having been trimmed down to make room for the warfare state. More important still is the spiritual connection. Black America, whose political actions have a complex impact on poor-white America, is at the moment being driven toward total alienation from white power and total solidarity against a system whose hypocrisies have never before been so nakedly on view.

In sum, the uncommon military resistance and moral visibility of the enemy, the virtual impossibility of resolving the conflict within America's present political environment, the increasing influence of the militarists within the increasingly militarized political economy, and the coincident heightening of racial and class unrest all combine to stimulate the corporate society's inherent impulses toward totalitarian reaction. The problems that loom before us now are, after all, scarcely the sort that have tempted other authoritarians to experiment with democracy or tolerance or political freedom.

Moreover, the apparatus by which the society can be totalized exists and is in running order: The corporate state has effective control of key elements of the communications system, exclusive control of the primary ganglia of political and economic power, and access to a matured nationalist ideology pregnant with violence and capable of justifying any reasonably sophisticated or adroit authoritarian action against organized dissent. If the central feature of the fascist state is the political alliance or identity of big government and big business, and the power of such an alliance to work its will without significant restraints other than those it chooses to impose on itself, then it minces words to say that an American fascism is possible. Such a fascism may or may not be internally vicious. The point is that its style will be determined essentially by its executives' unchecked will. They will somehow contrive to do what they will determine should be done. The corporate state can plant dynamite in a SNCC office, then stage a police raid to discover this dynamite; it has done this. It can plant narcotics in an SDS office, then stage a raid to discover these narcotics; it has done this. It can tacitly direct its right-wing policemen to stand by while a right-wing gang assaults a few war-protesters and then jail the protesters; it has done this. It can refuse to bring racist murderers to justice and thus produce an effectively state-sponsored Terror; it has done this. Whatever the state decides to do, it can do without check or hindrance. It is alone on the commanding heights of power.

What is to be done?

The central issue must be understood. The one and only basic question which Americans now have to ask themselves is whether or not they want to be politically free. The imperial house of bondage can give them wealth, security, and order; it can give them victories and certify these victories to be authentically glorious. It may even have the grace to let some people live in a subcultist absentia from the political society, sequestered from history in the undergrounds of LSD, suburban sex, pure research, or the quaint little magazines of provisory dissent, anonymously in solitude with like-spirited solitaries. The superstate may even turn a half preoccupied ear to the murmurs of the dispossessed; may give of its bounty to those who will ritually humble themselves before it. But the state cannot give political freedom. It is neither in the nature of the state that it can give political freedom nor in the nature of political freedom that it can be given. Political freedom is not a license to be purchased or petitioned from a higher power. It is not a gift. It does not exist as a fund under the superintendency of privileged offices. Political freedom is in political man, in his life, and it exists when he claims it. It is an elemental condition of the individual will. The state may deny it or obstruct its flow, but the state may neither take it nor give it because it does not lie in the capacities of the state to hold, to possess, so mercurial an entity as the political freedom of men. Only men, not states, can be free, can produce and exhibit freedom.

Whether or not Americans will choose to be free is the

transcendent political question, the one question that coordinates and subsumes all the searing issues of foreign and domestic policy. If Americans choose freedom, there can be no totalitarian America, and without a totalitarian America, there can be no American empire.

This central question is not clarified, it is obscured, by our common political categories of left, right, and center; it is not clarified, it is obscured, by the traditional American debate about socialism versus capitalism versus the Keynesian mixed economy. The socialist radical, the corporatist conservative, and the welfare-state liberal are all equally capable of leading us forward into the totalized society. Whether central planning should be coordinated by government or corporate hands is a question whose realism has disappeared. The urgent question is about the locus of power in the community: Is it in the state or is it in the people? And in our American time, our American place, the main principle of the radically humanist politics is this: *Any decision not made by the people in free association, whatever the content of that decision, cannot be good.* If the American humanist must mellow his intransigence and move from his Utopian principle to meet the realities of life in the technological society, it is nevertheless that main principle which sets his goals, gives him his style, and motivates his work; it is that principle which he proceeds to elaborate and enrich through human exchanges in the context of human situations. The humanist does not say: "We shall accept this dismal house of bondage and try to redecorate it." He says rather: "We shall insist on the priority of man's freedom and ground our social invention in the ethic of the social contract freely made." The primary task of the humanist is to describe and help to realize those political acts through which the power of the central authoritarian monolith can be broken and the political life of man reconstituted on the base of the associational, democratic, nonexclusive community. William Appleman Williams puts it this way:

> The core radical ideals and values of community, equality, democracy, and humaneness simply cannot in the future be realized and sustained—nor should they be sought—through more centralization and consolidation. These radical values can most nearly be realized through decentralization and through the creation of many truly human communities. . . . Such decentralization is technologically and economically possible. Such decentralization

is essential if democracy is to be maintained and extended. And such decentralization is psychologically and morally mandatory. Our humanity is being pounded and squeezed out of us by the consolidated power of a nationalist corporate welfare capitalism.[6]

This is not merely a leftist's challenge to other leftists. As much at it is in the grain of American democratic populism, it is also in the grain of the American libertarian right.

The right wing in America is presently in a state of almost eerie spiritual disarray. Under one and the same banner, joining the John Birch Society, out on the rifle range with the Minutemen, chuckling through the pages of the *National Review*, the conservative right wing of imperialist, authoritarian, and even monarchist disposition enjoys the fraternity of the libertarian right wing of *laissez faire*, free-market individualism. These two groupings could not possibly have less in common. Why have the libertarians conceded leadership to the conservatives? Why have the traditional opponents of big, militarized, central authoritarian government now joined forces with such a government's boldest advocates?

They have done so because they have been persuaded that there is a clear and present danger that necessitates a temporary excursion from final values. They should know better. They should know that for the totalitarian imperialists there is *always* a clear and present danger, that it is pre-eminently through the ideology of the Foreign Threat, the myth of the tiger at the gates, that frontier and global imperialism and domestic authoritarianism have always rationalized themselves. Three outbursts of exemplary candor on this point:

First, from a 1938 report authored by the United States Office of Naval Intelligence: "Realistically, all wars have been fought for economic reasons. To make them politically and socially palatable, ideological issues have always been invoked. Any possible future war will, undoubtedly, conform to historical precedent."[7]

Second, Senator Arthur Vandenburg's belief that to win their acceptance of a militant and expensive Cold War policy it would be necessary "to scare hell out of the American people."[8]

Third, the testimony of General Douglas MacArthur:

> Talk of imminent threat to our national security through the application of external force is pure nonsense. . . . Indeed, it is a part of the general pattern of misguided policy that our country

is now geared to an arms economy which was bred in an artificially induced psychosis of war hysteria and nurtured upon an incessant propaganda of fear. While such an economy may produce a sense of seeming prosperity for the moment, it rests on an illusory foundation of complete unreliability and renders among our political leaders almost a greater fear of peace than is their fear of war.[9]

It would be a piece of great good fortune for America and the world if the libertarian right could be reminded that besides the debased Republicanism of the Knowlands and the Judds there is another tradition available to them—their own: the tradition of Congressman Howard Buffett, Senator Taft's midwestern campaign manager in 1952, who attacked the Truman Doctrine with the words: "Our Christian ideals cannot be exported to other lands by dollars and guns. . . . We cannot practice might and force abroad and retain freedom at home. We cannot talk world cooperation and practice power politics."[10] There is the right of Frank Chodorov, whose response to the domestic Red Menace was abruptly to the point: "The way to get rid of communists in government jobs is to abolish the jobs."[11] And of Dean Russell, who wrote in 1955: "Those who advocate the 'temporary loss' of our freedom in order to preserve it permanently are advocating only one thing: the abolition of liberty. . . . We are rapidly becoming a caricature of the thing we profess to hate."[12] Most engaging, there is the right of the tough-minded Garet Garrett, who produced in 1952 a short analysis of the totalitarian impulse of imperialism which the events of the intervening years have reverified over and again.[13] Beginning with the words, "We have crossed the boundary that lies between Republic and Empire," Garrett's pamphlet unerringly names the features of the imperial pathology: dominance of the national executive over Congress, court, and Constitution; subordination of domestic policy to foreign policy; ascendency of the military influence; the creation of political and military satellites; a complex of arrogance and fearfulness toward the "barbarian"; and, most insidiously, casting off the national identity for an internationalist and "historic" identity—the *republic* is free; the *empire* is history's hostage.

This style of political thought, rootedly American, is carried forward today by the Negro freedom movement and the student movement against Great Society-Free World imperialism. That these movements are called leftist means nothing. They are of the grain of American humanist individualism and voluntaristic associational action; and it is only through them that the libertarian tradition is activated and kept alive. In a strong sense, the Old Right and the New Left are morally and politically coordinate.

Yet their intersection can be missed. Their potentially redemptive union can go unattempted and unmade. On both sides, vision can be cut off by habituated responses to passé labels. The New Left can lose itself in the imported left-wing debates of the thirties, wondering what it ought to say about technocracy and Stalin. The libertarian right can remain hypnotically charmed by the authoritarian imperialists whose only ultimate love is Power, the subhuman brown-shirted power of the jingo state militant, the state rampant, the iron state possessed of its own clanking glory. If this happens, if the new realities are not penetrated and a fundamental ideological rearrangement does not take place, then this new political humanism which has shown its courage from Lowndes County to Berkeley will no doubt prove unworthy of more than a footnote in the scavenger histories of our time. And someone will finally have to make the observation that the American dream did not come true, that maybe it was quite an idle dream after all and the people never really had a chance. The superstate will glide onward in its steel and vinyl splendor, tagging and numbering us with its scientific tests, conscripting us with its computers, swaggering through exotic graveyards which it filled and where it dares to lay wreaths, smug in the ruins of its old-fashioned, man-centered promises to itself.

Here stands the modern Western humanist, fruit of a long line, but perhaps already a useless and archaic item, superseded already perhaps by that very unsentimental rationality which he has for so long been pleased to honor. Increasingly estranged from those images of man which once sustained his work and informed his hopes, he slips his fantasies for a moment to wonder if there is not some easy way to recapture what seems to have been so easily lost. There is no use in wondering, however. What seems lost was not really lost; it came to an end. The frontiers are gone. There are no more barbarians to justify the basic conquests and salve the conscience. There is no easy way to make the old dream breathe in this new air, no buttons to find and push. The people are alone, as usual, with themselves. It belongs to Americans to claim again and try to reshape their country. Only the American people can do that. Only the people should.

NOTES

Chapter II: The Cold Warrior's Story

1. *Quoted in* Maurice J. Goldbloom, "The Fulbright Revolt," *Commentary*, September 1966.
2. Wilfred Burchett, *Vietnam, Inside Story of the Guerrilla War*, International Publishers, New York, 1965, esp. pp. 109–194.
3. Bernard B. Fall, *The Two Viet-Nams*, Frederick A. Praeger, New York, 1963, rev. eds. 1964, 1966; Pall Mall Press, London, 1963, p. 318.
4. *The New York Times* (*NYT*), August 10, 1966.
5. *In* Eric Robson, "The Namierist School," *The American Revolution*, ed., George Athan Billias, Holt, Rinehart & Winston, New York, 1965, p. 24.
6. Gary Porter, "Globalism—The Ideology of Total World Involvement," *The Viet-Nam Reader*, eds., Marcus G. Raskin and Bernard B. Fall, Random House (Vintage book), New York, 1965, p. 322.
7. *In* Isaac Deutscher, *Stalin, A Political Biography*, Random House (Vintage Russian Library), New York, 1960, p. xi.
8. *NYT Magazine*, January 30, 1966.
9. *NYT*, January 16, 1966.
10. *Political Science Quarterly*, April 1965.
11. *NYT*, February 1, 1966.
12. *NYT*, January 1, 1966.
13. Fall, "Viet-Cong—The Unseen Enemy in Viet-Nam," *in* Raskin and Fall, eds., p. 261.
14. *NYT*, February 27, 1966.
15. *NYT*, February 13, 1966.
16. *NYT*, February 1, 1966.
17. *NYT*, April 17, 1966.

Chapter III: Open Doors, Falling Dominoes

1. *In* D. F. Fleming, *The Cold War and Its Origins, 1917–1960*, 2 vols., Doubleday & Company, New York, 1961, p. 53.
2. *Ibid.*, p. 68.
3. *Ibid.*, p. 79.

4. Crane Brinton *et al.*, *A History of Civilization*, 2 vols., Prentice-Hall, Englewood Cliffs, N.J., 1955, vol. 2, pp. 482, 503.
5. Fleming, p. 17.
6. William Appleman Williams, *The Tragedy of American Diplomacy*, Dell Publishing Co., New York, 1962, pp. 197–200, 235–237. (Hereafter referred to as *Tragedy.*)
7. *Ibid.*, p. 251.
8. *Ibid.*, p. 252.
9. *Ibid.*, p. 258.
10. *Ibid.*, p. 258. Williams quotes without dating a London *Times* editorial.
11. *Quoted in* Deutscher, p. 328.
12. For a sustained "anthropolitical" development of this point, see Marshall D. Sahlins *et al.*, *Evolution and Culture*, The University of Michigan Press, Ann Arbor, Mich., 1960, pp. 110–122.
13. William Appleman Williams, *The Shaping of American Diplomacy*, Rand McNally & Co., Chicago, 1956, p. 35. (Hereafter referred to as *Shaping.*) This is a massive compendium of "Readings and Documents in American Foreign Relations 1750–1955," edited and with extensive commentaries by Williams. (In the following citations from this immensely useful book, I provide only page numbers for quotations drawn from the period "documents." For borrowings from the contributing historians' essays, author and title are given in parentheses.)
14. *Ibid.*, p. 15 (Max Savelle, "The Appearance of an American Attitude Toward External Affairs, 1750–1775").
15. *Ibid.*, p. 12 (Curtis P. Nettels, "British Mercantilism and the Economic Development of the Thirteen Colonies").
16. *Ibid.*, p. 82 (Louis M. Sears, "Jefferson and the Embargo").
17. *Ibid.*, p. 249.
18. *Ibid.*, p. 315.
19. *Ibid.*, p. 427.
20. *Ibid.*, pp. 217–224 (Charles C. Stelle, "American Trade in Opium to China, 1821–39").
21. *Ibid.*, p. 224 (Foster Rhea Dulles, "American Interest in China").
22. *Tragedy*, p. 26.
23. *Shaping*, pp. 433–434.
24. *Tragedy*, p. 66.
25. *Ibid.*, p. 78.
26. *Ibid.*
27. *Ibid.*, p. 133.
28. Department of State *Bulletin*, November 5, 1962, pp. 683–688.
29. *Tragedy*, p. 26.
30. Thomas R. Brooks, *To Build a New World*, League for Industrial Democracy, undated pamphlet, New York, p. 19.

31. *Ibid.*, p. 17.
32. *Shaping*, p. 434.
33. *Ibid.*, p. 382.
34. *Tragedy*, p. 27.
35. *Ibid.*, p. 66.
36. *Ibid.*, p. 123.
37. *Ibid.*
38. Department of State *Commercial Policy Series*, 1–70, 1934–41.
39. *The Public Papers and Addresses of Franklin D. Roosevelt*, vol. 4 (1935), Random House, New York, 1938, p. 463.
40. *Tragedy*, p. 233.
41. *Ibid.*, p. 239.
42. *Ibid.*, p. 237.
43. *Ibid.*, p. 235.
44. *Fortune*, June 1966.

Chapter IV: Free World Empire

1. *Tragedy*, p. 18.
2. Frederic L. Pryor, *The Communist Foreign Trade System*, MIT Press, Cambridge, Mass., 1963.
3. *Tragedy*, p. 234.
4. *In* Edmund Stillman and William Pfaff, *The Politics of Hysteria*, Harper & Row (Colophon book), New York, 1964, p. 97.
5. W. W. Rostow, "Guerrilla Warfare in Underdeveloped Areas," *in* Raskin and Fall, eds., pp. 110–112.
6. David E. Lilienthal, "The Multinational Corporation," paper delivered at the Carnegie Institute of Technology, April 1960.
7. Richard J. Barber, "Big, Bigger, Biggest: American Business Goes Global," *New Republic*, April 30, 1966.
8. *Wall Street Journal*, February 8, 1966.
9. Barber, *loc. cit.*
10. *Ibid.*
11. *Newsweek*, March 8, 1965.
12. Barber.
13. *Quoted in* Marshall Windmiller, "Viet-Nam and the Power Elite," *The Commentary of Marshall Windmiller*, TLD Press, Berkeley, Calif., March 31, 1966. The quotation is from Defferre's article in the April 1966 *Foreign Affairs*.
14. Barber.
15. *Forbes*, April 1, 1966.
16. Seymour Melman, *Our Depleted Society*, Holt, Rinehart & Winston, New York, 1965, p. 150.
17. "What U.S. Companies Are Doing Abroad," *U. S. News & World Report*, January 24, 1966.

18. For a good short review of these institutions and their shortcomings, see the memorandum "A Bank for Economic Acceleration of Backward Countries," by Morris Forgash, president of the United States Freight Company, published as Appendix D *in* Melman, pp. 342–352.
19. David Rockefeller, "What Free Enterprise Means to Latin America," *Foreign Affairs*, April 1966.
20. "Special Report on Multinational Companies," *Business Week*, April 20, 1963.
21. Paul Baran and Paul Sweezy, "Notes on the Theory of Imperialism," *Monthly Review*, March 1966.
22. John Gerassi, *The Great Fear in Latin America*, The Macmillan Company (Collier book), New York, 1965, p. 276.
23. *Ibid.*, p. 354.
24. Baran and Sweezy cite Standard's *1962 Annual Report.*
25. Gerassi, p. 355.
26. *The Economic Almanac 1964*, National Industrial Conference Board and *Newsweek*, New York, 1964, pp. 477, 480, 490, 511. (Referred to hereafter as *Almanac.*)
27. Gerassi, pp. 76–99.
28. *Ibid.*, p. 83.
29. Philip Siekman, "When Executives Turned Revolutionaries," *Fortune*, September 1964.
30. *NYT*, November 23, 1964.
31. *NYT*, November 25, 1964; March 21, 1965; October 11, 1965; October 28, 1965; November 8, 1965.
32. *NYT*, January 28, 1966.
33. *NYT*, October 2, 1964; December 24, 1964.
34. Besides the *NYT* citations in the text, the following magazine articles provide good immediate and general background on the Hanna Mining affair: *Fortune*, "Brazil: Hanna's Immovable Mountains," April 1965; *Fortune*, "Brazil's Battle with Inflation," December 1965; *Fortune*, "Brazil's Chief Miner," April 1966; *International Commerce*, "U.S.-Brazilian Guaranty Pact to Stimulate Private Investment," February 22, 1965; *Business Week*, "Harsh Curbs Generate Growing Discontent," March 27, 1965; *Business Week*, "Brazil: Some Success, Much Work to Do," January 22, 1966; Lincoln Gordon, "Brazil-United States: Partners in Progress," *U.S. Department of State Bulletin*, April 18, 1966.
35. Franz Lee, *Anatomy of Apartheid in Southern Africa*, Alexander Defense Committee, New York, 1966, p. 32. Lee is a South African political refugee.
36. *Ibid.*
37. *Ibid.*, p. 14.
38. Paul Booth and Christopher Z. Hobson, "Information on In-

volvement of U.S. Corporations in South Africa," Students for a Democratic Society, Chicago, 1966. This fact sheet summarizes continuing primary research on American corporate interests in South Africa being carried out by members of SDS and the American Committee on Africa. Data is continually accumulated at the SDS National Office in Chicago and is available on request. However, the best single, most convenient source on the subject is the January 1966 issue of *Africa Today*, "A Special Report on American Involvement in the South African Economy." Copies of this issue are available from the American Committee on Africa, 211 East 43rd Street, New York, N.Y. 10017.

39. *Ibid.*
40. *Ibid.* See also *New Republic*, "South Africa," August 13, 1966.
41. Booth and Hobson, *Africa Today.*
42. Kwame Nkrumah, *Neo-Colonialism, The Last Stage of Imperialism*, International Publishers Co., New York, 1965, p. 104. This book's cold, fine-grain research was surely conducted by the scholars of the Ideological Institute at Winneba, which was closed after the coup of February 1966.
43. *U. S. News & World Report*, November 22, 1965.
44. Booth and Hobson, *Africa Today.*
45. Nkrumah, pp. 147–149.
46. *Ibid.*, pp. 127–136.
47. *Ibid.*, p. 122; Booth and Hobson, *Africa Today.*
48. *Forbes*, "The Englehard Touch," August 1, 1965.
49. Lee, pp. 27–28.
50. *Ibid.*, p. 12.
51. *Ibid.*, p. 17. See also *New Republic*, August 13, 1966.
52. Lee, p. 19.
53. *The Military Balance, 1965–1966*, The Institute for Strategic Studies, London, 1965, p. 36. M. J. V. Bell, "Military Assistance to Independent African States," *Adelphi Papers*, The Institute for Strategic Studies, London, December 1964, p. 14.
54. Lee, p. 42.
55. *Almanac*, p. 505.
56. Gerassi, pp. 125–126.
57. *Ibid.*, p. 126.
58. *Ibid.*, p. 127.
59. *Almanac*, pp. 488, 490.
60. Gerassi, p. 192.
61. *Ibid.*, 191.
62. *Ibid.*, pp. 367–372.
63. *Almanac*, p. 492.
64. Gerassi, pp. 20, 32, 155–166.
65. *Ibid.*, p. 368.

66. Ross and Wise, *The Invisible Government*, Bantam ed., New York, 1965, pp. 116–121.
67. *Ibid.* Paul W. Blackstock, *The Strategy of Subversion*, Quadrangle Books, Chicago, 1964, p. 185. Gerassi, p. 241.
68. On Bunker and National Sugar's Dominican interests, see Joseph P. Lash, "Bunker Hits the Trail Again," New York *Post*, January 27, 1957; *Standard and Poor's* "Sugar—Basic Survey" and "Sugar—Company Survey" for 1963–1965; *Commodity Year Book* (annual) and *International Sugar Journal* (monthly); and Dana L. Thomas, "Richer Sweet," *Barron's*, September 27, 1965. On Harriman and National, see *Standard and Poor's Register of Directors and Officers* (annual) and any recent National *Annual Report.* On Fortas, Berle, and Sucrest, see Charles B. Seib and Alan I. Otten, "Abe, Help—LBJ," *Esquire*, June 1965; *Who's Who in America*; Sucrest *Annual Report.* On Farland, see South Puerto Rico's 1965 *Annual Report.* I am indebted for this data to Michael Locker of SDS.
69. A. Orlov, "The Philippines," *International Affairs*, November 1965.
70. Nkrumah, pp. 60, 66.
71. *NYT*, May 21, 1966.
72. *NYT*, June 19, 1966.
73. *NYT*, April 8, 1966.
74. Gerassi, p. 275.
75. *Ibid.*, p. 28.
76. *Fortune*, June 1966.
77. *Economic Affairs*, June 1, 1966.
78. Gerassi, p. 263.
79. *Wall Street Journal*, May 12, 1965.
80. Rockefeller, *loc. cit.*

Chapter V: The Vietnam Case

1. *Newsweek*, January 1, 1966.
2. Fall, p. 304.
3. *Fortune*, March 1966.
4. Fred J. Cook, *The Warfare State*, The Macmillan Company (Collier book), New York, 1964, p. 181.
5. Eugene J. McCarthy, "The U. S.: Supplier of Weapons to the World," *Saturday Review*, July 9, 1966.
6. *Ibid.*
7. *Ibid.*
8. *Ibid.*
9. *Ibid.*
10. *U. S. News & World Report*, July 11, 1966.
11. New York *Herald Tribune*, October 26, 1949; *quoted in* Cook, p. 183.

12. *NYT*, September 18, 1966.
13. *Almanac*, p. 470. U.S. export (and import) figures for 1933 and 1937–40 are as follows (in millions of U.S. dollars): Germany: 140 (78); 126 (93); 107 (65); 47 (52); and 0.2 (5). Italy: 61 (39); 77 (48); 58 (41); 59 (40); and 51 (23). Japan: 143 (128); 288 (204); 240 (27); 232 (161); and 227 (158).
14. Alex Campbell, "Japan Plays the Field," *New Republic*, March 5, 1966.
15. International Monetary Fund, *Direction of World Trade* (monthly). For an expert analysis of such trade figures, see Alexander Eckstein, *Communist China's Economic Growth and Foreign Trade*, McGraw-Hill Book Company, New York, 1966, pp. 200–212.
16. *Direction of World Trade.*
17. Fall, p. 194.
18. *Shaping*, p. 1119.
19. *NYT*, June 16, 1966.
20. *Ibid.*
21. Stillman and Pfaff, p. 40.
22. Pierre Vidal-Naquet, *Torture: Cancer of a Democracy*, Penguin Books, Baltimore, Md., 1963, p. 194.
23. *Ibid.*

Chapter VI: The Revolted

1. Gerassi, p. 45.
2. Robert S. McNamara, "Response to Aggression" (address delivered March 26, 1964), *in* Raskin and Fall, eds., p. 201.
3. *NYT*, October 28, 1965.

Chapter VII: Two Issues Revised

1. Quoted as epigraph in Charles A. Beard, *Economic Origins of Jeffersonian Democracy*, The Free Press, New York, 1965 (first published 1915).
2. Max Weber, *Politics as a Vocation.*
3. Thorstein Veblen, *The Engineers and the Price System*, Harcourt, Brace & World (Harbinger book), New York, 1963, pp. 72–73.
4. Max Ways, "Antitrust in an Era of Radical Change," *Fortune*, March 1966.
5. Beard, p. 8.
6. William Appleman Williams, "Policy for U.S. Radicals," *National Guardian*, November 27, 1965.
7. Harry Elmer Barnes, "Revisionism: A Key to Peace," *Rampart Journal*, Spring 1966.

8. *Tragedy*, p. 240.
9. Garet Garrett, *The People's Pottage* ("The Rise of Empire"), The Caxton Printers, Caldwell, Idaho, 1953.
10. Murray Rothbard, "The Transformation of the American Right," *Continuum*, Summer 1964.
11. *Ibid.*
12. *Ibid.*
13. Garrett.

PART TWO

Revolution: Heritage and Contemporary Option

by RICHARD SHAULL

VIII

Introduction

RECENT DEVELOPMENTS in our technological society have brought man to a new stage in his struggle to create more tolerable conditions for life through the ordering of his social existence. Social evils, once accepted as inevitable, can now be overcome by organized human endeavor; we have the resources and the power to create the type of society we want. Moreover, technological advances have served to awaken all classes and races throughout the world to the new possibilities before them, thus creating a mood of rising expectations, especially among the dispossessed.

Technology tends to shatter old forms of social organization and cause constant changes in our way of life. But it does not automatically create a society that offers increasing opportunities either for material well-being or for human liberation. To be sure, many people have known a marked improvement in their economic situation in the course of a few decades; yet nearly one quarter of our own population is still below the poverty line, and the distance between the standard of living of the rich nations and that of the poor nations becomes greater every year. It is now clear that the same developments that lead to improvements in our economic condition may also bring with them new forms of social domination, and limit even more than in the past our participation in the process of decision-making that determines our future. Moreover, so long as technological advance is incorporated into the ideological ethos now dominant in our society, those developments that make old social structures obsolete also provide them with almost unlimited power for self-preservation. In fact, so long as the power of a technological society is largely concentrated in the hands of those who profit most from the established order, such use of it is almost inevitable.

This problem constitutes one of the major challenges facing us today. Hopes once aroused cannot be easily suppressed; structures once rendered obsolete by events become more and more inadequate as time moves on. Our only hope lies in discovering, as quickly as possible, how fundamental changes can be brought about in the structures of our society, and how the resources of technology can be used to produce significant improvement in the lot of the dispossessed as well as increasing opportunities for human liberation. Otherwise, the prospects for the future will be dim indeed. Those in power will be tempted to develop more effective systems of domination in order to suppress discontent and revolt, and to maintain some semblance of order. On the other hand, those who become aware of the dehumanizing character of such an order will lose all confidence in the institutions of their society, and will be drawn toward resignation or acts of desperation.

Is there any chance that we can rise to this challenge? We have little evidence at the moment of any widespread awakening to its demands upon us. Those who benefit most from the present system and who are most influenced by its hidden ideology are not likely to take the initiative in this struggle. Other groups, such as organized labor, which served as an effective instrument for social change in the past, do not seem to be in a position to do so any longer. And the mass media offer unprecedented possibilities for preserving a mood of relative conformity among the great majority of people.

Nevertheless, a significant number of people of different ages and social classes are going through a gradual process of awakening. For some, this is the result of reflection upon the most recent developments in our industrial society; others have been shocked into awareness through their contacts with the dispossessed in our own land, or with the struggle of the peoples of the Third World. Many young people, who as yet have no stake in the system and are dissatisfied with the world around them, are free to understand the problem and do something about it. But we should not expect too much even from this minority. For those of us who belong to the older generation, this awakening is often a traumatic experience. The more progressive among us have thought about society in less radical terms and have worked for social change in more moderate ways. If events now reveal that our perspective is inadequate and that our strategy is ineffective, we may end up withdrawing from a struggle we cannot understand, or engage in efforts that never come to grips with the real issues. Promising as the new awareness among young people may be, it may not move beyond an attitude of rebellion and an early conformity with the established order.

There is, as I see it, one promising sign of a new day. Out of this same matrix of frustration and anguish, a new community is emerging, whose members not only understand the problem and are convinced that radical changes are urgently needed, but are also committed to working for such changes and are seeking a strategy by which to do so. I refer to the new revolutionaries and the new movements in which they are involved.

If we here single them out and set them over against the progressives of a former generation, we do not thereby pronounce judgment upon the one, nor affirm the moral superiority of the other. The new revolutionaries are probably not any more concerned about the world and the people who suffer in it than were their counterparts of an earlier decade; they may not be any more anxious to change society than we have been. But they do represent the response, on the part of a new generation, to a new historical situation. In their efforts to express their concern for man and to change society, they have been led to take a revolutionary stance, and have gradually worked out the implications of it for their understanding of the modern world and the definition of their responsibility in it.

If our analysis of the present crisis is correct, then this deliberate choice of revolution could become a turning point in the history of our nation. It could provide an occasion for the rediscovery of our American revolutionary heritage and of its relevance to the problems now confronting us, not only at home but also in relation to the Third World. And the emergence of revolutionary movements here could break our present drift toward increasing alienation from the peoples of Asia, Africa, and Latin America, and free us to participate creatively in the "Third-World century."

Many young people who have been formed by their

participation in the civil rights struggle or in new movements on the university campus have already found that they are identified, in outlook and concern, with a growing number of men and women in many parts of the world and in widely different situations: revolutionary students in the developing nations; a number of unusual people in almost every sphere of life in Western Europe; students and writers in communist countries. In all these areas, the new revolutionary mood can be found; in some places, such as Latin America, it is very widespread. But, strange as it may at first appear, it is only in the United States that we are confronted simultaneously with the full impact of the various major revolutions of our time—as young people brought up on the front lines of the technological-cybernetic revolution have become involved in the civil rights struggle, the fight against poverty or the free speech movement, and have also discovered, as a result of North American involvement in Vietnam and the Dominican Republic, the revolution that is on the way in the relations between the rich and the poor nations.

It is this new fact, this choice of a revolutionary posture—and its implications for American participation in the century of the Third World—which here concerns us. We shall attempt to examine it without, I trust, falling into undue generalizations. In the type of dynamic, pluralistic world in which we now live, it would be absurd to suppose that all situations are revolutionary, or that the only authentic response to the challenge of our time is that which the revolutionaries are making. I, for one, have no desire to force contemporary reality into a narrow and rigid rational scheme. But I make no pretense at having arrived at a detached, purely empirical analysis of this phenomenon. In order to live and to act, I have had to attempt to make some sense out of what is happening in the world today, in the light of our own history. I have also spent the greater part of two decades in Latin America in close contact with a revolutionary situation there, and have been forced to come to terms with it. These experiences have led me to certain conclusions about the significance of revolution and the contribution which those who take this position can make to our society at this time.

I therefore find myself in the unenviable position of being caught somewhere between two worlds. Having spent most of my life working for reform within the established order, I am now obliged to give priority to revolution. And much as I sympathize with the new mood of the new generation, I cannot forget the fact that I belong to another one. I have attempted to turn this handicap into an advantage by undertaking the task of interpretation and mediation. Perhaps from this vantage point, it will be possible to help some of those who are confused and upset by revolutionary developments to understand better what these movements represent. And we would dare to hope that reflection on revolution from such an ambiguous position may make some small contribution to the present efforts on the part of the new revolutionaries to find a solid foundation for fruitful thought and action.

IX

The Search for a New Style of Life

ONE OF THE main focuses of concern in our modern world is the search for a new style of human existence. The ideal of the "bourgeois man" has lost much of its power, and the peoples of Asia, Africa, and Latin America have discovered the inauthenticity of a pattern of life imported from and imposed by the West. Existentialism has developed its own models for the new humanity, and the Russians speak constantly of "the new Soviet man." The appearance of beatnik or rebel in many different cultures testifies to the seriousness of the problem. There is a growing awareness that the context in which human life is shaped has changed, and that only if a new style of life soon develops will modern man be able to find meaning in his existence and act responsibly.

The new revolutionary is in an advanced position in this search, because of his sensitivity to what is going on around him and his responsible involvement where the decisive issues about the future of man are being raised. I realize that this cannot be empirically demonstrated; it has more of the character of an affirmation of faith. Many of those who are most active in these movements are quite confused, and are often unable to articulate even what is most central in their own experience. Any attempt to outline the main elements in this new revolutionary posture will probably not offer an adequate description of any one particular group. However, my experience in very diverse revolutionary situations indicates that a specific style is emerging, the main lines of which are clear:

1. Much attention has been given to the process of

secularization as it has developed in the Western world in recent centuries, and that has now reached a climax, expressed by the intensity of concern on the part of modern man with existence within history. The new revolutionary has a heightened awareness of this; at the same time, his actual participation in the revolutionary struggle intensifies his concern for man and what happens to him within a concrete historical process. The change that has occurred in the attitudes of SNCC (Student Nonviolent Coordinating Committee) workers in Mississippi is paralleled by the experience of Catholic and Protestant students in Latin America. Their involvement in revolutionary movements quickly exposed the irrelevance of the traditional metaphysical world-view, and forced them to recognize that the old, abstract concepts no longer meant anything to them. If these absolutes have vanished, then the future is open; man has the freedom and responsibility to determine his own destiny. Nation and community provide the context for human fulfillment; and their transformation, in the light of certain predetermined goals, is the important thing.

In this situation, it is only natural that many people whose former attitude was one of cool detachment now have a new sense of involvement. Here the experience of the revolutionary is accentuated by the atmosphere accompanying recent developments in technology. As Marshall McLuhan points out in his book on *Understanding Media: The Extensions of Man:*

> In an electric age, when our central nervous system is technologically extended to involve us in the whole of mankind and to incorporate the whole of mankind in us, we necessarily participate, in depth, in the consequences of our every action. It is no longer possible to adopt the aloof and dissociated role of the literate Westerner.[1]

To live responsibly means to take a stand, to put one's life on the line; to act even though one cannot be entirely sure of the results of one's action, or guarantee its success.

Along this road of participation, the nature of the intellectual effort is redefined. Creative thought about a problem cannot come solely from abstract rational analysis of it. It is only from within the situation, in which the concrete stuff

[1] New York: McGraw-Hill, 1965, p. 4.

of reality is constantly changing, that we can work out our perspective or engage in serious reflection. The search for truth is a question of finding some patterns of meaning in the richness and variety of elements making up concrete reality. If the experience of former generations and the wider human perspectives are to mean anything, it is not enough to present them in books or university courses; the attempt must also be made to relate them to the present moment. Only thus can academic work be an exciting adventure rather than a meaningless burden.

Decisions must be made from within the situation, and help in decision-making can only come from those who are in some way identified with it. When someone who does not share this involvement takes it upon himself to warn of dangers and to offer advice, he should not be surprised if no one pays attention to him. If he is not willing to pay the price of the struggle, why should anyone take him seriously? Moreover, if he is not free to enter into the situation, and understand the ethical dilemmas as they are raised *there*, in all probability his insights will be of little assistance.

One of the interesting developments here, and for some the most disturbing, is the revolt against authority-structures and the repudiation of anything that smacks of paternalism. This should not surprise us; it is the almost inevitable result of the process we have described. As a metaphysical world-view loses its hold upon us, all patterns of authority that depend upon it are undercut. In a dynamic situation moving toward the future, the past may offer resources for our orientation, but it cannot impose its solutions upon us. When young people or the underprivileged begin to take initiatives to change their society, they are on the road to the discovery of authentic selfhood, and to the type of maturity that will repudiate all traditional paternalistic relationships.

This concentration on historical existence is the source of the strong humanistic emphasis in the new revolutionary movements. Young people of the upper and middle classes have become aware of the tremendous amount of suffering and injustice in the world and of the dehumanizing situation in which so many people are caught. To know the Negro as a human being is to know the dehumanizing conditions under which he lives. To establish contact with the peasants in Latin America is to be shocked by their subhuman existence. To take seriously the new developments in the technological revolution means to see the new possibilities and threats to human life that are latent in it. Thus, a deep moral passion is a major element in the revolutionary posture. Action is urgently needed and it cannot be delayed indefinitely by questions of prudential calculation. To be realistic cannot mean to limit oneself to what now seems politically possible, but to undertake the impossible in an attitude of daring and of trust.

We have no way of knowing whether this humanism will continue to play a central role in these movements in the years ahead. Nor do we know whether our culture can provide the resources needed to sustain such action. But one of the reasons why the new revolutionary movements are so important for our society is that they do incarnate this concern. Although they do not yet have the support of large numbers, they have succeeded in many instances in winning those young people who are most sensitive to the human situation, and who are prepared to do something about it. Thus they provide the context not only for the development of a new style of life, but also for the formation of a dynamic leadership, so badly needed at the present time.

2. Many of those who have taken their participation in historical existence seriously and are concerned about man and his future have been shocked to find that the order under which they live is almost intolerable. Among the colonial peoples of the world as well as the dispossessed in our own country, this has meant a keen awareness of their own exclusion from the enjoyment of the benefits and experiences that our society considers most important. The promise of material well-being is one thing; the way the economic order operates is another. The myths about a democratic society are appealing; the hard realities of political power are something different.

For many belonging to the privileged classes in the more advanced countries, this dissatisfaction has another dimension: the feeling that society, and especially the older generation, has failed to provide the possibility of a rich and meaningful life, yet cannot face the fact of its emptiness. A poignant sign of this malaise is a brief passage from a recent Russian novel, quoted in *The New York Times Magazine*:

"Your life, Victor, was devised by papa and mamma when you were still in the cradle. A star in school, a star in college, graduate student, junior scientific worker, master of arts, senior scientific worker, doctor of philosophy, member of the academy, and then . . . a dead man, respected by all. Never once in your life have you made a truly important decision, never once taken a risk. To hell with it! It's better to be a tramp and fail than to be a boy all your life, carrying out the decisions of others."[2]

What is striking about this statement is that it parallels so closely what many of the leaders of the new student left in our own country are saying.[3] They express the same rebellion against being treated as children indefinitely, the same feeling that the world in which they live "is a complete mess, a world which in their eyes preceding generations have botched up"; the same protest against a society which, possessing such extraordinary potential, "is simply no longer exciting." As Mario Savio put it, we in America are part of an automated, sterilized order, in which all the rules of the game "have been made up, which one cannot really amend" and the " 'futures' and 'careers' for which American students now prepare are for the most part intellectual and moral wastelands."[4]

This deep dissatisfaction with the *status quo* is hardly enough, in itself, to produce revolution. At the most, it could create a new sense of urgency about social change and a desire to move more quickly toward solutions. What makes the present situation so revolutionary among the younger generation is their discovery that when they begin to work for change at any specific point, they are confronted by a total system—a complex of attitudes, institutions, relations, and power alignments—which blocks fundamental changes in society.

Catholic students in Latin America respond to the incredible poverty of the masses by initiating social service programs in the slums or literacy projects in the rural areas. They soon awaken to the fact that all such efforts are ineffective palliatives; only by getting to the roots of the problem

[2] Quoted by Deming Brown, "The Man from S.M.O.G.," March 20, 1966, p. 88.

[3] See, for example, *Thoughts of the Young Radicals*, a collection of recent articles from the *New Republic.* Also Mitchell Cohen and Dennis Hale, eds., *The New Student Left* (Boston: Beacon Press, 1966).

[4] "An End to History," in Seymour Martin Lipset and Sheldon S. Wolin, eds., *The Berkeley Student Revolt* (New York: Doubleday, 1965), p. 219.

can any significant change come about. This leads them to recognize that they confront a feudal-colonial system, and that only a fundamental change in the nature and direction of that system will make it possible to meet these problems. Negro youth in the South take part in a few demonstrations. As they do so, they see that they are up against a whole way of life that must be changed if the Negro is to occupy a new place in society. The poor in our Northern slums who are encouraged to take initiatives in solving their problems understand that they will find no solution for them until basic changes occur in the economic order. And those who try to do something about our official policy toward the poor nations of the world, cannot long ignore the fact that capital *and* labor, the military *and* the State Department are in many ways working together to preserve the present situation, and that it is this order that must be changed in the interests of peace and justice. In other words, participation in movements for social change leads many young people to take a revolutionary position *vis-à-vis* the whole established order. As one Berkeley student stated, their experience exposed "not merely a vast and inept bureaucracy, but a coherent ruling-class structure."

If those in positions of power in our society were prepared to understand this phenomenon, admit the elements of truth in it, and struggle honestly with it, then our situation might not be so explosive. But all too often what stands out is the way all this is hidden by ideologies and myths that make it impossible for us to see what is happening, although facile rationalizations are provided to justify the preservation of the *status quo*. Certain basic presuppositions, it is assumed, should not be challenged, and when any significant group of students dare to do so, they are considered to constitute a threat that must be neutralized as quickly as possible. How else can we explain the facility with which some of our more liberal political leaders spoke of communist influence among those who protested against the acceleration of the war in Vietnam? So long as this situation continues to exist, participation in the struggle toward a better society will in itself constitute a process of radicalization for those so involved, and young social idealists will rapidly be transformed into revolutionaries.

Under these circumstances we should not be surprised if

the new revolutionaries conclude that the established order is incapable of bringing about the changes now demanded, and no longer trust in the traditional means of working for social transformation. In many places, the former dispersion and balance of power, which kept certain structures open, is no longer evident. They see the close identity of interest of the large corporations, labor, and government in the United States, which goes under the name of "consensus politics." In many of the developing nations, the political power traditionally concentrated in the hands of a very small minority—to the almost complete exclusion of other classes—now seems to be even stronger with the support of Western economic and political alignments. And, what is even more frightening, as Carl Oglesby has indicated, is the possibility of a *Pax Russo-Americana*, which would attempt to preserve more or less the present relationships between the rich and poor nations at the moment when fundamental changes are desperately needed.

Within the present order, those new forces which could make the greatest contribution toward social change find that they have been effectively excluded from the exercise of political power: the students in the university, the new leadership in the developing nations, the poor in the "inner cities." New developments in technology in our society have produced a situation in which the average citizen or worker is increasingly excluded from significant participation in the decision-making process within those institutions that determine his destiny. At the same time, technology provides extraordinary resources which can be and are being used to preserve the present system.

Intense awareness of this situation can only have drastic consequences in the orientation of young people and of the dispossessed in our own country and elsewhere in the world. It leads, on their part, to an almost complete breakdown of confidence in the institutions of the society to which they belong. As Mario Savio put it, university students question whether they can be committed to the society into which they were born. Negro young people are no longer interested in imitating whites; the colonial peoples are not attracted to the Western way of life; and the poor in the cities do not want to become middle-class. From a revolutionary perspective, institutions which were once the object of unquestioning loyalty, no longer occupy that position. Those that are open and flexible enough to adjust rapidly to new conditions, may offer an opportunity to work for their renewal from within. To work in the same way for the transformation of those that are more rigid, may simply not be worth the effort. If we want to serve the cause which they represent, then we may be called to make a concerted effort to subvert them from within, or to challenge them from without. Only thus can we hope for their survival and renewal. Otherwise, we can serve the future best by allowing them to die.

3. Many young people who have been led to this conclusion now adopt an attitude of defeat or rebellion; they try to find some way to escape from an impossible world, or at least to steer clear of the adult community. For the revolutionary, however, this situation is the occasion for the gradual shaping of a new vision of a new social order. In this sense, he is the authentic expression, in our time, of that which has been most central in the Western revolutionary tradition. As Hannah Arendt describes it in her book *On Revolution*,[5] this tradition represents the coincidence of the idea of freedom and the experience of a *new beginning*. It is an attempt to liberate man and to build a new order—the *novus ordo saeclorum*—by means of daring human initiative. The most surprising thing is that this has occurred at the very moment when all utopias have been exposed and all visions of a new order debunked. Our dominant myths are those of estrangement, not of hope—*1984, Brave New World*, and so forth; and many of our most outstanding intellectuals reflect a mood of cynicism and despair, or place great emphasis upon realistic calculation of the possible as the only basis for action.

This concern for a new order cannot be understood if it is seen as a return to a former type of superficial optimism and liberalism. The new revolutionary is very much aware of the failings of human nature and of the power of evil in society. He cannot avoid seeing them. But he also is confronted by the fact that modern technology has given man the resources he needs to create the type of society he wants. And the breakdown of all the old authority structures forces upon us the freedom to determine the shape of the future.

[5] New York: Viking Press, 1963.

The question is whether or not we have the will to act in such a way that we can build a new society.

In this context, what is called for is creativity, imagination, plus the constant willingness to risk all. Utopia becomes an explosive force in the present, and the only way to act intelligently and responsibly is to repudiate narrow rational calculations about what things can and cannot be done. To allow politics to be determined by what appears to be possible means to limit our possibilities and render the political struggle petty and uninteresting. In the Port Huron Statement of the Students for a Democratic Society, the consequences of this ineffectual posture are recognized and repudiated: "It has been said that our liberal and socialist predecessors were plagued by vision without program; while our generation is plagued by program without vision."

This revolutionary vision of a new society may still be somewhat blurred. Certainly it is conditioned by the specific character of each revolutionary struggle. And yet, the diagram of a new society is gradually taking shape, one in which certain specific elements can already be distinguished.

One of these is the growing conviction that society can and must assume responsibility for ordering its economic life, by determining the goals of economic development and the means by which these can best be reached. It is now clear that the economic realm is not a mysterious order of nature which we must allow to go its own way; it is simply one of those structures that a community can use for the ends it determines. With the resources now at our disposal, the material poverty that still exists is an evil we need no longer tolerate. The wastefulness of the free-enterprise system—even with the restrictions now placed upon it—and its orientation toward production for profit rather than attention to the most basic needs of man and society, represent luxuries we cannot allow much longer without disastrous consequences. Thus, the construction of a new order involves a certain degree of socialism, not in terms of the adoption of the Marxist philosophy, but in the most basic sense of the concept itself: *control of the economic order by society itself*. Rather than wasting any more time on the hackneyed, sterile debate between capitalism and socialism, we must meet today's challenge to create new models for the ordering of economic life by society, and engage in the type of experimentation that will blaze the way toward the future.

A second element in the revolutionary vision of the new society is indicated by the emphasis upon participation of all groups and classes in the life of community and nation, and especially in the process of decision-making by which their future will be determined. Hannah Arendt sees this as the major emphasis which has emerged spontaneously in the revolutions of the West. In her analysis of Jefferson's revolutionary outlook, she points out that it was his conviction "that no one could be called happy without his share in public happiness, that no one could be called free without his experience in public freedom, and that no one could be called either happy or free without participating, and having a share, in public power."[6] The recognition of this fact is almost universal today. Classes, groups, and races that have been marginalized in the past, are now coming to see that they are part of a history in which something has been and is now happening. As they awaken to this reality, they gradually understand that they can have a meaningful life only as they become *participants* in this history, and that their situation can be altered only if they take part in the struggle to change it.

In the developing countries as well as in those more advanced, the limitations of many of our so-called democratic institutions have been exposed. The new democratic society must be one in which young people and students, the dispossessed as well as the ordinary citizen, can have a share in the use of public power within the institutions in which they live their lives: the political structures of local communities and nation, *and* the factory or office in which they work. Many people may be quite happy without this opportunity, and no organization will be able to offer a perfect balance between the demands of order and efficiency and such participation. But our present structures are woefully inadequate, and human imagination and creativity can go a long way toward opening up new possibilities for participation in these spheres.

Third, the new revolutionary is gradually coming to understand that a basic change must occur in the relationship between the rich nations and the poor nations. He can see that almost all our attitudes and approaches are vitiated by paternalism, and that the programs of assistance we have so

[6] *Ibid.*, pp. 258–259.

far developed do not go far enough. Our attempts to work out an adjustment between our national self-interest (as now understood) and the interest of the developing nations are highly ideological, and shot through and through with myths and illusions. On these foundations, international peace and stability will be impossible; and the situation of the poor people of the world will become more desperate each year.

New problems call for new solutions. Our economic resources are such that we can encourage and support new models for development in the less advanced nations, and experiment with new patterns of relationships—economic and political—with them. In the younger nations, leaders are emerging who have been trained in the technology of the West and are free to work for authentic solutions for their national problems. But they are not inclined to accept the peripheral position to which their countries were condemned during the colonial period. They are committed to working for a new international order. They are now being joined in this struggle by a number of people from the West who realize what the nature of our economic and political relationships with the colonial peoples has been. Modern technology has made a new international order possible and necessary, and created a situation of unrest, hope, and interdependence which can be met only as such an order takes shape.

Ultimately, the revolutionary is searching for a *new form of personal existence*, for himself and for others. The realm of history has become the center of his concern; with this comes an intensification of human self-awareness. Technology and bureaucracy constitute a tremendous threat to man; they also create conditions never before imagined for freedom, human relatedness, and self-realization. It is within our power to meet the basic material needs of everyone; at the same time, full personal existence involves much more than the satisfaction of these needs. This leads to the paradox that the revolutionary who is committed to the struggle to better the economic condition of the poor can also repudiate the materialism of bourgeois society. It is not surprising that both capitalism and communism have lost their attraction. A new generation calls for a vision of personal existence that reaches beyond both these systems.

All this does not mean that anyone has a clear blueprint for the future. But one thing is clear: To build a new society requires a "new beginning." We must develop new ideas and perspectives on life and society by the cultivation of the creative imagination. So often the social thinking of many of us is sterile because we allow ourselves to be boxed in by a logic of our own making. We remain bound by presuppositions that are no longer valid, and are slow at finding alternatives for obsolete institutional patterns. The new revolutionary rightly senses that our historical experience has not exhausted all the possibilities that exist for the ordering of society. He shatters our complacency and challenges us to forge new models and respond to the impact of the future.

New thoughts about society must be accompanied by new politics; a new game calls for new rules. We may not know just what these rules should be, but for the civil rights worker in Mississippi or for those trying to bring about fundamental changes in urban society, it is all too clear that the old rules no longer suffice. To the liberal as well as the conservative, this conclusion comes as a shock. It creates a situation in which many who are working for the same objectives as the revolutionary find it difficult to communicate with him, and almost impossible to participate with him in the same struggle. Those who live by the old rules quickly forget that their way of acting was once an offense to the generation that preceded them. They cannot understand that the profound changes in recent decades may require an even sharper break with earlier ways of doing things.

Because of the nature of his vision and commitment, the revolutionary finds himself caught in an almost unbearable tension. He has been captivated by a vision of a different society; he is also aware that the *status quo* stands in sharp contradiction to it and represents an integrated order with great power. Only a fundamental change in this structure can open the way to even an approximation of the revolutionary's goals, but there is no obvious way by which such change can be brought about.

In the long run, a satisfactory solution of this problem depends upon a basic transformation in the structure of our institutions. Only as they are oriented more toward the future than toward the past, and have built into them the machinery for constant self-renewal, can we hope to have a stable and more human society. The revolutionary struggles of today may be an important factor in bringing about such a change if this generation of revolutionaries has the courage, wisdom, and persistence demanded of it.

Whatever the personal resources required for this effort, it is not likely to succeed unless the revolutionary has a clearly defined strategy by which he can expect to bring about significant changes. Here too he faces a serious dilemma. A previous generation of reformers worked for the renewal of society by serving the given structures according to the established rules. The new revolutionary is convinced that this will not produce results fast enough. But the logical alternative to this strategy seems even less promising. To move out of the Establishment and attack it head-on will also accomplish very little. To attempt to develop new institutions to replace those now existing in each major area of society—a new church or university system, a new labor movement, new political parties—would be an impossible task. Even if such an undertaking were to succeed, there is no guarantee that it would produce institutions any less rigid or more open to the future than those that now exist. Little wonder that so many young people assume an attitude of rebellion; while others who were most radical during their early years give up the struggle, and concentrate on their personal life and careers.

Modern revolutionary experience has developed another strategy, the importance of which we have been slow to apprehend, due partly to its origin and associations. In the face of the massive military power of an established order, *guerrilla warfare* has, under some circumstances, proved effective. But the strategy of guerrilla warfare need not be restricted to its military expression. At this stage in the development of a technological society, *its political equivalent* may offer a valuable instrument for bringing about changes in our major institutions.

The focus here is on the formation of small groups and movements which, whether based inside or outside an institution, force it to accelerate its own renewal. By means of many limited attacks at various points, a small group of people may be able to liberate large institutions for more effective service. This can be accomplished by a variety of techniques: the concentration of effort on limited objectives for a short period; flexibility and freedom of operation, which make it possible to advance to new fronts whenever blocked;

the maintenance of initiative and the element of surprise; and the attempt to bring about those relatively small changes that will set a much wider process in motion. Institutions which, as a whole, are unable to act in new ways, can support movements which do have the freedom to do so. One small team, with a certain amount of autonomy and freedom, can transform a large organization; while the renewal of one institution in the center of society can affect others related to it.

Many examples of the effectiveness of this approach could be mentioned. The Freedom Democratic Party may be able to bring about changes in the political order in Mississippi that would be almost impossible within the Democratic Party. One of the reasons for the surprising success of some aspect of the civil rights movement is that it tends to erupt at times and places where least expected, and to move on to new frontiers whenever it is stopped at any one particular point. The participation of the poor and dispossessed in projects of urban renewal may have unforeseen consequences in city life and politics.

Revolutionary movements in this country have developed, almost spontaneously, a variety of guerrilla tactics that have proved more or less effective. What is needed is more systematic reflection on the significance of these developments, and a clearer understanding of the best ways to take advantage of the potential here available for social change. Greater attention should be given, within this framework, to the question of the relationship of those working for radical change to the institutions of the established order. Service in the framework of a particular institution does not necessarily demand complete subservience to it; nor is there any virtue in maintaining one's independence. The question is rather how, in each particular situation, to contribute to the renewal of the institution being served. In some cases, this can best be achieved from within; in others, by working from outside it. At the present time, the essential thing is for those who have adopted a revolutionary position to preserve a certain degree of group identity. Thus they may be able to run the risks of being "in" but not "of" the structures, and live as "exiles" within the society to which they belong.

Those who are accustomed to a more traditional pattern of institutional loyalty will probably look upon the strategy we have just suggested with deep suspicion. But for those committed to revolution, it may be the one ground for hope that powerful interdependent institutions of a technological society can be changed. In fact, we may eventually discover that in this way a dynamic process can be set in motion that will bring about more fundamental transformations than have occurred as a result of previous forms of revolution.

We shall return to this issue later on. What we have tried to indicate here is that in our world today, a significant number of people are deliberately choosing *a revolutionary style of life*, and that it represents a type of thought and action that stands in sharp contrast to our former ways of reform. For many, this is a disastrous development that threatens our whole social fabric. But it will not go away, and we have no choice but to try to understand it and deal with it.

For many others, the choice of revolution is the only road to authentic and responsible existence. Those who take this step face a quite different task. They confront difficult human problems and must discover how to act responsibly in relation to them. Their own concerns and attitudes, as well as the specific situation in which they live, have been shaped by a particular cultural and spiritual heritage. Today, however, the forms in which that heritage is expressed are so identified with the old order that the revolutionary finds little or no meaning in it. What is even more serious, those institutions that could perform this mediating task—family, school, church, *et al.*—have by and large failed to do so. In some instances they seem to exist in order to preserve the old forms. Where this is not the case, they often reflect the same uncertainty and confusion the younger generation knows so well.

If we are to understand ourselves and live responsibly in this new era, the question of the relationship between the revolutionary posture and our Western cultural heritage and history, must receive our attention. Is this spirit of revolt a foreign growth, which now appears as a virulent cancer threatening to destroy us? Or does it represent the natural flowering of certain ideals and hopes that are at the heart of that tradition?

X

Social Revolution and Technology: The Paradox of Our Heritage

THE NEW REVOLUTIONARY has made his appearance at the moment of most extraordinary advance in technology. Thus we have two prototypes of the new man who is emerging in our time: the revolutionary and the technocrat. They look at the modern world from very different perspectives and represent two sharply contrasting styles of life; and both are products of our Western history.

They have not always existed side by side in our culture, nor are their positions of equal strength. Whatever may have been the role of revolution in our early history, in recent decades technology has dominated the scene. Our reactions to it have been mixed. For many scientists as well as for the technocrats, technology offers almost unlimited possibilities for a new and bright future. In the minds of others, it has evoked apocalyptic visions of "1984" and the "Brave New World." In the last few years, however, a new generation has arrived which is not content to observe and lament these prospects for the future. It has decided to challenge directly the hidden ideology of the system, to confront it head-on in a revolutionary struggle. And this is happening precisely in the United States, where technology is most advanced and where the ideology of a technocratic society has so permeated our thought that it is almost taken for granted.

So far the struggle is very unequal. It is difficult to imagine a sharper contrast than that between the Secretary of Defense and those students who burn their draft cards or organize protest demonstrations against United States policy in

Vietnam. Mr. McNamara is the very picture of self-confidence. He is convinced of the rightness of his cause, is the master of a vast amount of information, and has at his disposal almost unlimited power. The students, on the other hand, are apparently very weak, all too aware of the limitations of their knowledge, perplexed and confused in the face of irrational forces they cannot hope to understand or to control.

Now that this rift in our soul has been exposed, we shall be able to live with ourselves as individuals and as a nation only if we find some way of dealing with it honestly and openly. To do so ultimately means to come to terms with our own history; that is, with the forces out of our own past that have made us what we are. This is a long-term project which can be carried out only as those who find themselves involved existentially in this situation are provided with adequate resources for such reflection. It is a task primarily for the intellectual and for the university, a task which, in large part, still remains to be done. Most of us, in the meantime, must come to some sort of preliminary conclusions which will allow us to make sense out of our own situation, and prepare us to act responsibly in it.

In my own attempts to do this, I have been greatly influenced by a Dutch scholar, Arendt van Leeuwen, whose recent book, *Christianity in World History*,[1] has made quite an impact in some circles. He contends that something unique has happened in Western history which has prepared the way for both technology and revolution, and that a better understanding of this history would free us to relate these forces creatively to each other and find a way out of our present impasse. As a student of ancient cultures and religions, he has come to the conclusion that they were all dominated, to a large extent, by an "ontocratic" understanding of life and reality. By this he means that they conceived of all aspects of reality—nature and society, the temporal and the eternal, the divine and the human—as parts of one total cosmic order. In this framework, nature, as well as all major aspects of man's historical existence, was essentially identified with the divine, and thus sacralized. King and father, the political and social order, possessed an absolute authority which could not be tampered with. Under these

[1] New York: Scribners, 1965.

conditions, life was stable and secure; it was also relatively static. Social structures were rigid, and the past dominated over present and future.

In the early experience of the people of Israel, however, something happened that challenged this entire outlook, and that opened the way for a different view of reality. As they attempted to make sense out of what was happening to them in everyday life, the conviction grew upon them that they were constantly coming up against a Power that was active in their midst. They could not avoid the conclusion that this reality was personal in character, and that He was calling them to fulfill a particular mission within history. Out of the intensity of this experience, they gradually came to other conclusions of profound consequence. The concern of religion was shifted from the eternal to the temporal realm, and focused more on social and historical existence than on the inner experience of the individual. The relation of this sovereign power to the temporal order could only be conceived of as that of a *Creator* to His *creation*, and thus nature as well as society gradually lost their sacral character. As this God continued to be active in history, He stood over against every established order, and shattered all the pretensions of rulers and of social institutions.

This new attitude did not achieve an easy victory in Jewish or, later, in Christian circles. The Old Testament tells the story of a long and bitter struggle on the part of the prophets against repeated attempts to revert to the old ways. Much later, medieval Christendom represented an extraordinary effort to work out a compromise between the theocratic and ontocratic perspectives. Nevertheless, as this Hebraic revolution spread and permeated Western European culture, conditions were created which contributed to the emergence of science and technology. The realm of nature as well as the social order were seen as temporal realities which man was free to study and understand. He could harness nature to serve him and shape social institutions according to the goals which he determined.

Two other elements in the Judaeo-Christian tradition have played important roles in the development of our modern world. One of these is the *messianic undercurrent* that has broken out time and again across the centuries. Its origin is found in the early Israelitic experience of the Exodus and the

Promised Land. Out of it they concluded that the God with whom they had to do was leading them toward a new day, in which they would find new opportunities for human fulfillment within a new social order. Thus the dominance of the cyclical view of history was shattered, and men were free to look toward the future expectantly, as the place where new things could happen at any moment. Closely associated with this was Israel's sense of vocation as a "chosen people." This new order would not come spontaneously. It would be the result of a disciplined and sustained effort of a particular people to whom this historic mission had been entrusted. And because of this fact, the elect nation would be able to live with itself and find meaning in its historical existence only as it was faithful to this vocation.

In our most common North American perspective on life and the world, a rather amazing synthesis of these three motifs has occurred, in which technology is not only central but has been supplied with the support of a powerful ideology. Our pragmatic, functional way of dealing with reality is tied up with a belief in the power of technology to create almost unlimited possibilities for the betterment of human life, and with the conviction that America has been "chosen" for the mission of bringing these benefits to the rest of the world.

We are not interested here in arguing the relative importance of this Judaeo-Christian heritage in shaping our society, as over against other cultural forces. And we certainly would not defend this present synthesis as a faithful expression of that heritage. We are only trying to make the point that these elements have been important in shaping our self-understanding, and must be examined much more carefully if we hope to respond creatively to the problems we now face. Otherwise, we shall concentrate our attention on the pragmatic and the technological, while ignoring the context in which they have arisen and developed. And we will allow our extraordinary technological development to proceed within a highly ideological framework, which is more dangerous because we are by and large not conscious of it.

If we are free, however, to reflect upon these central elements in our own history, we shall soon discover that any such naive assumptions run into serious difficulty. At least, this is what happened among the Israelites. The same experience of being a chosen people, which made it possible for many not only to justify the *status quo* but also to be proud of it, produced some very troublesome characters. *For these men, liberation from old authorities, concern for human emancipation, and a sense of destiny led them to look critically at their own society and to become very dissatisfied with it.* They saw that when the power of the ontocratic pattern was broken, men were not only set free to create a new order; they could also use this freedom to satisfy their own individualism and collective ambitions in a way that was not possible in a more controlled society. They became aware that messianism can easily be perverted to serve other goals than the emancipation of man, and that if a chosen people is necessary for the transformation of the world, it can easily become an obstacle to it.

Unpleasant as these conclusions were, they were eventually strengthened by historical events. If Israel had been brought out of slavery in Egypt to the Promised Land for the sake of "the restoration of the nations," something apparently had gone wrong. The new era which they had hoped to inaugurate had not appeared; and the chosen people found themselves involved in social conflict and continuous warfare that eventually ended in political annihilation. But out of the profound crisis of self-understanding that this produced, the prophetic vision emerged. For these men, the sovereignty of God implied not only freedom but also judgment. When structures created to serve man become rigid and stand in the way of human fulfillment, they must be torn down. Only in and through their collapse can a new order be built. When a chosen people, even after its arrival in the Promised Land, is disobedient, it will be scattered—to rediscover its destiny in the Diaspora. In other words, *the prophets become the first revolutionaries.* What is even more important for our discussion here, *the same attitude toward reality which, as it took shape among the people of Israel, opened the way for the eventual development of science and technology, also prepared the way for revolution.*

No matter how hard we try to ignore this second element we cannot hope to succeed, for it is an integral part of the complex of ideas and attitudes, concerns and hopes, which make us what we are. Those aspects of the Judaeo-Christian heritage that we have mentioned were incorporated into our Western culture, developed and reshaped by it. As a result, technology and revolution not only exist side by side, but act upon each other in a constant state of dynamic tension. Whenever technology allows itself to be dominated by a heretical messianism, the revolutionary arises to expose it precisely at those points where technology has made the greatest impact. The destruction of the ontocratic order that makes technology possible—and is also carried forward by technology—leads men to call into question the authority of all structures, and sets them free to change them. The same messianic undercurrent that produces in some a passion for a technocratic society can lead others to expose and challenge its dehumanizing elements. And if the secularized myth of the chosen people provides those in power with a sense of destiny, it also makes it possible for those committed to building a new order to struggle with a similar sense of vocation.

Technology and revolution may represent contrasting perspectives that are in tension with each other. But we can safely affirm that neither would be what it now is without the other. The original impulse for the desacralizing of an ontocratic world may have come from the Judaeo-Christian message; but in modern times its triumphal march across the entire world, which has made revolution possible, has been produced by technology. On the other hand, it is social revolution that creates the type of open society in which technological advance can go forward and contribute most to human well-being. Revolution is the force that shatters the old ideologies standing in the way of technological advance. In point of fact, the greatest flowering of technology has occurred, not in the ontocratic societies of the East, but in those countries in which the revolutionary spirit has made a profound impact.

One of the central themes in Western history is the gradual working out and universalization of these two processes in a relationship of mutual support and tension. On the one hand we have those developments associated with technology, which gradually undermine all authority structures and all the old foundations of stability, and in their place establish an emphasis upon functionality and rationality in the ordering of one sphere of life after another. Simultaneous with this, the revolutionary struggle goes on. It aims at the overthrow of the old order in order to build a new one that will create new opportunities for human emancipation and well-being. This process also seems to unfold in ever-widening circles, touching new classes, institutions and peoples.

In an interesting chapter on "The Revolutionary West," Professor van Leeuwen traces this development from the time of the Roman Empire to the present. He contends that the two great symbols of an ontocratic society in the early and medieval period of Western history, the empire and the feudal system, were gradually undermined by forces working from within. The set of ideas referred to above acted "like a charge of dynamite," exploding the pretensions to divinity on the part of old authorities and institutions, and opening the way for the new to emerge. Out of this came new ideas and institutions that have revolutionized the West. At the end of the medieval period new, independent cities appeared, whose citizens were emancipated from the dominance of the old order, and who desired to control their own political life and concentrate their attention on the rational development of commerce and industry. New nation-states arose to challenge the waning authority of the Holy Roman Empire and to provide an opportunity for the major ethnic groups in Europe to order their life in the same way.

As time went on, the struggle for emancipation and rationality expressed itself in the economic sphere, through the development of capitalism and the Industrial Revolution. In the political order, the citizens of the nation affirmed their sovereignty as well as their vocation to make their nation an instrument of universal liberation. In order to fulfill this calling, they insisted that the people must be guaranteed the exercise of certain inalienable rights. In England, North America, and France, the struggle for these goals led to revolution. At the present time, this Western revolution has moved one step further. Its focus now is on the emancipation of the proletariat, which includes not only the dispossessed and marginalized classes in our societies, but also the external proletariat of the Western world—the vast populations of Asia, Africa, and Latin America.

With this, the development of the West and its impact upon the rest of the world has reached a climax. The process of secularization has undercut all old authority structures and opened all areas of life so that they may be rationally ordered by man. Technology has provided the means by which man can create the future he wants. It is in his power to shape society in accordance with his will, and to distribute economic resources and political power as he chooses. At the same time, the revolutionary spirit has become universal. The hope for liberation and fulfillment, for economic well-being and an opportunity to participate in the use of public power, has now touched all peoples. They are aware that such a life is possible, and they are gradually discovering that they must take the initiative in the struggle to achieve it. Moreover, technology, by shattering all autocratic structures and by creating a situation of interdependence of all areas of life and all parts of the world, has transformed revolution into something total. We thus have before us almost unlimited possibilities both for bringing about social change and for transforming life on the one hand, and for creating conflict, chaos, and social disintegration on the other.

In spite of all the changes that have taken place in our world at the end of the colonial era, the West still has tremendous economic, political, and military power, and will continue to play a decisive role in the human struggle as it is now defined. But will the West be able to accept the consequences of its own history, and do its part in carrying through the revolution it has forced upon the rest of the world? Certainly at present the prospects are not bright, for this would require sympathetic support of those who have opted for revolution, greater concern for the transformation of our economic and political structures, and bold new initiatives in education, welfare, and urban renewal.

In relation to the developing world, the task seems even more overwhelming. We have accepted the end of the colonial era in a political sense, with the rise of new independent nations in Asia and Africa. But we have hardly begun to imagine what will be required of us if we take seriously their demand for a new economic relationship with us and for a new role in international affairs. Until we discover how to reverse the trend by which each year the distance between the rich nations and the poor nations increases, we cannot hope to meet the present impasse or avoid eventual disaster.

It is not difficult for those of us who are North Americans to realize that the choice is posed most sharply for us. Because of the fact that technology has advanced so far in our society, our power is greater, and the nations that are anxious to speed up their own development are in one way or another dependent upon us. Historically speaking, our technological progress is closely related to the fact that revolution has had such a central place in our history. Many of the early colonists were products of the Puritan movement in England. They not only adopted a revolutionary attitude toward society, but came to America with a sense of destiny as a chosen people, called to build a new order and to be agents of universal emancipation. Our existence as a nation and our basic political institutions were shaped in a revolutionary struggle that constituted as great a threat to the established order of that time as the new revolutions represent for ours. Metternich, the nineteenth-century Austrian statesman, understood this when he declared:

> These United States of America have astonished Europe by a new act of revolt, more unprovoked, fully as audacious, and no less dangerous than the former. . . . In . . . fostering revolutions wherever they show themselves, in regretting those which have failed, in extending a helping hand to those which seem to prosper, they lend new strength to the apostles of sedition, and reanimate the courage of every conspirator. If this flood of pernicious example should extend over the whole of America, what would become of our religious and political institutions, of the moral force of our governments, and of the conservative system which has saved Europe from complete dissolution?[2]

But something has gone wrong. We have allowed our understanding of technology to be dominated by a heretical ideology of messianism, and this ideology now blinds our eyes to events around us. We find it difficult, if not impossible, to understand the contemporary dynamics of revolution—at home or abroad—and are thus unable to meet its challenge. As the situation becomes more revolutionary, we appear to the people in the developing nations as the symbol of anti-revolution. Consequently, we are considered partially responsible for the frustrations they feel when they are unable to change the structures of their society.

In the past we have been able to respond to new challenges because of the existence of a liberal vanguard in our midst, which has helped to interpret events to us and provide a basis of political power for change. As our present situation becomes more revolutionary, however, liberal ideologies seem

[2] Quoted by Dexter Perkins in *The United States and Latin America* (Baton Rouge: Louisiana State University Press, 1961), pp. 46–47.

less able to meet the challenge. Herein lies one of the major reasons for the crisis of confidence in our society that is so evident among progressive young people in our own country, and that is at the heart of the pessimism in the developing countries regarding our leadership in the world today. Tom Hayden, one of the leaders of the new student left, has expressed this failure of our liberal leaders and his reaction to it, in these terms:

> Their themes purport to be different but always the same impressions emerge: Man is inherently incapable of building a good society; man's passionate causes are nothing more than dangerous psychic sprees . . . ; ideals have little place in politics—we should instead design effective, responsible programs which will produce the most that is realistically possible. . . . You false liberals are suffering from the failure of your youthful dreams; you are eviscerating the great optimistic tradition of liberalism from the Enlightenment to the twentieth century; you are justifying disinterest in morality; you are eliminating emotion, dissent, outrage and, yes, the wellsprings of life itself.[3]

Over against this background, the spontaneous development of new revolutionary movements today could well be one of the most significant events at this stage of our national history. They offer us a new opportunity to understand the contemporary challenge we face and respond to it creatively; to be incorporated once again into our own revolution and to clarify our vocation in the world in relation to it.

This emphasis upon the importance of revolution at this particular historical moment does not imply that all revolutionary action is good and everything else bad. The new order toward which the revolutionary is moving cannot be identified with any specific political or social structure. Every revolutionary struggle brings with it both the possibility of a more human order and new threats of dehumanization. But in the perspective on Western history that we have presented here, the battle for the future of man focuses at times on the frontiers of revolution. When that happens, we should not waste our time trying to decide whether or not we will support revolution. The real issue is whether we have anything at all to contribute to it.

[3] "A Letter to the New (Young) Left," in Cohen and Hale, *op. cit.*, p. 4.

XI

Ideology and Theology

THE MODERN technocrat need not be unduly perplexed about events in our society nor about the nature of his own responsibility. He is committed to the use of the scientific method for the constant expansion of knowledge about nature and society, as well as the application of it. And his efforts are sustained by an ideology that makes it possible for him to assume that the continued application of technology will, in a relatively stable society, lead to the solution of major social problems, and create possibilities for a better life for an increasing number of people. This was recently put to me very sharply by a young atomic scientist at the University of Michigan. Taking issue with my thesis that a new radical leadership was needed for the building of a new society in Latin America, he insisted that I was concerned with the wrong issue. What is important, he said, is to provide an abundance of nuclear power for the production of electricity in the underdeveloped countries. With this will come industrialization and the creation of a strong middle class, capable of such leadership. By these steps, the problem will be solved.

Those who choose the path of revolution will not have such an easy time of it. They must have an understanding of what is happening today that will make is possible for them not only to break with this ideology, but also to develop an alternative perspective. If they want to get anywhere, it will be necessary for them to think about old problems in new ways, and pose new questions. They should be prepared to define their goals, suggest how these goals can be attained, and provide a reasonable ground for hope that such social transformation is possible. This is a formidable task.

It is further complicated by the fact that often those most aware of this responsibility see no clear way of meeting it. For centuries, our action in society has been oriented by a general philosophical world-view, which was based on the assumptions that reality was ultimately rational and that man, by the use of reason, could unravel its mysteries. Within this framework, it was not only possible to formulate a general view of man and society, but also to come to definite conclusions about the future as well as the best ways to move toward it. Today, all these metaphysical perspectives have lost their attraction for us. We are no longer sure that reality is rational, and have even less confidence in the ability of human reason to reach a trustworthy synthesis of it. More than that, we are now aware that the concreteness of social reality will never fit completely into such abstract schemes, and that the accelerated pace of social change makes them obsolete by the time they are formulated. Orthodox Marxism represents the last great effort to order society by such a total world-view; yet even there the situation is changing. New stirrings in Marxist intellectual circles around the world clearly indicate that the old formulas have lost much of their power and are gradually being replaced by new approaches to historical reality.

Our North American pragmatic and empirical approach to the problem also leaves much to be desired. We have logically assumed that if it is impossible for us to find answers to ultimate questions or have a total integrated world-view, then what must concern us is the empirical study of restricted spheres or fragments of reality. In this way we can arrive at limited but useful knowledge and be content with what it offers for the ordering of our society. This attitude has served to liberate men from old ways of thinking, and has opened the way to advances not only in knowledge, but also in the transformation of society. Today, however, especially for the revolutionary, this approach has serious limitations. Affirming that ideology is no longer necessary, it has fallen victim to a hidden ideological ethos that restricts our areas of interest, limits the questions we ask, and may close our eyes to the range of possibilities latent in a situation. When our scientific investigation of the social order is not related to an attempt to understand who we are as human beings and where we are going, this ideological distortion of our perspective is inevitable, and we are quite likely to end up by subordinating our "scientific" concerns to a restricted view of individual and national self-interest. Max Weber's insight into the consequences of this approach speaks to our condition. In his *Sociology of Religion* he declares that only two alternatives are still open to Western society: a spiritual renewal—brought about by wholly new prophets or by a powerful renaissance of old thoughts and ideals—or "mechanized petrification varnished by a kind of convulsive sense of self-importance." In the latter case, our society will produce "specialists without spirit or vision and voluptuaries without heart."

When this happens, there remains only one short step to the point where those who take pride in their scientific, non-ideological research allow themselves to be used by the government or the CIA for very definite ideological purposes. Technology and science become tools by which conflicts are managed and young people are kept under custody until they are without passion. And, as Tom Hayden has put it, a managed society "is a paralyzed one, in which human promises go unrealized, dreams die, people stop hoping for anything beyond the necessary evil."

Is there any way out of this impasse? Is it possible for us to recognize the limitations of reason and at the same time make the maximum use of it in order to understand our social experience? Can we be agnostic about the ultimate nature of social reality and still be free to do everything within our power to change it? Can we discover a way of thinking about our social existence and our prospects for the future that will combine the most complete openness to the complexity and concreteness of an ever-changing situation, empirically observed, and the insights provided by our historical experience, by the artist and philosopher, the ethicist and theologian? In the concluding paragraph of his essay on "'Objectivity' in Social Science and Social Policy," Weber predicts that a time will come when this will be absolutely essential. He writes:

All research in the cultural sciences in an age of specialization, once it is oriented towards a given subject matter through particular settings of problems and has established its methodological principles, will consider the analysis of the data as an end in itself. It will discontinue assessing the value of the individual facts in terms of their relationships to ultimate value-ideas. Indeed, it will lose its awareness of its ultimate rootedness in the value-ideas in general. And it is well that should be so. But there comes a moment when the atmosphere changes. The significance of the unreflectively utilized viewpoints becomes uncertain and the road is lost in the twilight. The light of the great cultural problems moves on. Then science too prepares to change its standpoint and its analytical apparatus and to view the streams of events from the heights of thought. It follows those stars which alone are able to give meaning and direction to its labors.[1]

Today we are badly in need of such "heights of thought" and "stars" to give meaning and direction to our labors. But we have no philosophical system or set of ultimate values that are able to do this. The type of insight and understanding we now need can only be supplied by *ideology*. For ideology is the product of thought about the concreteness of man's life in the world in the context of his wider historical and human experience; it offers the possibility of explaining something of the latent meaning in the history that is to be made. It represents an attempt to look at particular social developments in the light of the past as well as the future; a search for understanding in order to define goals and work for change. Because ideology provides an opportunity for such self-understanding—on the part of individual, group, and nation—it can help to sustain those threatened by change, at the same time that it serves as a dynamic factor in the social struggle. Ideological thought stresses involvement in a particular situation as an essential condition for arriving at true insight; it is the result of a collective enterprise, in which the masses can also participate and contribute to a gradual process of social awakening and reflection.

Such positive ideological developments will not occur spontaneously. We do not have much experience with this type of intellectual effort, and may not be willing to accept the discipline it requires. A revolutionary movement may begin with creative reflection on the events in which it participates but soon tire of the effort, become satisfied with its earlier conclusions, and end up repeating irrelevant clichés. The demands of a revolutionary struggle may tempt its leaders to absolutize their own position. When this happens,

[1] In *Methodology of the Social Sciences* (New York: The Free Press, 1964), p. 112.

ideology stands in the way of the type of social understanding that constituted its original reason for existence.

The fact that these dangers exist is not sufficient reason for abandoning the effort, especially when there is no clear alternative. In the era in which we are now living, we either go courageously about our task of producing the best ideologies we can or we will be enslaved by the unconscious ideological ethos around us. The question that should concern us is whether those engaged in the empirical study of our society, as well as those dedicated to the task of its renewal, will be open to—and have at their disposal—all the insights and experiences that can offer clues to the understanding of man and his history, the nature of human fulfillment, and the future prospects for the human enterprise.

As the reader is well aware, my approach to the problem is from the perspective of theology. It is out of this context that my involvement in revolution has developed, as well as my attempts to reflect upon its significance. This fact has been in the background of all that has been written here thus far; I shall now deal with it more explicitly. I am well aware that most people are not inclined to turn in this direction for orientation on revolution. In fact, the church and its thought have been so identified with the old order that many modern revolutionaries have felt compelled to become atheists. The conservative position of the church and the irrelevance of much theology are so evident that nothing can be accomplished by attempting to cover them over; we can only confess what one Asian student recently described as the "profound humiliation" of the Christian in the midst of modern revolution.

And yet, this is not the whole story. A closer look at our Western history would seem to indicate that certain elements in the Judaeo-Christian tradition push us in another direction, and upset the inner stability of Christian thought and life from time to time. It is widely recognized that our Western perspective on history, with its emphasis on development, progress, and social change, is closely related to this theological undercurrent. In a recent essay, "The Priest and the Jester,"[2] a young Polish philosopher, Leszek Kolakowski,

[2] In Maria Kuncewicz, ed., *The Modern Polish Mind* (New York: Grosset & Dunlap, 1963).

shows how all the basic questions about man and society that now engage our attention are re-formulations of theological questions. And the distinguished Marxist philosopher Ernst Bloch has given a great deal of attention to the prophetic and apocalyptic elements in the Bible, as well as to those revolutions that found their primary inspiration in Christianity. He goes so far as to declare that "even Christians know . . . that all the utopian aspirations of the great movements of human liberation derive from Exodus and the messianic parts of the Bible."

One of these revolutions is carefully analyzed and evaluated in a fascinating book, *The Revolution of the Saints,*[3] by Michael Walzer, a young professor of politics at Princeton University. Setting out to examine Puritanism as a political movement, Walzer arrived at the unexpected conclusion that it represented "the earliest form of political radicalism": "The Calvinist saint seems to me now the first of those self-disciplined agents of social and political reconstruction who have appeared so frequently in modern history. He is the destroyer of an old order for which there is no need to feel nostalgic" (p. vii). This revolutionary posture was the authentic expression of his theology. The Calvinistic stress on the sovereignty of God over all life and history set the Puritan free to relativize all lesser loyalties, see through the pretensions of social and political institutions, and cut away the metaphysical framework in which the old order was set. This, according to Walzer, undermined "every earthly authority" and pushed toward "the radical devaluation of the conventional world, of the political, legal, and intellectual *status quo*" (p. 100). Out of this emerged, in the Puritan movement, the first modern ideology, organization, and discipline for social revolution.

These historical examples, of course, do not prove that theology has any contribution to make in the present situation. But they may help us to perceive something which might otherwise go unrecognized: When we strip off those layers of metaphysics and religiosity behind which Christian faith is so often hidden, what remains is a perspective on history and on the possibilities for the fulfillment of human life that is radically oriented toward the future. And this

[3] Cambridge: Harvard University Press, 1965.

is very close to what an ideology of revolution is concerned about.

Theology attempts to look at our historical experience in the light of a particular history—that of the people of Israel; and to reflect on possibilities open for human fulfillment in the light of the humanity of one man—Jesus of Nazareth—and those most directly influenced by him. This implies that Christian faith ascribes a special significance to certain events in the past; they possess the character of a "revelation." By this we do not mean that a past experience has been absolutized, nor that belief in its significance must lead to claims for the superiority of this dogma or religion. The basic idea of revelation is that of "removing the veil" behind which reality is hidden. If there is any truth in the Christian claim, it will be indicated by the possibility which such reflection on the past offers for understanding what is going on now, and for apprehending the real possibilities open for the future. To deal with social problems in the light of this perspective need not lead us to defend our own theology or to insist that everyone adopt our total view. What it can do is provide us with a way of thinking about the concrete issues we face in working out an ideology of revolution that we can use openly and freely. If this perspective is valid, then it should provide insights into the human predicament and possibilities that can be accepted by those who do not share these same presuppositions.

Any such attempt to interpret what is going on in the world can hardly be expressed in an abstract theological system, in spite of the tendency of theologians to do just that. The Bible itself presents us with a wide variety of concepts and symbols, images and parables, specific experiences and their interpretation. These are more adequate instruments for communicating the variety and richness of dynamic historical existence; but they also confront us with a difficult problem. We will be able to carry on a meaningful dialogue between a previous historical experience and the present situation only if we have some principle of interpertation, some conceptual formulation of the central meaning of that experience in relation to our own. Thus, we must run the risk of developing a hermeneutical principle, recognizing that no such principle can be entirely adequate, and that it must be subject to constant re-examination and revision.

At the center of the Old Testament is the pilgrimage of the people of Israel from Exodus and slavery to Promised Land and freedom. In the New, it is a movement from the first to the second Adam, from our present state to the new humanity. This suggests that historical existence is a continuous struggle toward liberation, in the midst of which man is time and again surprised by new possibilities of meaning and fulfillment—in individual and collective life. When we look at contemporary reality from this perspective, several elements emerge which seem to me particularly relevant to our present reflections on revolution.

Messianism and Power in the Shaping of History

For those who are seeking some perspective on history as a basis for their reflection on revolution, the immediate prospects are not encouraging. Within the limitations that modern philosophy has imposed on itself, there is not much room for dealing with this question. Marxism has a clear answer. It speaks of the shape of the future with confidence, affirms that history is inevitably moving in the direction of greater humanization, and provides strong rational grounds for its historical interpretation. But it is too schematic and rigid, places too much trust in the rationality of history, and ends by being essentially deterministic. Existentialism also wrestles with the problem, is sensitive to the great complexity of each historical situation, and affirms the freedom of man. But it sees no possibility of meaning in the historical process, and can provide no solid ground for hope in either the present or future.

A number of philosophers and historians—Toynbee, Jaspers, Bloch, Butterfield—have worked on this problem and present us with a variety of perspectives, which interest us at the same time that we recognize their limitations. Even a superficial reading of these studies, however, reveals that the Judaeo-Christian perspective on history has played an important role in our Western self-understanding and is still, to some degree, a factor in contemporary attempts to answer our most pressing questions.

As suggested earlier, the Christian attitude toward reality opened the way for the development of an unusual perspective on history. It expressed the conviction that something positive was happening in the historical process, and thus made it possible to assume an attitude of trust in the face of perplexing and complex developments. It implied that man can achieve some understanding of what is going on around him, and thus work toward greater intelligibility without needing to rely on a total world-view for security. He can act in a way he hopes will contribute to the well-being of man without waiting until all the evidence is in, and without a total scheme of things to guarantee the results of his efforts. Action can be taken in trust that new insight will come along the road, and that mistakes can be corrected. In this context, it is possible to be realistic about human nature and about any particular situation, yet not fall victim to despair.

At the heart of this outlook is what can best be described as thorough-going *messianism.*[4] As the people of Israel reflected on the meaning of their experience, they came to the conclusion that history was going somewhere. Their entire life as a nation was oriented toward the coming of the Messiah, a ruler whose appearance would mean the establishment of a new order in the world. Thus, history is not merely a constant struggle for human liberation; it is a struggle that is moving forward toward its goal. But if the hopeful expectation of the Messiah was the central element of faith, there was no way to know for certain when and where he would come, and no sure method to guarantee his eventual appearance. In fact, the messianic king would appear after the House of David had been destroyed; he was the new shoot that would sprout from a dead trunk. In the messianic perspective, new possibilities for human life appear in history after all human possibilities have been played out.

The messianic hope, however, was not identical with our liberal doctrine of progress. Much as the Jewish people wanted to believe that God's favor would mean increasing national security and prosperity, such a facile view was always being upset by events; the efforts to bring in the messianic age and establish a new order constantly ran into trouble. *Principalities* and *powers*, to use the words of some

[4] I am well aware that this word usually suggests to us something quite different from its original meaning. But the concept is an important one, and I know of no other way to express it. Perhaps the time has come to rehabilitate the word and distinguish between authentic and false messiansim, between movements which are the bearers of messianic humanism and those which are "messianic" in a different sense.

of the biblical writers, always got in the way. On the political level these terms referred to those structures of society that were essential for human existence, because they held society together and prevented chaos. The trouble was, they were always getting out of hand. Instead of being content with a limited, functional role, they made absolute claims for themselves and pretended to give ultimate meaning to life.

As the messianic concern became more clearly defined and intense, the struggle with these powers came to the fore. It was not a question of doing away with them, but of forcing them to accept their rightful place as servants rather than lords. This meant breaking their ultimate power and authority over man. The tremendous seriousness of this struggle is typified in the crucifixion of Jesus. At that moment, state and church joined forces, and the resources of law, piety, and religion combined to get rid of one accepted by many as the Messiah.

This apparently simple task of removing someone who had become a threat to the established order produced unexpected results. Those who had joined the battle on the side of the Messiah concluded that this struggle between the powers and the Messiah provided them with a clue to what was going on in history. They also became convinced that, in this struggle, the powers were exposed and defeated. The sharpness and vividness of the New Testament description of this is extraordinary. Jesus is seen as having "discarded the cosmic powers and authorities like a garment." He "made a public spectacle of them" (Colossians 2:15)—put them out of commission, stopped them in their tracks. The remarkable thing about such an affirmation is that it was made at a time when it appeared quite clear to everyone else that the powers had been successful and that the messianic movement had been completely destroyed. Thus, what the early Christians were saying, in essence, was that appearances are deceptive. Especially where power is involved, an overwhelming victory may in the long run turn out to be a defeat, whereas weakness and defeat may be the road to ultimate victory.[5]

[5] The Apostle Paul expressed this in his own decisive way in a passage in the first chapter of I Corinthians: "Jews call for miracles, Greeks look for wisdom; but we proclaim Christ—yes, Christ nailed to the cross— . . . the power of God and the wisdom

What is even more surprising, the powers here exposed and defeated are not the worst institutions of society, but the best: the Roman Empire as the representative of law and order, the religion of God's chosen people, and the piety of their most devout sect, the Pharisees.

What we have here, then, is the matrix out of which a revolutionary view of history could eventually emerge. In the context of Christian theology the belief that God was acting in this way meant that historical reality functioned in these terms, that such a view of history was the most realistic one and provided the best opportunity to understand what the future would bring. The revolution in thought which this occasioned and still represents can be stated this way: If we want to understand what is really happening in history at any particular moment, or to assess correctly the impact of the future upon it, we should focus our attention at those points where *messianic movements are arising and challenging the power structures of society.*

This is not the way in which politicians and statesmen usually look at the world around them. They are engaged in an effort to assess the powers correctly as the representatives of the interests of diverse groups in society, balance them and use them for specific goals which may contribute to social well-being. Within this framework, any group that represents a messianic concern and wants to change the social order in the interests of human emancipation is something of a nuisance. It upsets the prudent calculations of politicians and can easily be considered subversive. In fact, even more progressive representatives of the Establishment are never quite able to understand why such groups are around, or what to do with them. When young people from wealthy aristocratic families in Brazil join the cause of the impoverished peasants, when students in this country go to Mississippi to work with the Negroes there, or Presbyterian ministers take the initiative in community organization in the Northern urban ghetto, the reaction is often similar.

We can, of course, continue to act politically within a

---

of God. Divine folly is wiser than the wisdom of man, and divine weakness stronger than man's strength. . . . To shame the wise, God has chosen what the world counts weakness. He has chosen things low and contemptible, mere nothings, to overthrow the existing order" (v. 22–29).

framework of understanding that excludes this dimension. But we can also accept the possibility that few things are more important for statesmen and politicians who want to act realistically than for them to take this messianic humanism into account, and deal with it in a perspective that can make sense of it. Decisive as self-interest is in the shaping of the politics of community and nation, it is not the entire picture. Over against it, and equally important in the long run, is the fact that community and nation exist in a world in which the accommodations of self-interest are time and again upset by pressures from outside and protests from within. In a world in which poor nations are seething with revolution because of their poverty and their exclusion from the centers of international life, any definition of our national self-interest that fails to take seriously these currents of messianism works against our own interest. Any national policy narrowly defined in these terms also ends up by alienating those groups within the country whose concern for human emancipation makes their participation within the power structures of society urgent and necessary.

In the context of messianism, no country or community can be understood merely in terms of its past. If we are interested in knowing what the chances are that America will respond creatively to the challenge of world revolution, it is always helpful to look at our past and try to discover those elements there which give us some assurance that we can understand and deal with such a reality. More important is the fact that we are not bound to act in the same way that we have until now. We can respond in new ways to a new challenge as it is mediated to us through unprecedented contacts with the underdeveloped world and constant confrontation with small messianic communities in our midst.

In a society in which these movements of human liberation are a dynamic force and people are confronted with a clear witness to the strange and paradoxical relationship between power and weakness, new possibilities open up for understanding what is happening in history, and for estimating the prospects for revolutionary change. The economic, political, and social structures of the *status quo* have tremendous power, and nothing is gained by underestimating it. But they also have a tendency to appear more powerful than they really are, and to make claims that are unjustified. So long as they remain unchallenged, they can maintain this illusion. But when movements of human emancipation arise which point to the real shape of the human, these powers are exposed. It becomes evident that they have exceeded their mandate and for this reason are on unstable ground. The powers can no longer hide the difference between their pretensions and what they really are; between what they claim to offer and what they actually do to human life.

The life and teachings of Jesus exposed the moral bankruptcy, the spiritual inadequacy, and the ultimately dehumanizing consequences of the legalism and piety of his time. Today something similar happens when messianic movements appear. A segregated society can maintain all sorts of myths about itself for a long time; but when Negro teen-agers are willing to risk violence and imprisonment to protest against it, these myths are undercut. And when this society finds it necessary to rely on hatred, violence, and murder to protect itself from such threats, the precariousness of its situation becomes evident. We may accept without questioning the policy of our government in Latin America and its support of the most reactionary regimes there—until the moment when significant numbers of Catholic students give up everything else to organize peasant leagues, or decide that there is no way to work for change except through participation in guerrilla movements. Then some people at least begin to see through the empty clichés used to defend such a policy. When a revolution relatively under control in a small Caribbean country leads us to send in 12,000 troops and support a military elite that shoots defenseless workers and students, it is not long before we begin to have doubts about the stability and power of the present order.

As this process continues, those who see urgent need for change gradually lose their confidence in the old order and refuse to accept its authority over them. The Negro in a segregated society is no longer dominated by the old patterns of relationship which he had taken for granted; the university student learns to question his former attitudes toward the authorities; the Brazilian peasant suddenly sees that he need not be bound by the whole ethos of the patriarchal system that has dominated rural life for centuries. And some of those who most desperately want to preserve the *status quo* perceive that these powers are leading them into a blind alley and making ultimate claims upon them that can only prove destructive.

Confronted by this exposure of their pretensions, the powers can either accept this judgment upon them and adjust to the new reality or use the power which they have in self-defense. When they choose this second path, they can often keep control of the situation and eliminate all immediate threats. But in so doing they show how insecure they are, go to extremes which provoke more enlightened and organized opposition, and take steps which reveal to an increasing number of people how dehumanizing the whole order is. By overreacting to the situation, they make the problem worse, and set forces in motion which it is increasingly difficult for them to control. In the end, their effort to stop change makes a more radical solution almost inevitable.

On the other hand, those who are working for change find themselves in a paradoxical situation. Since they are the ones who have exposed the instability of the old order and its dehumanizing character, they can expect to be violently attacked by those in power. They may be the objects of the hatred and fury of desperate men. And in the face of this use of naked power, the revolutionary will be well aware of the weakness of his own position, and discover that his movement is destined to suffer one defeat after another.

This same revolutionary is also in a unique position to see the instability of the old order and to recognize that it is fighting a hopeless battle. Because of his sensitivity to the shape of things to come, he can perceive that this reliance on power hides the inability of the old order to respond creatively to new challenges. The revolutionary may discover that his own weakness is stronger than he imagined, and that persecution, suffering, and defeat contribute to eventual victory. His freedom to take such an attitude of trust toward the future, and to act accordingly, may be an important factor in determining the outcome of the struggle, for it liberates the revolutionary from excessive preoccupation with the immediate future and what is happening to him, and makes it possible for him to concentrate on the job to be done. As most of us are not inclined to think about history in these terms, one of the most important elements in a revolutionary struggle is the presence of small communities of men and women who are engaged in parabolic action. By this I mean that they put this perspective to the test time and again on the most important frontiers in such a way that others are provided with signs that suggest that things do work out this way.

This perspective on history could, I believe, offer us a way out of the ideological dead end in which we are now caught in this country in our efforts to deal with two fundamental issues: the relationship between stability and change, and the role of violence in social transformation. Thus far, the consequences of this have been most evident in our policy toward the developing nations; given the revolutionary situation we face internally, it is quite possible that the same ideology will appeal to many people here, with even more unfortunate consequences. The fact that the liberal seems almost as prone to fall prey to it as the conservative makes the problem even more urgent.

Our present policy is partly motivated by a legitimate concern for stability and order, and the recognition that social disintegration and violence can easily prepare the way for totalitarianism and delay both economic development and improvement of the lot of the impoverished masses. But it is dominated by an ideological perspective that so distorts the whole picture that it leads to an obsession with stability, minimizes the need for change, and is willing to go to any length to eliminate the threat of violence—except in defense of the established order. The end result of this ideological blindness is our failure to see that such stress upon stability may make an explosive situation more unstable, and that this way of dealing with violence can make a violent solution more probable.

In the perspective of biblical messianism, stability and order take shape *on the other side of change*. When any particular structure of society becomes so rigid that it blocks change indefinitely, its destruction may be necessary. The more rigid an institution is in a dynamic society, the greater the likelihood of eventual institutional discontinuity. In the long run, it is not change but the opposition to it that constitutes the greatest threat to order and stability. Those who help to preserve a segregated society in this country or the patterns of feudal-colonial exploitation in Latin America are the real enemies of stability, not the revolutionaries. Therefore, an authentic concern for order should encourage us to run the risks of change and to realize that the sooner this is done, the better. It should also lead those who are more conservative to be in contact with and encourage those who are working for change, for only this sort of relationship and effort at dialogue can contribute to the stability of the type of society in which we now live.

In our own society, we have accepted the possibility that violence may erupt from time to time at those points where the situation is most desperate. At least our government has not decided that it should train a large part of the armed forces to deal with internal unrest, or rely on massive military occupation of our slums to remove the problem which there exists. But in Latin America as well as in other parts of the world, where the need for revolution is greater, we act quite differently. We have helped to transform the traditional armed forces in many countries into antisubversion units, and have involved our own military and even social scientists in this effort. As a result, we have greatly strengthened those groups in power who have effectively blocked nonviolent efforts at change, and have helped to create a situation—in Latin America, at least—in which an increasing number of those most aware of what is happening conclude that guerrilla warfare offers the only hope for basic social change.

Our Western influence in the rest of the world has created a situation which we now seem unable to understand or help others to understand. In a static society, where there are no messianic pressures for change, the problem of violence is usually not a serious or complicated one. But in a world in which people have awakened to hope, they are constantly pressing toward a new order that of necessity implies a "violation" of the old. As such expectancy becomes more universal, violence can be an important element, both in blocking change and in bringing it about. Those who are called on to handle this problem will be able to do so wisely only if they are free to face it openly and to understand its full dimensions.

It is our contention that the messianic perspective to which we have pointed here does offer one such possibility. It creates a sensitivity to the dehumanizing character of violent struggle; at the same time, it opens our eyes to the urgent need for movements that do violence to the old order. In this paradoxical situation we have the freedom to understand our own history, and also to face realistically the options before us in the midst of revolution. We can accept the fact that our nation was born in an act of violence; that the Negro was emancipated and our national unity preserved by means of violence. We are free to admit the possibility that acts of violence may have their place in the struggle of the dispossessed peoples in our urban ghettos and in the underdeveloped world. At the same time, we can concentrate on the type of study and action that will help minimize the necessity of violence, and limit its destructiveness in the process of social change.

There is one further element in our understanding of history that will influence our political ideologies. Our world is becoming increasingly pluralistic and interdependent. All peoples of the world are in contact with and dependent on each other; and in almost every country, people of all classes are directly confronted by individuals and communities representing other languages, cultures, attitudes, and ideologies. This forced interrelatedness is not sustained by a common history, ethos, or world-view; in fact, the constant expansion of knowledge and experience seems to lead us in the opposite direction. At the same time, we witness the rapid deterioration of all structures of authority. No group or class of people, no moral or legal code, can maintain order on the basis of implicit trust in and respect for it. Young people no longer accept without questioning the authority of their parents; the poor do not trust the paternalistic concern of the wealthy and powerful; and the external proletariat of the Western world have rebelled against their colonial status. As a result, many despair of any possibility of social integration, and see only chaos ahead; others boldly affirm their uniqueness and independence, and stop at that.

From the point of view of a theology of messianism, this whole process looks quite different. We begin by accepting it, because we see here the work of God. The Christian belief in creation and in the subordination of all nature, history, and human life to an ultimate sovereignty, desacralized all these spheres and undermined all authority structures. Gradually this influence has penetrated deeper and deeper into society and also into man's self-understanding. This development is not an end in itself. Rather, it is the essential precondition for messianic fulfillment. Man has been set free to move ahead toward the new humanity, and he is provided with an increasing number of elements that contribute to it. In fact, we might go so far as to affirm that the recent history of the West makes our choice clearer and more inescapable: between chaos and new efforts at social integration, in quite different terms from those of the past.

If all authorities are losing their ultimate power, all life and society must be ordered by the future rather than the past. A nation or a community must decide what type of world it wants, what goals it will set for the future, and then join in a common effort to achieve it. People come from very different backgrounds, experiences, and cultures, but they can engage in dialogue about the possibilities of human fulfillment that lie ahead of them, and be united in the experiences and hopes out of which a new ordering of life will emerge.

Our political background and theories may be widely divergent, but we can participate in a common effort to define the type of political relationships most adequate for the situation in which we find ourselves, and to engage in a common search for new models and new political strategies. We may be in favor of different economic systems, but this is not an insuperable barrier to the recognition that we now have no choice but to determine how best to develop our resources and distribute the goods we produce in the closest approximation to the common good. In such a society, in which difference, tension, and conflict are inevitable, we can accept them for what they are and work constantly toward reconciliation. In this process we may discover that reconciliation rather than the suppression of conflict opens the way to new relationships and a new richness of individual and social life. Discipline is essential. But discipline, for the community, represents the effort it is willing to expend and the price it is willing to pay, in order to move toward the goals it has established. For the individual, discipline is a matter of willing to so order one's life in the present as to keep the door open to wider fulfillment in the future.

All this may justify one concluding remark: Theological

reflection on history will be most relevant to the ideological struggle when it is willing to become something of an ideology itself. Scholars can provide us with insights into the patterns of historical understanding found in the Bible and in the works of the great theologians. But all of this means very little to us until it is related directly to the more immediate history of which we are a part. This cannot be done today by a mixture of theology and philosophy in some new system. It can come as the result of a running conversation between our theological heritage and the events of our time that gives us new freedom to understand what is happening around us and to respond to it more creatively. By its very nature, such reflection must always be seeking for meaning in a dynamic and flexible situation; thus it must always remain tentative and open to constant revision. This is what should characterize ideology. The freedom of Christians to revise their own ideology of history may, in the long run, be their most significant witness to those engaged in the ideological struggle.

Social Revolution and Human Fulfillment

The above phrases suggest an inner tension that manifests itself frequently in the life of the revolutionary and in the history of revolution, and which will probably never be completely resolved. The revolutionary, whether he be the natural leader of the oppressed in their struggle for emancipation, or a member of another class who has decided to cast his lot with the suffering and exploited, often has a deep human concern that is the main driving force in his life. At the same time, something seems to happen in the midst of the revolutionary process that dulls this concern. It is very easy to be intensely concerned about the well-being of man and blind to what is happening to men and women. Moreover, there is something about the revolutionary struggle itself that is dehumanizing, and that releases forces which work against the goals previously established. One of the most common and unfortunate products of this is the disillusioned and embittered ex-revolutionary, of which there are so many examples today. And ideology with which we hope to orient our revolutionary action must give attention to this problem.

In spite of all that theologians have done to obscure the fact, theology is concerned to interpret certain events and images which witness to the liberation of man and the renewal of human life in the midst of such an ambiguous struggle in history. They affirm that man's historical existence is a movement toward a liberation which is fulfillment. But the peculiar dynamic of this position is the result of the association of this hope for man with a particular historical person, Jesus of Nazareth, in whom we have a concrete indication of what such a new humanity can mean. Jesus, the Messiah—a political; in fact, a revolutionary figure—is the instrument of human emancipation. The Messiah has come in the past, yet still continues his work; thus, liberation is both an actuality and a possibility toward which we are moving. The Messiah was crucified; our hope for liberation is realized in and through struggle and suffering, when our messianic efforts to build a new order are frustrated. And the crucified Messiah is the new man, the second Adam. Human fulfillment in the midst of suffering and defeat is a reality; it has occurred in the life of one man, and is now at our disposal. From the time of the early disciples until today, interest in and response to this person has led men and women to a wager regarding the ultimate prospects for man's historical existence, and the meaning of our present time in relation to it.

Within this framework, the tension between revolution and humanization is defined and accentuated in a striking way. Attention is focused on what Paul Lehmann has described as "the political character of the divine activity." The new humanity takes shape in the world where the battle for man is being carried on over against the powers. When these forces are challenged, put to rout, and forced to reorganize, men find the freedom to develop new forms of life. As these powers are kept under control and made to serve those goals which we set for them, we *make room* in the world for greater human fulfillment. It is therefore nonsense to talk about the spiritual and moral renewal of man without giving due attention to this element. The use of religion, psychoanalysis, or the mass media, as instruments by which people are helped to adjust to a dehumanizing social order without being challenged to change it, is essentially a betrayal of man. All these efforts contribute to a situation in which the powers gradually increase their destructive rule. Responsible concern for the inner well-being of the person must therefore lead to action that seeks to control and use political power in order to make room for greater freedom in community. Along this road of political involvement, it also becomes clear that very often our deepest experiences of meaning and fulfillment come to us in the midst of this struggle when we least expect them and are preoccupied with other things. In these circumstances, we are reminded that he who seeks to save his life shall lose it, and he who loses his life shall find it.

This political figure, the Messiah, is also the new man; he represents a new form of human existence in the world. Thus, politics and revolution are set in a context in which they can contribute to human well-being only if they are kept in their proper place, as servants of the new humanity. As soon as we come to rely on them to answer the ultimate questions about life and its meaning, we make demands on the political order that it cannot fulfill, and thus pervert it. This temptation is especially serious for us today because the whole process of secularization has destroyed our confidence in the old absolutes by which we once lived, and it is much easier for us to make an idol of our political struggle than it is to learn to live precariously without idols.

A political movement will be able to contribute to the ultimate goal of authentic messianism—i.e., to human fulfillment—only if those who participate in it do not expect too much of it. The best revolutionaries are those who are free men in the sense that their self-identity and personal stability does not depend on their political role. Especially in the type of world in which we are living today, significant success in the revolutionary struggle tends to diminish the importance of revolution; and effective political action can create the type of society in which politics becomes less important. Only the revolutionary whose political commitments are related to a broader vision of human life and history can cope with this situation, and thus contribute significantly to the humanization of contemporary society. Very often, participation in revolution is a means by which people are able to transcend their petty personal anxieties and problems as they discover a new realm of personal freedom in obedience to a higher loyalty. It is, however, this very experience that can also increase their dependence on the political order and lead to easy disillusionment with political movements. In the long run, politics cannot contribute to personal liberation unless we recognize its limitations and make room, even in the midst of a revolutionary struggle, for those institutions and forces that meet other human needs. So far, at least, modern revolutions have not distinguished themselves on this point and, perhaps for this reason, have had such limited success.

The association of the messianic imagery of the Old Testament with the historic person of Jesus of Nazareth leads to a further affirmation: The *crucified* Messiah is the new man. Crucifixion occurs along the road toward the emergence of the new humanity. It is this that opens the way to an unusual combination of sensitivity to the profound ambiguity present in every revolutionary struggle and hope regarding its outcome. In this perspective, all determinism is shattered. In the long run, the most overwhelming concentrations of power cannot succeed in their efforts to preserve the *status quo*; and the revolutionary process itself does not follow an inevitable course. A revolution offers the opportunity to build a new social order—on the brink of social disintegration—and it may also open the way for new manifestations of social evil. But the important thing is, that this very ambiguous process provides recurring opportunities for the creation of new and more human forms of social organization. Thus, it is possible to be quite realistic about what is going on and at the same time take advantage of every new occasion to push toward the ultimate goals of social revolution.

The Messiah was crucified by His own people—by those in positions of power in the messianic society and those striving most intensely to bring in the new age—and abandoned by His disciples at the moment of greatest need. This suggests that we should have no illusions about political movements or their leaders, about revolutions or about revolutionaries. Revolutionary leaders misunderstand the situation, and make mistakes in judgment and strategy; human weaknesses are as prevalent among them as in any other group. At certain moments, the revolutionary struggle may be just as dehumanizing as the old order. But if crucifixion is an inescapable element in social transformation and does contribute to this goal, then we are free to accept this fact and get on with the job. We can constantly expose and attempt to correct those things that threaten the revolutionary cause. without losing hope. And the fact that the revolutionary struggle itself becomes dehumanizing at certain moments is not sufficient reason for abandoning it. In an oppressive situation, in which all efforts at change are easily blocked, a movement of racial integration can easily become rigid and extremist. Yet such a movement may be the instrument by which that society is broken open and begins to move toward a greater degree of justice. Violence is always destructive. Under some circumstances, it becomes terribly dehumanizing; under others, it serves as the necessary midwife of a new social order. No abstract set of principles or values will be of much help in decision-making in such a situation. But the illumination we seek may come as we attempt to evaluate the alternatives before us in terms of their potential contribution to a more open and more just future.

The crucifixion of the Messiah also reminds us that the struggle between the old order and the new goes on throughout history, in the social order that emerges from revolution as well as in the old order that preceded it. Unfulfilled hopes, frustration, and suffering are part of our lot even when the cause of revolution triumphs. At the same time, we may discover that some of the most significant steps forward occur under difficult and ambiguous circumstances, and that, in the light of the future, even partial victory may prove to be an important gain for the cause of man.

Revolution, Transgression, and Transcendence

There is one other complex of problems that places a heavy burden on revolutionary ideology. By its very nature, revolution implies a "violation" of the old order in the name of the new. It requires a transcendent critique of the *status quo*, a refusal "to accept the given universe of fact as the final context of validation," and an attempt to "'overshoot' the established universe of discourse and action toward its historical alternatives."[6] If this herculean effort succeeds, the

[6] These expressions are from Herbert Marcuse's *One-Dimensional Man* (Boston: Beacon Press, 1964), a book which has some important things to say about this problem.

revolutionary then faces the danger of becoming enslaved by his own ideology. The history of modern revolution thus far provides little evidence that such idolatry, and its consequences, can be avoided.

As we have seen earlier, this attitude of transgression and transcendence over against the society in which man finds himself is not a very common occurrence. In the West, it was a product of the metaphysical world-view that arose as the result of the synthesis of Greek philosophy and Christian theology. In this framework, human life and society are related to an order of Being that transcends the finite. The Eternal stands over against the temporal, and all social institutions are judged and reshaped by an ideal order to which they should conform.

These metaphysical entities have gone, and with their disappearance we face a new and difficult challenge. Placing stress on the functional and operational can easily lead to a view of reality in which entire dimensions are lost, while the present tendency in the empirical sciences provides us with no clear rationale by which critical theory can transcend this society, no basis for qualitative change. When this is accompanied by an ideology of rationality that is geared to the preservation of the established order, and by the happy consciousness that has no sense of radical guilt or judgment, we can quickly become burdened with the dead weight of the old order, yet have no foundation from which to challenge it.

Those who see through all this may rebel against it. But rebellion in itself cannot produce the new, nor liberate man; it may be only a negative sign of his enslavement to the establishment order. The repudiation of old categories of thought about North American foreign policy will not provide us with the tools to forge a new one; and protests against the enslavement of man will not make us free human beings. What we need are the resources for radical transcendence: those insights into and perspectives on life and society that break the power of the old, stand in judgment on the *status quo*, and provide us with a universe of discourse in which new models and new "projects" can develop. Here philosophy and art, literature and drama, the stimulation and enrichment of historical memory, all have their place.

The words *transgression* and *transcendence* have, above all else, a religious dimension, and suggest that theology should make some contribution at this point, if we can pry it loose from the world-view with which it has been associated. As a matter of fact, this close identification with a metaphysical order is not so much an indication of the nature of theology as it is of the advanced stage of acculturation of Christianity in a former era. The type of transcendence we find in the Bible is more eschatological than metaphysical; it refers not so much to an Eternal Order above man as it does to the Future which transgresses against and transcends the present. The supreme reality in history is the Kingdom of God which is coming and which is present now as an explosive force in our midst. We may no longer believe in Utopia, but we can trust that new and surprising possibilities for the ordering of human life and society can appear on the road to the future. In that case, we act most responsibly when we are engaged in a constant effort to create new "projects," and strive to make them reality. Potentiality stands in sharp tension with actuality because the potential is a historical possibility. We are able to achieve the possible only as we undertake the impossible in trust that the future is open. We easily betray and limit reality when we restrict our understanding to the actual, as empirically observed. Reality is that which is coming-into-being as our historical existence moves to the future: as Ernst Bloch puts it, "What *is* cannot be true."

The coming of the Kingdom is a question of the reordering of human relationships and social structures; thus, the judgment of the future upon the present is not a matter of claiming allegiance to certain abstract, eternal values or ideals, but of quite specific technological and political goals. They are defined, and given concreteness, in the midst of the dialogue between our vision of man and of what he can become and the situation in which we find ourselves. What stands out here is the *concreteness* of our goals for the future. "Values" are transformed into human needs, specific changes necessary and possible in society, specific technical possibilities which we now have before us. As we fit these diverse elements together in a more comprehensive picture of our goals, the future breaks the finality of our present structures and institutions, and opens the way for the increasing use of technology in the service of man.

Admittedly, the Christian Church has not always demonstrated this freedom to break with that which "is" in loyalty to that which is coming-to-be. When it has occurred, it has been nourished by a certain way of thinking about reality, expressed in a variety of theological concepts and images. Basically, it represents a wager that these symbols and concepts provide a clue to what is really going on in the world and thus point the way to meaningful and responsible living. History is understood as not self-contained; it is not determined by absolute laws which work themselves out inevitably. Rather, history is the realm of freedom and responsibility where human communities are constantly being confronted by new prospects for the future. Human life is seen as most human when it is lived in response to a higher loyalty than self, and expresses the trust that reality—coming-to-be—is ultimately favorable to man. In every sphere of collective existence, men are most free to struggle for the betterment of the human condition when they do not attribute absolute value to what they are doing. Most paradoxical of all, man is free to be a transgressor against the order in which he lives when he is perturbed by an unhappy conscience; that is, when he realizes that he is called to a way of life and a standard of action which stand in judgment upon him.

The moment we think in these terms, we run into tremendous difficulties, as the biblical writers, and especially the Old Testament prophets, clearly understood. For them, this radical transcendence and transgression could have only one of two sources. It could come as the result of ascribing infinite value to one aspect of finite reality. This absolute loyalty to a new ideal or vision of a new social order can provide the basis for dynamic revolutionary action. But in the end it fails because it is idolatrous: It is a human creation that tends to violate reality and thus to enslave those who are most loyal to it.

The second alternative, suggested by the Christian imagery of transcendence, reverses this whole process. The object of loyalty is not some element of the finite which has been absolutized, but the Creator who relativizes and at the same time sustains all created reality. We are challenged to trust in a purpose and initiative at work in life and history, in relation to which life is free and the struggle to change the world makes sense. The prophets understood very well that the line between idolatry and trust in sovereignty is a very fine one indeed; yet they insisted that it represented the fundamental choice that determines human destiny.

Today we face an unusual situation. We are very much

aware that all our idols have feet of clay, and also that all the symbols of theological transcendence have lost their meaning and power *at the very time when new resources for transgression and transcendence are indispensable for the revolutionary struggle.* In this situation, it would be fatal to turn in desperation to new idols. And it would be futile to spend our time arguing the case for Christian transcendence. But the old biblical imagery does affirm that history is open to a more promising future; that we are free to be transgressors in our service to our neighbour; and that men and nations can create new models for a new society, and do something effective to transform them into reality.

We can still make this wager. When we do so, we may eventually be surprised and shocked by a new language and imagery of transcendence which could have far-reaching implications for the renewal of society.

XII

A Word About Strategy and Tactics

THE FACT THAT this essay is already long might provide an easy way out of a difficult dilemma: Because of his interest in the *achievement* of certain goals for man and society, the theologian cannot be indifferent to questions of revolutionary strategy and tactics. But he is not prepared to discuss these questions because they require a type of social and political analysis of which he is not capable. The most he can hope for is to participate in a wider dialogue on these issues—which is not possible here. However, as I learned long ago in Latin America, we have no right to urge people to become revolutionaries unless we can give some concrete indication of how the goals of revolution are to be reached. Otherwise, we share responsibility for their frustration and despair, as well as the results of it, if they abandon the struggle or are led to act irresponsibly. We thus have no choice but to make at least some preliminary observations about the present prospects for the revolutionary struggle.

In recent years I have been impressed by the way in which the rapid advance of technology seems to create or intensify certain paradoxes in our society:

1. By the integration of systems, it provides the established order with almost unlimited power for self-preservation. At the same time, this integration of systems represents a very precarious balance that can easily be upset, and the changes produced by technology seem to contribute to the emergence of forces intent on upsetting it. The recent repercussions of a one-man crusade for auto safety is only one example of this.

2. In the past, the authority and stability of social structures meant that even violent revolution could make only a

limited impact, usually in one restricted sphere of society. The collapse of authority structures and the dynamics of social change now create a situation in which change can affect all areas of society and penetrate very deeply into it. This offers a unique opportunity to build a *new* society. But these same developments mean that revolution can also cause total social disintegration and make new forms of regimentation necessary. This, in turn, may hinder the achievement of revolutionary goals. In the past, revolution had to bring about *quick* changes before the old stabilities once again set in; today, revolution may represent a constant threat of chaos over a long period of time.

3. Technology creates a mentality that is concerned about the analysis and control of the *given* order, and that provides the power and techniques by which this can be done. The same technology creates a dynamic social situation which can only be understood in the light of the future, and renders ineffective all institutions that cannot adapt to the new. Under these circumstances, the task of the revolutionary in the long run is not so much that of *replacing* the total system of the present by a totally new system, but that of breaking social institutions open and keeping them in motion so that they can better serve man as they respond to new realities. In this effort, revolution as *class* struggle has only a relative place. Lines are drawn more sharply between those who understand what is going on and respond to it, whatever the class to which they belong, and those who do not. Very often there are many people, leaders as well as others, within the Establishment, who can respond to the challenge of the new or who have already done so, but are unable to act because of the inertia of the institutions they serve.

If these developments are taking place, then a new strategy of revolution is urgently needed. The attempt to change society by destroying the entire power structure and replacing it by a new one may be not only an increasingly difficult task, but also a most unlikely way to achieve the goals that the revolutionaries have. There are some situations in which the rigidity of the old order and its resistance to change may permit no other alternative. But if we hope to contribute effectively to the transformation of advanced technological society, new strategy and tactics more appropriate to that task will have to be devised.

These new factors suggest the main lines of an alternate strategy, and help to create the conditions for its success. Instead of *total* revolution in the sense of a head-on assault on the total structure of the established order, we can work for *permanent* revolution, by which the entire structure is confronted by an increasing number of challenges at those points where changes are most imperative. Our goal is not primarily that of overthrowing the present structures but rather of forcing them to be more open and flexible, and to respond to new problems in more creative ways. Our efforts will not be oriented so much toward one moment of total victory some time in the distant future, but toward a large number of small victories all along the way, which may disturb the precarious balance of power where it is not in line with reality, and bring about the type of changes that will push the revolutionary process forward to new stages.

Throughout this study, we have suggested that a theological perspective on revolution frees us from historical determinism; at the same time, it assures us that we are part of a revolutionary process moving in a certain direction. For this reason, our action should possess something of the quality of a *witness* to the future which is even now invading the present. Our belief that the future is on the side of revolutionary change liberates us from obsession with the defense of our systems and ideologies, or even of the territory under our control, as so often happens with the defenders of the *status quo*. We can cooperate with the future that is becoming a reality in our midst, in full openness to the concrete demands of it, whether they fit into our ideologies and schemes or not. What becomes important is the exposure of specific injustices in the old order and of its failure to meet the new issues demanding attention; the awakening of people of different social classes to what is going on around them and to responsible action; and the initiation of those changes that will offer the greatest potential for further change. If the action of the revolutionary is in line with reality, then he has the advantages of initiative and creativity, of surprise attacks and the choice of strategic places and moments for each battle. A small victory prepares the way for a more advanced struggle, and defeat in one specific effort is the occasion for the regrouping of forces on two or three new fronts.

This is what we had in mind in the first chapter when we suggested that strategy and tactics of revolution today should concentrate on the development of a *political equivalent to guerrilla warfare.* To the degree that such an attempt succeeds, the revolutionary may find it possible to sustain a difficult struggle with hope; our society may discover that profound and necessary changes in the social order can take place without the threat of total social disintegration. Along this road, the possibility exists of combining realism about society, and about the power of the forces blocking change, with optimism about the prospects for revolution, confirmed again and again by small victories and the acceleration of the process of change. We are provided with a strategy based on the spontaneous response of small groups on many different frontiers, which can be coordinated in an over-all strategy without destroying local initiative. If this strategy succeeds, the ultimate result will not necessarily be the control of certain spheres of society by revolutionary movements, but the type of change in social institutions—in the direction of openness, flexibility and response to the needs of men—which could eventually make revolution unnecessary.

We have no guarantees that such a strategy will succeed. To argue that it has a chance represents an affirmation of faith regarding the basic health and potential creativity of our society. A venture of this sort calls for revolutionary movements that are free to explore new ways, avoid the traps into which many past revolutions have fallen, and persevere during a long and arduous struggle. It can only occur in a society that is able to respond to new challenges rather than take refuge in desperate attempts to resist change at any price.

The verification of this hypothesis, as well as the working out of its implications, will depend on those who have the tools of social analysis and the revolutionary experience to do so. In conclusion, I should like to discuss briefly the relation of this approach to several questions that have frequently arisen in revolutionary movements and are with us now:

1. The question of whether it is better to work for social renewal from inside or outside the structures has always plagued reformers. Today it seems even more difficult to answer. The size of institutions and the concentration of power which each represents create a situation in which it is

very difficult to conceive of doing anything effective except from within. On the other hand, the weight of the past and the relative inertia of large bureaucratic structures, the pressures to conformity, and the necessity of playing the game according to pre-established rules, all militate against rapid and effective action for change. Many people have given the best years of their lives to such a struggle in government or business, the university or the church, only to discover that their efforts have accomplished very little at those points where fundamental changes were most urgently needed. This is a mistake that the younger generation is not inclined to make.

But the prospects of accomplishing anything outside the structures are not any more encouraging. It is possible for such groups to take a more radical position, have a clearer idea of the goals toward which they are working, and preserve their integrity as revolutionary movements. But they will probably have no base for effective operations, and can end up at the margin of the struggle for change. In fact, they may eventually wake up to discover that the battle for the very issues which most concerned them has been going on elsewhere. Even if they do become powerful enough to make an impact, they may find that they are soon threatened with the same tendency to inertia and inflexibility that they originally rebelled against elsewhere. Our experience in the church today is probably not very different from that of people in other institutions: We see little possibility of doing anything effective by working from within the present bureaucratic structures, but few prospects are less promising than that of starting a new church, which would very soon be nothing more than an ineffective sect.

A strategy of guerrilla action offers the possibility for a redefinition of the problem. In this perspective, the important thing is not whether a group is working for radical change inside or outside the structure, but whether or not it has its own self-identity and base of operation, a clear definition of its goals, and a relevant plan of action—whatever its relation to and position in a particular institution. From such a base, it may be able to challenge an organization to do what needs to be done, and carve out certain small spheres of relative freedom—within the structure, where that is possible—from which to get on with the job.

The important thing here is for those who are most committed to working for change in our society to have their own self-identity; that is, for them to be related to each other in such a way that they can take a position over against the ideology, rules, and pressures in the area in which they are working. Only to the degree that this happens will it be possible to analyze a specific situation, develop a new perspective on it, create new models, and work out an effective strategy for action.

For those who do this, there is no special merit in being outside the structures. The important thing is to *use them* for the purposes of social transformation, wherever this is possible. We may have very little hope that, in the foreseeable future, these structures will take the initiative in making the changes needed. But at some points, they can be used effectively. An organization may give its official support to a new project which is attempting to solve an urgent social problem; or it may tolerate the existence, within its midst, of groups that are working in a creative and dynamic way. In some institutions, there are leaders who see the need for change and who will be able to act more courageously because of the existence of movements that create new pressures for change.

Such an approach should avoid doctrinaire attitudes. Where structures are sufficiently open and flexible to respond creatively to new challenges, revolutionary movements are not justified. These people who have chosen to fight the battle for renewal from positions of power within the structures should not be condemned simply because they have chosen this road. The contemporary revolutionary will be inclined to doubt the possibility of working for effective change in this way, and will choose another alternative. For him, priority now must be given to the development of new perspectives, the creation of new models, and the freedom for wide experimentation. When one effort to do this fails, he must be free to admit failure and start again elsewhere. To the degree that social institutions today permit such groups to function within them, they contribute to their own renewal and provide the revolutionary with the most effective channels for the eventual achievement of his goals.

This strategy of placing stress upon small, radical groups with their own self-identity and program moves in quite the opposite direction from consensus politics. It is not interested primarily in uniting large groups on the basis of the lowest common denominator, but in forming a small nucleus that is free to work on a serious problem, research for new solutions, and develop a new strategy of action. A group that achieves this will be interested in finding the largest possible number of allies for a specific program of action; it will seek and accept the support of all those who can, for one reason or another, cooperate on limited objectives. An example of what we mean by this is provided by present efforts to do something about United States policy toward Latin America. There are many people and many different organizations concerned about changes in it. What is now required, however, is the type of study and reflection that can get to the heart of the matter, develop a new perspective on it, and provide new suggestions for meeting the present challenge. It is most unlikely that this task can be undertaken by a broad, heterogeneous group. At this stage it is important to find those who are free to explore new ways. If and when these succeed, many different individuals and groups can be brought together to study and support at least some items in a new program.

2. Modern revolutionaries have not been very successful in solving the problem of the participation of the masses in the revolutionary process. Since they are working for the betterment of the lot of the underprivileged classes, the revolutionaries naturally assume that their efforts should be supported by the masses, who can be forged into an effective instrument for social change. In some instances, this happens; in others, it does not. Frequently, those who stand to profit most by revolution are unable to understand it and afraid or unwilling to support it. On the other hand, modern revolutions have been the occasion for the spontaneous appearance of all sorts of organizations of workers and peasants in leagues, communes, and soviets—an expression of their deep longing for participation in the use of public power. Yet such groups have not usually been encouraged or tolerated by revolutionary governments.

If the central element in revolutionary strategy is the formation of small units for a guerrilla-type political struggle, we may have some chance of breaking out of the old impasse. A political strategy that depends on small guerrilla units cannot succeed unless it is authentically related to the masses and supported by them; yet it need not have illusions about their reliability nor demand more of them than they are prepared to give. Peasants, even in the most desperate situations, are often dominated by the authority patterns and the paternalistic ethos of the old society. Some of the workers who migrate from rural areas find their new situation so much better than the old that they are not inclined to revolution; others are so threatened by the total insecurity in which they live that they will pay almost any price for some small guarantee of stability. Wherever the resources of the mass media are used to control elections "democratically," or where the political structure does not permit a real choice between different ideologies and ruling groups, the whole electoral process is vitiated and its significance for social change limited. In fact, the basic problem today is not that of getting the masses to participate more actively in the present political order, or even to transfer political power from one group to another, but rather to move toward the creation of new political institutions.

For this to happen, it will be necessary to give attention primarily to the formation of those most basic political organizations which can be the authentic expression of the participation of diverse groups and classes of people in the transformation of their society. Since these people have been alienated from what is happening and excluded from the decision-making process, this requires a long and intensive process of awakening of men and women to the sociohistorical situation in which they live and to the nature of their responsibility for it. Such elementary political organizations thus provide the context for an educational process in which a new sense of self-identity and a new vision of the future can take shape. In most instances, this can probably occur only in groups quite different from the traditional political organization, but it will be effective in the long run only as it is related to these larger structures—and contributes to their transformation. Perhaps it will take movements with this sense of identity and relative independence of the present political structures to bring about any significant change in them.

3. Revolution has brought the issue of conflict and its resolution once again to the center of attention. For a long

time, society has been so successful in hiding the suffering and discontent of the underprivileged and covering up the violence of those in power that many people have been unaware of the place of conflict in social life, and are unprepared to deal with it. In recent years, periodic explosions of violence, in the developing nations as well as in our own country, have confronted us with this reality—and left many upset by what they have seen. Suddenly aware of the instability of society today and the potential for conflict in it, they easily turn to and support those political movements that promise to eliminate the problem by the effective suppression of subversive elements. The revolutionaries, on the other hand, may also be unprepared and unequipped for their encounter with conflict. They are very much aware of it, because their struggle brings it to the surface. As violence is used against them and they discover how difficult it is to achieve change under such circumstances, their tendency may be to formulate an ideology of conflict that exaggerates its importance and conceives of revolution in terms of total struggle. Unless we succeed relatively soon in meeting the most urgent demands of the Negro in this country, the civil rights movement may well provide a number of examples of this.

In the present revolutionary struggle, a coordinated strategy of guerrilla action on a variety of fronts could, I believe, indicate an alternative. By providing an instrument for the effective use of limited conflict, it might make it possible to avoid an ideology of total conflict, and thus save us from the sort of social disintegration or total resistance to change on the part of the established order which delays the achievement of the goals of revolution.

A theological perspective would support efforts in this same direction. Biblical realism is free to see the place of conflict in society and accept it. It does not believe that the social order must inevitably fall apart when conflict is allowed to take place. In fact, a type of realism that cannot conceive of peace and stability independently of justice recognizes that, in certain situations, conflict must not only be permitted but also encouraged.

This same theological approach sets all conflict in the context of a movement toward reconciliation. Conflict is not ultimate; it cannot be an end in itself. And reconciliation involves the establishment of new relationships in and through conflict, not its elimination. Thus, conflict is accepted simply for what it is: an element that is essential in certain situations if new relationships are to be established between groups and classes in society.

Ultimately, conflict is controlled, not by constant attempts to suppress or limit it, but by its integration into a strategy of reconciliation. This implies that those on both sides of a revolutionary struggle have the freedom to perceive and take advantage of opportunities for the resolution of conflict through understanding and dialogue. It is only thus that those who want change can see what is possible at a particular moment, and that those who are against it can be led to accept the changes that are most urgent. In this framework, the impasses created in conflict situations can be overcome; and those on both sides of the struggle can engage in a search for new ways of thinking about a particular problem and new solutions for it, and thus begin to move confidently toward the future. Among those who are concerned about social change today, few things are more important than further exploration of the possibilities that a strategy of reconciliation offers.

For those who are disposed to combine a commitment to revolution and a dialogue with theology, the most important issue regarding strategy may well be of another order. The person who lives this dialogue soon becomes aware of a mounting tension within himself. He comes to see more clearly the importance and significance of his option for revolution, and moves toward more complete involvement in it. At the same time, he develops a greater sensitivity to those external and internal factors that block the achievement of the goals of revolution by movements dedicated to it. These factors are many; among them: the tremendous burden of the task itself; the demand for new ideas and rules; the sharp and difficult ethical questions that arise; the inevitable tendency of movements of this type to absolutize their position and to be uninterested in critical judgments on their outlook and work; and the fact that, in the dynamic situation in which we find ourselves today, creative thought requires a continuous process of idealogical revision. In other words, the most authentic revolutionary is one who can unite full commitment with a certain degree of detachment, who can keep a sense of humor that allows him to laugh at himself, and who can maintain a critical attitude toward all revolutionary thought and action.

In the past, this could be partially achieved by insistence on certain ethical ideals that expressed both the type of society for which the revolution was striving and the means by which it could be approximated. Today these elements are much less helpful. The new rules that are needed cannot be worked out abstractly. A set of general ethical ideals and values are of very little significance except as they become more concrete in particular historical situations.

In spite of the fact that this emphasis on ideals and principles has a special appeal to religious people, biblical imagery suggests quite a different approach. The possibility of combining participation in efforts to transform society with an attitude of relative freedom and critical judgment *comes from being part of a community which has a point of reference beyond the immediate social struggle;* in biblical terms, a "chosen people," fully involved "in" but not entirely "of" the world; constantly open to the "Kingdom of God" which is now "coming" in our midst. In such a community, the evolving picture of the new order somehow or other calls into question the highest human achievements; and those movements that are the most important instruments of social change are seen as neither perfect nor completely indispensable.

Moreover, the shape of the new order becomes most clear, not through the definition of a set of ideals, but in a living community, which expresses and at the same time points to a new reality of social existence, and provides a laboratory in which its diverse aspects can be experimentally worked out. To the degree that this happens, such a community provides a sign, in the midst of the revolutionary struggle, of the possibilities that are open there and of the way by which they can become reality.

Surprising as it may seem to many people today, the original reason for and purpose of the *church* was precisely this: to be a people *called* into existence and *called out from* their immediate context, in order to be *for* man there, serving him in freedom. Obviously, a massive program of church development today would not fulfill this purpose in the contemporary revolution. However, all revolutionaries and revolutionary movements, be they Christian or not, need to make room in their strategy for some sort of community that can undertake this task and provide the framework for reflection, criticism, and freedom. The exact form of such communities will have to be determined by study and experimentation. Perhaps today the study center and similar nuclei on the local level indicate one possibility. One of the most encouraging signs of a development of this type is the plan for the Radical Education Project of the Students for a Democratic Society. It proposes to encourage, on local, regional, and national levels, constant study and reflection upon what is happening in America today, the type of society that can and should be built in the future, and the best strategy for arriving at this goal. If this plan can be carried forward with the participation of those who have most to contribute to it, and in radical openness to ideological confrontation and free discussion among those committed to social revolution, it may offer a new model for the type of community we are here suggesting.

For those who are Christian or have some interest in the dialogue with theology, a final word should be added. Any hope for a significant Christian contribution to the revolutionary struggles going on around the world will depend, I believe, on the emergence of new forms of Christian community on the front lines of revolution. Such groups can have no pretension of being political movements; they need make no claims to special authority, nor exclude anyone interested in their objectives. But they can offer the context for a continual running conversation between our theological and ethical heritage and the major human issues that arise in the attempt to transform society. It is just possible that in such weak and informal communities new ideas and questions may take shape which will be of significance for the revolutionary movement as a whole; and the resources available for such a struggle may become more visible through such an effort.

My own conviction on this is the result of some years of work with the Latin American Student Christian Movements, and the Commission on Church and Society in Latin America, both of which have been working at the task of creating such communities on the revolutionary frontiers. They have been engaged in a long and difficult struggle, not without some encouraging results. In both organizations, the formation of small nuclei on the local level, as well as the structuring of much wider contacts, has offered an opportunity for analysis of the Latin American situation and reflection on it, and has helped to sustain those who are in the midst of the present struggle. More than this, a number of people and movements with no special interest in or relationship to the Protestant religious community have recognized the significance of the work of these groups for themselves and for the struggle in which they are involved.